the MIRROR —— *of the* —— WORD

DAILY DEVOTIONS TO REVEAL AND REFINE

C.E. WHITE

THE MIRROR OF THE WORD:
DAILY DEVOTIONS TO REVEAL AND REFINE
Copyright © 2024 by Connie E. White

Paperback ISBN: 979-8-9850311-4-0
Hardcover ISBN: 979-8-9850311-5-7

cewhitebooks@gmail.com
www.cewhitebooks.com
www.facebook.com/cewhitebooks
www.instagram.com/cewhitebooks
First Edition, October 2024
Cover design by Jenneth Lead
Edited by E.J. Kitchens

INTRODUCTION

"But prove yourselves doers of the word, and not just hearers
who deceive themselves. For if anyone is a hearer of the word
and not a doer, he is like a man who looks at his natural face in
a mirror; for once he has looked at himself and gone away, he
has immediately forgotten what kind of person he was.

But one who has looked intently at the perfect law, the law
of freedom, and has continued in it, not having become a
forgetful hearer but an active doer, this person will be
blessed in what he does."
—James 1:22–25

These verses tell the tale of two paths. I've taken both, and I'm here to
tell you that being a doer, not just a hearer really is the path to finding
all the blessings God promises us. The "law of freedom" looks con-
stricting on the front end, but it always brings us out into the "open
place" on the other side (Psalm 18:19).

Years ago, I dreamed someone gave me a gift. It was mysterious—
a jumble of pieces that changed from foam to plastic, and finally, to
wood as I struggled to assemble it. I couldn't even tell what it was supposed to be.

At last, I realized it was a wall shelf, only for it to vanish, replaced
by a headstone engraved with the words, "Seek ye first."

My gift had become my gravestone . . . only I wasn't dead.

When I woke, I understood that the gift symbolized my faith. Ini-
tially fragile and vague, it grew sturdier as I matured, becoming something that was presentable to others and purposeful to me. But just as
I thought it was complete and ready to display, it transformed again.

My faith, in its wholeness, wasn't just a nice addition to my existing life or something for me to use and display my earthly treasures and trinkets on; it was a reminder that I was already dead, and my life hidden in Christ (Colossians 3:3). It was a call for me to put to death the things of the flesh (Romans 8:13) and seek God's kingdom and righteousness first (Matthew 6:33).

My real-life transformation didn't occur until I put feet to my faith, examining my reflection in the mirror of the Word and striving to obey it daily. I always would've said I believed God's Word was absolute truth, but before this, I often half-heartedly followed its instructions, treating them like potentially helpful but unpleasant, unattainable, or impractical suggestions.

Living like this renders the Word useless in our lives, just like looking in the bathroom mirror in the morning is pointless if we don't then comb our hair, shave, or fix the shirt we've buttoned askew.

And I'm not just talking about clearing out all our raging, obvious sin. I looked pretty good on the outside. But I frequently looked into the mirror of the Word and still went away bitter, resentful, anxious, unforgiving, complaining, easily provoked, envious, selfish, and a host of other attitudes the Bible says God wants to heal and correct.

This kind of faith will always be weak and easily crushed, like an unexercised muscle. We have to train it if we want it to be strong (1 Corinthians 9:25–27).

Faith is supposed to mean we're planted, rooted, unshakeable, and able to withstand storms and drought (Psalm 1:1–3; Isaiah 58:11; Matthew 7:24–27).

So I wrote the words, "Try it HIS way" on a notecard and stuck it in my morning devotion as a bookmark.

Trying it his way meant a lot of hard things. I had to figure out how to forgive people—even (especially) the ones who didn't deserve or ask for it. I had to set my mind on things above instead of scrambling to try to get what I wanted right now. I had to give up some sins I'd convinced myself were okay. I had to stop disguising and ignoring my pride and try to figure out how to actually stop being prideful. I had to set aside my selfish ambition and start considering others more important than myself (Philippians 2:3).

But it also meant learning how to rest and stop worrying about meeting society's expectations, how to stop trying to fight all my own battles, and how to stop letting this world's storms sink me.

My faith slowly became more concrete and heavier. Now, it's truly the most real, solid thing in my life. I'm finding the rest, the easy yoke (Matthew 11:28–30), the love, joy, peace, patience, kindness, goodness, faithfulness, gentleness, and self-control (Galatians 5:22).

I'm not telling you I'm perfect; none of us are. But the things all of us want and hope for in our faith are coming alive in me; I'm living the true abundant life (John 10:10).

The path isn't for the faint of heart. Many of my devotions hit hard, because faith must be challenged and trained if it's going to get stronger.

If we want to find our lives, we have to lose them (Matthew 10:39).

My prayer is that every one of you will fight the good fight, walk the narrow road, and find the abundant life on the other side of the crucible as you examine yourself in the mirror of the Word and try it HIS way.

JANUARY 1

"Do not call to mind the former things or consider things
of the past. Behold, I am going to do something new, now
it will spring up; will you not be aware of it? I will even
make a roadway in the wilderness, rivers in the desert."
—Isaiah 43:18–19

In the new year, our focus is usually on how we can make this year better than the last. This pressure sometimes brings more discouragement in our circumstances than hope for our future. It can remind us how far we are from where we want to be rather than motivating us to try and get there.

But we can take heart—God is always doing a new thing in a new way—something that we never could have expected.

When Joseph's brothers sold him into slavery and he was falsely imprisoned, he didn't know that God was doing a dramatic new thing and saving nations from starvation. But he was faithful with the life he'd been given.

When Ruth's husband, brother-in-law, and father-in-law died and she left all she knew to move to Israel and care for her mother-in-law, she didn't know that God was doing a dramatic new thing by bringing her into the lineage of Jesus Christ. But she was faithful with the life she'd been given.

We might feel hopeless and abandoned in the lonely wilderness or the dry desert Isaiah mentions, but God is always making a way where there seems to be no way and quenching thirst when there's no water in sight.

Instead of dwelling on the disappointments of the past, we can know God is doing a new thing in and around us. We can choose to live the life we've been given faithfully.

"Then Moses said to the Lord, 'Please, Lord, I have never
been eloquent, neither recently nor in time past, nor since
you have spoken to your servant; for I am slow of speech
and slow of tongue.' But the Lord said to him, 'Who has
made the human mouth? Or who makes anyone unable to
speak or deaf, or able to see or blind? Is it not I, the Lord?
Now then go, and I myself will be with your mouth, and
instruct you in what you are to say.' But he said, 'Please,
Lord, now send the message by whomever you will.'"
—Exodus 4:10–13

By "whomever you will," Moses actually meant, ". . . whomever you
will except me." In modern terms, he was saying, "Please send someone else!"

This came from his insecurity.

We know our own faults—that we're weak and fallible people—
and we generally know what talents we have or don't have.

But we've seen God's power, and if we believe the Bible, we should
know that he is capable; yet somehow, we think he cannot overcome
our own weaknesses.

Sure, he can turn a stick into a snake and part the sea . . . but our
inability to speak well? That's surely too much for him!

But he created us; he knows all about our limitations, and he's not
worried about whether we're capable or not. He just wants our willingness. If God can overcome even the finality of death, our inabilities
and weaknesses are no impediment to him. He can work through us
just as he sees fit no matter how capable or incapable we are.

God lets us be a part of what he's doing not because of our skills
and abilities, but because of our obedience.

"How often I wanted to gather your children
together, just as a hen gathers her young under
her wings, and you were unwilling!"
—Luke 13:34

Our Lord invites, woos, and pursues us. He defends, upholds, and provides for us.

But not if we will not come to him.

Like the prodigal son, though we're offered an inheritance, provision, and love in our Father's house, we too often leave its protection.

We don't want to yield to the authority that comes with that inheritance, provision, and love or the responsibility sonship requires.

We decide the Father doesn't really have our best interests at heart, so we run out from under the protection, warmth, and plenty he gives.

We want to do what we want when we want, so we leave.

We trade the fullness of joy in the Lord's presence that leads to pleasures forever (Psalm 16:11) for the temporary pleasures of sin (Hebrews 11:25) that lead to our soul's destruction (Galatians 6:8).

The Father wasn't restricting us from good things; he was giving us the true prize while protecting us from everything that masquerades as good.

When we've wandered long and far enough to see the shiny veneer wear off the world's offerings, our Father is still there waiting and wanting to welcome us home.

He longs for it, just as a good earthly father would always want his wayward son to return home.

When we're feeling lost and exposed in this world, earthly pursuits have tarnished, and we remember the beauty of all we left behind with our Father, we don't have to hesitate to return.

He wants to gather us under his wings.

"Watch over your heart with all diligence,
for from it flow the springs of life."
—Proverbs 4:23

Sometimes we miss the point; we forget that our hearts should be flowing with life (John 7:38).

While we do need to put our faith into action (James 2:14–17), many of us try to "act right" but never get around to working on our hearts. We might look okay on the outside, but inside, we're hurting, exhausted, irritated, overwhelmed, anxious, and lonely.

God cares about our hearts. He wants them flowing with the springs of life. If we are empty, flowing with disappointment, bitterness, and anger, we need to take time for healing that. We need to sit with the Lord like Mary did (Luke 10:39), to rest from our strivings, recognize the lies that are controlling our thoughts and feelings, and battle against them in a spiritual war for our hearts. We must learn the biblical truths that counteract those lies so we have ammunition against them.

As we do these things, eventually, the springs of life will begin to flow more freely. Jesus is the source of those springs, and the more we draw near to him and he draws near to us (James 4:8–10), the quieter the thoughts, feelings, and words of death will grow. We'll never totally get there in this life, but learning who the Lord is and who we are in him will take us further and further along that path.

Spend time healing your heart. The world needs our hearts springing with life, not only our hands doing good works out of duty and obligation.

"Commit your works to the Lord,
and your plans will be established."
—Proverbs 16:3

When we ask ourselves what we can do to honor God and love others in our daily actions, the Holy Spirit gives us confidence and guidance in our plans for the future.

Perhaps this is why so many of us feel confused and uncertain. We make our own plans without ever committing them to the Lord, or we've decided we're supposed to attempt grand things for him before we've ever committed our current duties to him. Maybe we're still doing many of our daily tasks with bitterness, anger, or carelessness, but Luke 16:10 says, "The one who is faithful in a very little thing is also faithful in much; and the one who is unrighteous in a very little thing is also unrighteous in much."

Committing our works to the Lord ensures that our plans will also be his plans, and through our faithfulness and commitment, they will be established in our lives and for his kingdom.

So many people in the Bible were simply living faithfully where they were—Ruth, Joseph, Daniel, Paul, David, Esther, Mordecai . . . the list could go on. And because they were faithful in the small things, the Lord established their plans, and they did great work in the kingdom of God.

When we dedicate all our works to him, he will establish our plans when the time is right. We may not know what he is guiding us toward, and the way might not be easy. His timing may not be what we would like or plan for ourselves, but he will give us everything we need to do his will when we've committed all our works to him no matter the circumstance.

"Things which eye has not seen and ear has not heard,
and which have not entered the human heart, all that
God has prepared for those who love him."
—1 Corinthians 2:9

───────◆───────

None of us can truly comprehend heaven or eternity. We can't understand how amazing and wonderful it will be, nor grasp the fathoms of infinity.

But though we can't understand it fully, if we don't find the idea of eternity with Christ motivating or helpful to our Christian walk, it's time to change that.

The Bible tells us over and over that our hope doesn't lie in this world, and this word "hope" is synonymous with waiting and expectation (Psalm 62:5–6; Psalm 40:1; Psalm 33:20 . . . the list could go on). All of this is temporary and fading away (Isaiah 40:7–8; 2 Corinthians 4:18).

Since everything the Bible says to hope in is eternal, if we don't have an understanding of eternity, we don't have a firm grasp on our hope.

If what God is preparing for us is so wonderful that ideas of it have not even entered the human heart, can you imagine its grandeur and how quickly it will wipe away all our earthly sorrows?

Paul writes that our earthly troubles won't even tip the scales against the weight of glory we will experience there. He isn't downplaying the suffering; he's expressing the immense wonder of heaven! The sorrow won't even rate as anything that matters to us anymore. Indeed, the "light and momentary affliction" here is helping produce the glory there (2 Corinthians 4:17).

If our understanding of eternity is dim, let's spend some time learning about it and why it should be a beautiful light that spurs us on when we're feeling defeated by this world.

"He has no stately form or majesty that we would look at him, nor an appearance that we would take pleasure in him. He was despised and abandoned by men, a man of great pain and familiar with sickness; and like one from whom people hide their faces, he was despised, and we had no regard for him."
—Isaiah 53:2–3

Reading this prophetic passage about Jesus, we would not want to be this man.

We want to be attractive and look powerful. We want people to admire our appearance. We want to be loved and embraced by men; we don't want to live with pain. We want to be considered important and to gain success in the eyes of others.

But the servant is not greater than his master. We must be willing to live like unappreciated servants (John 13:15–17) and to endure persecution (John 15:20).

And yet we're surprised and offended when we, in all our brokenness and imperfection, are rejected or mistreated. Jesus is the human embodiment of everything that is good, true, perfect, holy, lovely, and loving, yet rejection and mistreatment is how we, in our humanity, received him.

Even if we're walking perfectly according to the Lord's plan, there will be those who hate and mistreat us. It's our duty to make sure their only reason is our association with Christ, not because of any wrong we've done to them or others. "For what credit is there if, when you sin and are harshly treated, you endure it with patience? But if when you do what is right and suffer for it you patiently endure it, this finds favor with God" (1 Peter 2:20).

We can endure injustice as Christ did—for the eternal joy set before us (Hebrews 12:2).

"Above all, keep fervent in your love for one another,
because love covers a multitude of sins."
—1 Peter 4:8

The church has largely lost the concept of fervent love for one another, but this wasn't a casual request. Peter says we're to love fervently "above all." He's not forgotten that the greatest commandments are to love God with all your heart, soul, and mind, and to love your neighbor as yourself (Matthew 22:36–40).

We often think this fervent love will require too much of us or be too invasive. Sometimes, we're just plain scared because fervent love requires truly knowing and being known. We may either be afraid to reach out or afraid others won't like us once they really know us.

But fervent love also "covers a multitude of sins" both on the giving and the receiving end.

If we're fervently loving, we will be obediently forgiving others as God has forgiven us even where offense has been done (Matthew 6:12–15). And if others are fervently loving us, we will not be easily provoked at the smallest slights nor allow misunderstandings to fuel conflict (1 Corinthians 13:5). We will trust that since we see them loving us well in other ways, they didn't mean to hurt us.

"Fervent" means unceasing, intent, and earnest; this is not a halfway action. It requires that we step outside of our comfort zones and stop keeping each other at arm's length. It's not always easy, just like loving the members of our family is not always easy.

It may require some of our deepest sacrifice, but it may also open us up to some of our greatest blessings. Others need us, but we also need them.

"But Moses said to God, 'Who am I that I should go to
Pharaoh and bring the children of Israel out of Egypt?'"
—Exodus 3:11

When Moses was favored in Egypt, he wanted to free the Israelite slaves. He believed he had the skills, power, and position to do so, and he relied on those abilities. But his anger and pride led him to do it his way in his time, and he had to flee Egypt, leaving his people enslaved.

Moses spent the next forty years as a shepherd, probably feeling like he'd wrecked that task and lost the chance to save his people.

But after all those years, God reminded him of the true calling he'd recognized as a young man.

This time, Moses wasn't arrogantly deciding how to do it by worldly means. His response to God's call now was, "Who am I? Why would you want me? I don't have what it takes."

In his humility, he was finally ready to follow God's lead.

Most of us have times we feel like we've failed in our lives and in our service to God. We tried and just made a big mess of it.

But perhaps, like Moses, this season is working a humility in us that we need for our own good and for the kingdom of God. Even if it seems like we had all the earthly advantages and lost them through poor decisions, our only concern should be to get back up and follow the Lord once more; he never needed our power—only our obedience.

May we always seek God's purpose, wait on his guidance, and ask, "Who am I?" each step of the way, directing all the glory to our Lord.

"Blessed are those who hear the word of God and follow it."
—Luke 11:28

We short-change the building of our faith when we don't obey Christ and the Word even when we don't like or understand it.

Logically, it made no sense for Jesus to tell Peter to go back out and try again though he'd been fishing all night with nothing to show for it (Luke 5:4–6). It would've been easy for him to think Jesus was just cheering him on (and was ignorant of fishing) or to think Jesus was being hard on him. He'd been fishing all night and was surely ready for a break. But Peter obeyed, and the result was not only a lot of fish, but a confidence that Jesus's words were trustworthy.

When we prove God's Word in our lives by obeying it, it strengthens not only our own faith, but that of those around us.

If Peter had not cast his nets again, he might've wondered for years why Jesus had told him to do so. Only through obedience did he begin to see the divine power of Christ and have his faith built because of it.

Perhaps, instead of obeying like Peter did, we spend a lot of time contemplating the nice things Jesus says. Or we might believe he's being too hard on us by asking us to keep going in the face of failure or hardship.

But when we take steps of obedience, we actually see that his words are true and purposeful. The more we see that, the easier obedience becomes.

> "Do not be afraid, for those who are with us are greater
> than those who are with them."
> —2 Kings 6:16

The king of Syria had sent a great army to kill the prophet Elisha, surrounding the city with horses and chariots. While Elisha knew there was more to the battle than what they could see with their human eyes, his servant was afraid.

Elisha prayed, and God opened the servant's eyes; he saw that the Lord's army, "full of horses and chariots of fire," was protecting them.

Sometimes we look at our circumstances with human eyes instead of eyes of faith. Things seem impossible, and with only our earthly resources, they would be.

Elisha didn't have the power to overcome those armies, the Israelites didn't have the strength to challenge Pharaoh, and we don't have the ability to save ourselves from sin.

But God and his armies are always greater than whatever or whoever is coming against us. We can't always see what he's doing, but as it says in Exodus 14:14, we can be sure that "the Lord will fight for you, while you keep silent."

We don't have to depend on earthly advantages or abilities. "Some praise their chariots and some their horses, but we will praise the name of the Lord, our God" (Psalm 20:7).

Whether our spiritual eyes are opened to what's going on around us or not, let our confidence always be in the Lord's faithfulness.

The problem may be big, but our God is bigger.

"Now about midnight Paul and Silas were praying and singing hymns of praise to God, and the prisoners were listening to them; and suddenly there was a great earthquake, so that the foundations of the prison were shaken; and immediately all the doors were opened, and everyone's chains were unfastened."

—Acts 16:25–26

———◆———

Paul and Silas had been attacked by crowds, stripped, beaten with rods, and chained in the innermost cell. Yet they sang.

Can we imagine ourselves there? The other prisoners watched Paul and Silas hauled in past all the other cells—they were bloody, bruised, and maybe still naked. Yet they sang.

The prisoners must've listened with confusion, shock, and not just a little curiosity.

And then the miracle came—all the doors opened, and all the chains came loose. Yet in Paul and Silas's faithfulness and hope, they convinced the other prisoners to stay right where they were.

When we pray and praise in the midst of a trial, bonds are broken and chains loosed, but sometimes, prison is where we're meant to be. Many came to salvation because Paul, Silas, and the other prisoners stayed there.

It might look like we're defeated and in prison, but as long as we're in Christ, no circumstance can be bigger than his purpose. *No* circumstance. Not Paul and Silas's bloody, bruised bodies. Not an illness, financial troubles, a struggling marriage, or a lagging career.

What song are we singing when we're mistreated and all the circumstances seem against us? Is it despairing self-pity? Vengeful anger? Or is it prayer and praise that will bring freedom and salvation to both the jailed and the jailer?

Let's praise him in the midst of our trials and be prepared to see him work.

"After he was baptized, Jesus came up immediately from
the water; and behold, the heavens were opened, and he
saw the Spirit of God descending as a dove and settling
on him, and behold, a voice from the heavens said, 'This
is my beloved son, with whom I am well pleased.'"
—Matthew 3:16–17

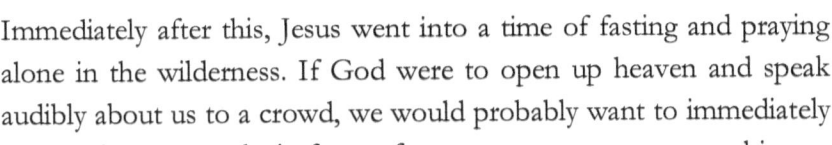

Immediately after this, Jesus went into a time of fasting and praying alone in the wilderness. If God were to open up heaven and speak audibly about us to a crowd, we would probably want to immediately go and do great works in front of everyone—to go on a preaching or healing tour.

But Jesus knew the most beneficial thing to do after God appears in our life is to go out where we can be alone and spend dedicated time with him.

When we have "mountaintop experiences" with the Lord, we tend to want to show them off, but, in reality, it's often a time we should retreat and prepare for the work he has for us next. Satan loves to come after us when everyone is watching and we're feeling invincible.

Had Jesus not spent his days fasting and praying in the wilderness, would he have been prepared to face the temptation that came? He was weak in body after that time but strong in spirit.

Let's take his example and retreat in prayer and fasting when the Lord moves in our lives so that when it's time to begin his work, we'll be ready for the spiritual attack the devil will launch against us, since "our struggle is not against flesh and blood" (Ephesians 6:12).

Public work requires private devotion. If we neglect that, our public work will be fruitless, and we will be vulnerable to temptation of all kinds.

"As iron sharpens iron, so one person sharpens another."
—Proverbs 27:17

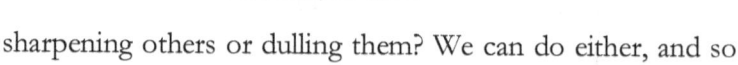

Are we sharpening others or dulling them? We can do either, and so much of that has to do with the words we say.

- Are we taking care that our speech is edifying and our words beneficial (Proverbs 12:25)?
- Are we speaking what is true, honorable, just, pure, lovely, commendable, excellent, and worthy of praise (Philippians 4:8)?
- Are our words life-giving and full of wisdom (Proverbs 18:4)?
- Are our words careless or thoughtful (Leviticus 5:4)?
- Is what we speak critical (James 4:11) and boastful (James 3:5) or kind (Proverbs 16:24) and gentle (Proverbs 15:4)?
- Are we speaking blessing or cursing (James 3:10)?
- Are our words true or deceitful (Psalm 34:13)?
- Do we speak words of flattery only to gain favor (Psalm 12:2)?
- Are we speaking God's good news (Psalm 40:9) or focusing on the dire stories of the world?
- Are we praising the Lord (Psalm 51:15; Hebrews 13:15)?
- Are we speaking biblical truth (John 17:17) and taking care that all our words are in line with the Word of God (Proverbs 5:2)?
- Are we guarding our words or speaking rashly (Proverbs 13:3)?
- Are we being transformed by the renewing of our thoughts (Romans 12:2) and training our hearts in truth and love so that is what we speak (Luke 6:45)?

These are just a fraction of the verses that talk about how we use our words. Proverbs 18:21 says, "Death and life are in the power of the tongue, and those who love it will eat its fruit."

Let us always speak and surround ourselves with those speaking life, not death, and thereby sharpen and be sharpened by those around us.

> "I will not drive them out from you in a single year, so
> that the land will not become desolate and the animals
> of the field become too numerous for you. I will drive
> them out from you little by little, until you become
> fruitful and take possession of the land."
> —Exodus 23:29–30

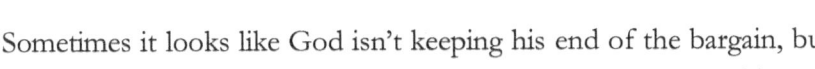

Sometimes it looks like God isn't keeping his end of the bargain, but he sees things we don't see and considers things we can't consider.

If he had driven the Israelites' enemies from the land too quickly, the cultivated areas would've become wild, and the herds would have become so large as to be unmanageable. The Israelites would've been left with an overwhelming workload.

But in his wisdom, the Lord did it little by little, so that not only did the Israelites take over the land, they benefited from the labor of their enemies.

If it looks like the Lord hasn't finished his work in our lives, it could be that he is not slow, but patient, giving all people the time to come to him in repentance (2 Peter 3:9) or maybe because it will be better for us in the end—or perhaps, both. Perhaps he is ordering things and preparing us for the responsibility so we're not overwhelmed by it when it comes.

God sees the end from the beginning and his plan will be established (Isaiah 46:10).

Our position is always to trust that he has a reason, continue following him, and faithfully bear the fruit of the Spirit while we wait so that when the time comes, we're able to take possession of what he's given us.

"There is one who scatters, and yet increases all the
more, and there is one who withholds what is justly
due, and yet it results only in poverty. A generous
person will be prosperous, and one who gives others
plenty of water will himself be given plenty."
—Proverbs 11:24–25

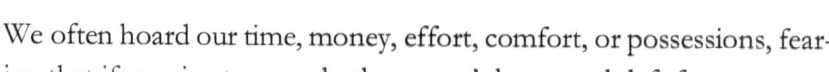

We often hoard our time, money, effort, comfort, or possessions, fearing that if we give too much, there won't be enough left for us.

God says that's not how it works. In his economy, if we withhold what we should give, we will be in want. If we water others where the Lord directs, we will be watered.

2 Corinthians 8:15 says it again, "The one who had gathered much did not have too much, and the one who had gathered little did not have too little."

We see this play out with the widow in 1 Kings 17:7–16 who fed Elijah from the last of her flour and oil, yet never ran out.

People will tell us we must limit our giving sensibly according to our worldly wisdom, but Jesus praised yet another widow for giving everything she had to live on (Mark 12:41–44).

So next time the Lord puts a need in front of us, let's not fear meeting it as he leads with whatever earthly resource we have, even if it feels like that resource is already stretched to its capacity.

God's resources aren't limited, and if he asks it of us, we can trust him with it.

"Lord, you have searched me and known me. You know
when I sit down and when I get up; you understand my
thought from far away. You scrutinize my path and my
lying down and are acquainted with all my ways. Even
before there is a word on my tongue, behold, Lord, you
know it all. You have encircled me behind and in front
and placed your hand upon me. Such knowledge is too
wonderful for me; it is too high; I cannot comprehend it."
—Psalm 139:1–6

What a beautiful reminder that the Lord knows us better than we know
ourselves. He knows our thoughts before we know them, our words
before we say them, and our steps before we take them.

David says this knowledge is "too wonderful"—so wonderful, in
fact, that he can't even begin to know it of himself. We may consistently be wrong about what we will or won't do, just as Peter did not
understand he was capable of denying Christ (Luke 22:31–34).

It's good to know ourselves and to have direction, but in this world
of self-discovery and "finding yourself," it's even better to remember
that there will always be depths within us and directions we need to go
that we cannot discern. This is too "high" for us. We're not smart
enough and don't have the full picture.

Proverbs 9:10 says, "knowledge of the Holy One is understanding."

It's wonderful to rest in the fact that when we don't know the right
way, God does, and we can gain that understanding by knowing and
following him.

He is ahead of us, behind us, and directing us in the way of truth,
life, hope, and peace.

"Not that I have already grasped it all or have already
become perfect, but I press on if I may also take hold
of that for which I was even taken hold of by Christ
Jesus. Brothers and sisters, I do not regard myself as
having taken hold of it yet; but one thing I do:
forgetting what lies behind and reaching forward to
what lies ahead, I press on toward the goal for the
prize of the upward call of God in Christ Jesus."
—Philippians 3:12–14

Jesus took hold of me; now it's my job to take hold of what he's given me. We are not the authors of our salvation, but it is our job to continue working with diligence, discipline, and self-control to attain the prize.

The Word implores us to pursue righteousness (1 Timothy 6:11). We will never fully attain it in this life, but we're never given permission to live in the flesh (Romans 6:12–14). Instead, we're constantly implored to put our whole will toward living righteously and putting to death the deeds of the flesh. True faith requires continually working toward obedience (Philippians 2:12).

This passage goes on to say that those who walk according to their fleshly appetites and whose minds are on earthly things are enemies of Christ. He does not say they are bad Christians; he calls them enemies (Philippians 3:18).

We may have lived as such in the past (1 Corinthians 6:11), but as believers, we do not dwell on what lies behind, return to slavery once freed (Hebrews 11:15), nor place our hope in our current circumstances. We press on to what lies ahead—our eternal inheritance with Christ, which we are promised as long as we abide in him.

"Through him then, let's continually offer up a sacrifice of
praise to God, that is, the fruit of lips praising his name."
—Hebrews 13:15

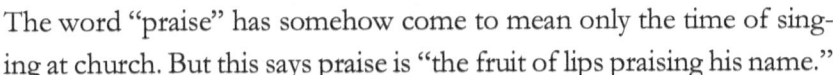

The word "praise" has somehow come to mean only the time of singing at church. But this says praise is "the fruit of lips praising his name."

So it's not simply praising his name, but the fruit that acknowledgement bears in our lives.

1 Samuel 15:22–23 says, "Does the Lord have as much delight in
burnt offerings and sacrifices as in obeying the voice of the Lord?
Behold, to obey is better than a sacrifice, and to pay attention is better
than the fat of rams. For rebellion is as reprehensible as the sin of div-
ination, and insubordination is as reprehensible as false religion and
idolatry."

Living a life that acknowledges God and his goodness is not only
something we do for half an hour before a sermon; that will be an
empty ritual before the Lord if we are not also allowing his Word to
transform our moments and our days.

If we praise the Lord with our lips in truth, that will cause us to live
our lives in a way that requires sacrifice. That is our praise—to do the
work of the Father and live according to his Word. Real praise will
never only be singing and speaking of his goodness; it will also transform our lives into fruit, which comes by obedience.

And it says to do this continually.

May we continually and intentionally use both our words and our
lives to acknowledge God throughout the week and praise him not
only with songs but in action.

"But I said, 'I have labored in vain, I have spent my strength
for nothing and futility; nevertheless, the justice due to me is
with the Lord, and my reward is with my God.'"
—Isaiah 49:4

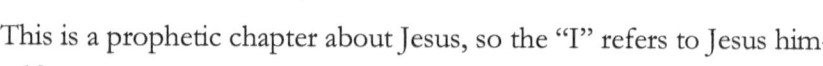

This is a prophetic chapter about Jesus, so the "I" refers to Jesus himself.

Isn't it comforting to see that even Jesus would be tempted to believe that his work wouldn't amount to anything? All the rejection he would face was discouragement even to him, but the verse ends with a statement of faith.

This tells us it's okay to say, "It feels hopeless and like I'm working for nothing, but God is with me, and my reward is from him."

It's not a sin to be discouraged, but it is a sin to allow that discouragement to keep us from obedience or lead us into sinful attitudes like anger or resentment; that's when it becomes distrust in the Lord's plan.

We can't always help how we feel, but we can acknowledge those feelings without shame, take them to the Lord, and take our thoughts captive by ending with those statements of faith. We can give ourselves grace in the discouragement and still act in faith.

When it seems like we're working for nothing, no one notices, others think we're not doing enough or not doing things right, and there's no tangible reward, we can know the Lord is right there with us, and our reward is with him. It's nice to be recognized and rewarded here on this earth, and sometimes that happens too.

But sometimes we don't get to see our impact until we reach eternity with him, and that's enough when he is our aim and we've put away the desire for this world.

"And some people came, bringing to him a man who was
paralyzed, carried by four men. And when they were
unable to get to [Jesus] because of the crowd, they
removed the roof above him; and after digging an
opening, they let down the pallet on which the paralyzed
man was lying. And Jesus, seeing their faith, said to the
paralyzed man, 'Son, your sins are forgiven.'"
—Mark 2:3–5

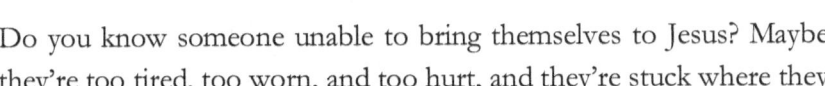

Do you know someone unable to bring themselves to Jesus? Maybe
they're too tired, too worn, and too hurt, and they're stuck where they
are.

We have a responsibility to bring those people to God in faith, and
he looks not only at them, but at the faith of their friends who carry
them to Christ in prayer and service.

There was nothing the man's friends could do except bring him to
Jesus. They couldn't heal him, and presumably doctors had given no
hope. They certainly couldn't forgive his sins. Sometimes we think, "I
wish I could do more than pray." But praying is bringing them to Jesus.
We can also do it through witnessing, encouragement, and speaking
the truth of the Word, but the final restoration is only going to come
with the touch of our Lord.

If it seems like there's no way to bring someone to Jesus, don't give
up. This man's friends tore off a roof to get him there. Can we pray
like we're tearing tiles off a roof in order to get our friends to Christ? I
think so. "A prayer of a righteous person, when it is brought about,
can accomplish much" (James 5:16).

"And a poor widow came and put in two lepta coins,
which amount to a quadrans. Calling his disciples to him,
he said to them, 'Truly, I say to you, this poor widow put
in more than all the contributors to the treasury.'"
—Mark 12:42–43

She put in "more than all." Jesus doesn't say more "considering" or more "in comparison to." He says she gave more—no qualifications.

Giving everything we have—whether in time, talent, money, or intelligence—may not look like much to others. It might look like a woman throwing two pennies into the offering plate. Others may ridicule how little we have to give and how we could think it even worth the trouble.

But that's not how God sees it. Jesus didn't look on the woman with pity and say, "Well, at least she did her best, poor thing. It doesn't amount to much, but we'll take it anyway." He commended her above all the others.

God doesn't need our riches; he owns the cattle on a thousand hills, after all (Psalm 50:10)! He wants us to give because it shows where our hearts are (Matthew 6:21). When we're willing to give all to the Lord, holding nothing back, it means all of our heart belongs to him.

When we give all we have, it might look like nothing to the rest of the world, but the Lord knows what it cost us. And in his great goodness, he honors what we give as a good father treasures a gift from his young child. God will multiply what we give for the good of his kingdom just as he multiplied the little boy's five loaves and two fish (John 6:8–11).

"The good person out of the good treasure of his heart
brings forth what is good; and the evil person out of the
evil treasure brings forth what is evil; for his mouth
speaks from that which fills his heart."
—Luke 6:45

If our heart-treasure is good, it will produce more good. If our heart-treasure is evil or vain, it will produce more evil and vanity.

Is reputation our treasure? First Samuel 16:7 says that man looks at the outer appearance, but God looks at the heart.

Is financial gain our treasure? First Timothy 6:10 says that the love of money is the root of evil and Matthew 19:24–26 tells us it's easier for a camel to go through the eye of a needle than for a rich man to enter the kingdom of God, though all things are possible through Christ.

Is safety our treasure? Matthew 10:28 says not to fear those who can harm the body, but rather fear him who has power over the soul and the body.

Is ease our treasure? John 16:33 says that in this world we will have trouble, but that Christ has overcome the world, and Romans 5:3–5 tells us we can rejoice in our sufferings knowing they produce godliness, perseverance, and hope in us.

Our only real treasure is Christ and eternity in his kingdom with him—the pearl of great price worth selling all other treasure to gain (Matthew 13:45–46). His treasure will see us overflowing with the fountain of living water, and there is no bottom to that fountain.

We should take great care to evaluate our treasures and what they are bringing forth in us and through us.

"Jesus said to him, 'Get up, pick up your pallet and
walk.' Immediately the man became well, and
picked up his pallet and began to walk."
—John 5:8–9

This isn't the only instance when Jesus gave someone a physical command in conjunction with healing.

John 9:7: "'Go, wash in the pool of Siloam' . . .. So he left and washed, and came back seeing."

Luke 17:14: "He said to them, 'Go and show yourselves to the priests.' And as they were going, they were cleansed."

And in the Old Testament, Elisha told Naaman, "Go and wash in the Jordan seven times, and your flesh will be restored to you and you will be clean" (2 Kings 5:10).

Like Naaman, we might be angry that instead of immediate healing, God gave us something to do that doesn't make sense (2 Kings 5:11–12).

But this is a picture of the type of faith we're meant to have: we believe what God says (his Word), therefore, we follow it in action.

The Word of God is living and active (Romans 4:12), and to follow it is to live and act on it, not simply contemplate its message. We need to contemplate it to know what it says and recognize our Shepherd's voice, but it does not end there.

Had these men not acted on what Jesus told them to do, they wouldn't have been healed, and their faith wouldn't have been built.

The Word of the Lord proves itself to us and builds our faith as we act on it. If we truly trust him, we will do what he says.

"Father, if you are willing, remove this cup from me;
yet not my will, but yours be done."
—Luke 22:42

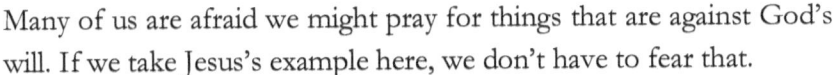

Many of us are afraid we might pray for things that are against God's will. If we take Jesus's example here, we don't have to fear that.

We can pray what we hope as long as we ultimately end with, "yet not my will, but yours be done."

That's not always an easy thing to pray. Even Jesus's experience shows that sometimes God's plan requires that the illness not be cured, the difficulty not be lifted, the thorn not be taken away, and the hurt not be healed in this lifetime. But it also gives us the understanding that he will use the illness, the difficulty, the thorn, and the hurt for good. He will transform our troubles into great good just as Jesus's suffering ushered in the greatest good of all time—our reconciliation to him, the guarantee of complete healing, and infinite joy in eternity with God.

In our prayers, we're like children begging for things which may do them and others very little good in the end. The parent may say no, but the child isn't wrong for asking.

The willingness to trust and obey the answer even if it's against our desire is what's important.

We may still long for the thing, but we can trust God's judgment. Sometimes that may take time and maturity; the child might be an adult before realizing why the father said no to a particular request.

We can never fully know the mind of God, but we will learn to accept even his difficult answers as we come to understand his goodness and love. We can ask for what we hope while yet trusting even his no.

"Never repay evil for evil to anyone. Respect what
is right in the sight of all people."
—Romans 12:17

Our human nature believes that repaying evil for evil is only fair, but God tells us differently.

He says we're to do what is good and honorable despite others' actions and to bless those who persecute us (Romans 12:14).

He says we're to love our enemies (Matthew 5:44) and treat others as we wish to be treated no matter how they treat us (Matthew 7:12).

We think in terms of phrases like, "Turnabout is fair play," "Karma will get them," or—if we do retaliate—"They deserved it."

But it's not for us to exact revenge. Our job is to love despite their wickedness and pray for God to reach them before it's too late, just as he did for us.

Christ is our example, and he gave us grace when we deserved punishment. If we truly understand that and what eternity looks like without the Lord, we will wish for even our most bitter enemies to come to the saving knowledge of him.

We're to leave thoughts of retribution to the Lord, for he says, "Vengeance is mine, and retribution; in due time their foot will slip. For the day of their disaster is near, and the impending things are hurrying to them" (Deuteronomy 32:35).

We pray for their repentance, but we know that for those who remain in their wickedness, the day of disaster is coming. They may prosper for a moment in this life, but that is all the good they will get.

They deserve our compassion rather than our revenge. May we walk in the same love Christ showed as he forgave those who crucified him (Luke 23:34).

"Your ears will hear a word behind you, saying,
'This is the way, walk in it,' whenever you turn to
the right or to the left."
—Isaiah 30:21

Sometimes when we talk about turning to God with every decision, people say things like, "But what about free will? Doesn't God allow us to make our own choices?"

The answer is, "Absolutely." We can always refuse God's path, and he also gives us great freedom within his will.

Much of God's guidance comes not with specific direction—"This is the career you must pursue"—but with nudges to grow spiritually—"This customer service interaction is where you can grow in the Spirit by denying yourself and your right to respond in un-Christlike ways even though you've been wronged."

Our character is more important than the jobs we work.

But the fact remains that we serve an infinite, omnipotent God who knows every winding step our lives will take. Why would we not want to include him in all our day-to-day decisions?

It's not about control; it's about inviting him into our journey and trusting that he is guiding us every step of the way.

We're often uncertain, and we might live in that uncertainty for a time, but God always has a reason for our waiting. The uncertainty often leads us to things we didn't even know to look for.

So if we've been asking, "Which way, Lord?", and not getting an answer, we can trust that he wants us to keep seeking him in that.

The answer will come, and in the meantime, he's leading us to grow deeper in our relationship with him. The more closely we're following him, the better we can hear his voice and recognize the guidance of the Holy Spirit.

"A precious cornerstone for the foundation, firmly placed.
The one who believes in it will not be disturbed."
—Isaiah 28:16

That word "disturbed" literally means "in a hurry" or "make haste."

As we read about the life of Jesus, it seems he was never in a hurry . . . never stressed about how quickly he got to the next place.

He was calm and diligent, but not hasty, anxious, nor constantly concerned about getting to the next thing on the list. It's following this example that leads to peace, confidence, and the work of the Holy Spirit.

We don't have to worry about getting enough done; we simply trust God to give us the time needed to do the things he has for us.

He doesn't want us frantically completing one task before rushing on to the next. He wants us present, settled, and confident in him.

The fruit of hurry is almost always frustration, irritability, stress, anger, sloppy work, and distraction. The list could go on.

It's doubtful if hurrying has ever made us more Christlike or brought out the fruits of the Spirit.

When our lives are full of this kind of hurry, we can know there is a misplaced priority somewhere. We're either committed to tasks the Lord never asked of us, or we're not trusting him to guide us in the work he's given.

If our lives are a whirlwind of hurry, we should take some time and ask God to show us how to change either our responsibilities or our attitudes so that we can be fully in his presence, present for those around us, and available when others need us.

"Therefore be patient, brothers and sisters, until the coming of the Lord. The farmer waits for the precious produce of the soil, being patient about it, until it gets the early and late rains."
—James 5:7

The verses just prior to these are speaking of evil men taking advantage of, cheating, oppressing, and murdering righteous men.

This is to be our attitude when faced with such men—patience like the patience of the farmer who plants and trusts that the Lord will bring the rain and, even when it looks impossible, a nourishing and fruitful harvest.

A bit further on, James 5:11 compares this type of patience to the patience of Job in his suffering: "We count those blessed who endured. You have heard of the endurance of Job and have seen the outcome of the Lord's dealings, that the Lord is full of compassion and is merciful."

Imagine if the farmer didn't trust that planting would eventually bring a good result. Would anyone ever persevere through the months of difficult toil and tending, pests and storms, if they didn't believe something nourishing would come from it?

We must have this kind of hope and patience if we're to endure the hardships and sufferings of this life. The Lord can use even those difficulties to plant something in us, in others, and in the Lord's kingdom; we can trust that his watering Holy Spirit will bring forth good fruit.

The Lord blesses those who endure even when they don't see how the fruit will come. He has compassion and mercy on them. He sees the difficulty and the pain. He hears the cries of the laborers (James 5:4).

Our trouble is a seed being planted, and God will not neglect to water and bring the harvest.

"And I will walk at liberty, for I seek your precepts."
—Psalm 119:45

Many people think following God is just a rigorous list of dos and don'ts. It's true that if we're following God, our obedience necessarily means there are some things we must not do and others that we must.

But in the truest sense, following God means freedom—freedom from man's expectations, from insecurity, from the world's definition of success, and greatest of all, from the slavery of sin and its consequences.

The guidelines God has set aren't made to keep us confined and suppressed but to help us live full lives in his protection.

He's like a parent who gives rules so we will be safe and healthy:

- No, you can't eat more ice cream.
- Don't touch the oven.
- Stay inside the fence.

A child doesn't understand that without these rules, he may be ill, injured, or even killed.

We also don't understand all God's rules, but we're his children, and he put them in place for our good. When we follow them, we are more free to enjoy our lives, not less so.

Satan had Eve looking at the one thing she and Adam couldn't have instead of all the wonderful things they could, and he still tries to deceive by convincing us that God is holding back something good and just wants to control us.

But a good parent doesn't want control for control's sake. They want their children to obey so they are protected from dangers they do not understand and cannot see.

Let's remember that the "do nots" are God's all-knowing hand of protection and keep our eyes on all the freedom he's given us instead.

"For I have had great joy and comfort in your love,
because the hearts of the saints have been refreshed
through you, brother."
—Philemon 1:7

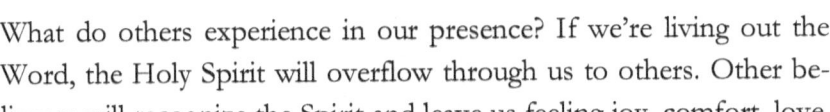

What do others experience in our presence? If we're living out the Word, the Holy Spirit will overflow through us to others. Other believers will recognize the Spirit and leave us feeling joy, comfort, love, and refreshment.

But there are times we drink from the wrong well, and what flows from us becomes tainted. A good way to check this is to consider what effect we're having on fellow believers.

Is it joy, comfort, refreshment, and renewal?

Or is it negativity, stress, and exhaustion?

Do they leave us feeling lighter, encouraged, hopeful, edified, and loved, or do they leave feeling down, fearful, frustrated, anxious, or unseen?

If our own lives are pulling from the wrong source, we need to dig in to discover what well we're drinking from. It may be the well of self-interest, arrogance, fear, fault-finding, complaint, anger, or a wealth of other worldly possibilities.

If we're pulling from broken cisterns that cannot hold water (Jeremiah 2:13) and cannot satisfy, what's missing in our own hearts will be missing from our interactions with others, and what they drink from our presence won't be very refreshing.

But if we quench our thirst with the living water of Jesus and the Word, allowing him to transform us as we study, grow, and obey, what we leave others with will always be joy, comfort, love, and refreshment.

"Taste and see that the Lord is good;
how blessed is the man who takes refuge in him!"
—Psalm 34:8

Notice that living in the Lord's goodness and protection requires action on our part. It is not an accident or something that happens automatically. We must actively taste and intentionally look for the Lord's goodness.

How do we taste? By eating. And we do not eat every once in a while; we eat multiple times a day. Partaking of the Word is an essential part of "tasting" who God is. The more we know of it, the more we know of him.

And knowing who God is fuels our confidence in his goodness; we begin to believe that we can trust him and take refuge in him.

We will not take refuge in a king we do not know and trust; that king might be evil or controlling.

But feeding on the Word reveals to us that the Lord is good, loving, and trustworthy. He doesn't show favoritism, never changes, doesn't lie, has our best in mind, and is willing to sacrifice himself for us.

This is a king we can depend on. If we know all this about him, we can trust that his laws are meant for our good and safety, not to keep us in subjection. We will be confident, then, in following his laws.

If, however, we feel uncertain of God's character and therefore uncertain we can trust his protection, we need to spend some time feeding on the Word. The knowledge that he is good will encourage us to take refuge in him.

"Though he slay me, I will hope in him.
Nevertheless I will argue my ways before him."
—Job 13:15

This is the statement of true faith—that no matter what horror comes in this world, we will trust him.

It's hard to think about the fact that Job is also saying, "Though he slay my children and all the servants in my household, and though he take my livelihood and my health, I will trust him."

All of that had already happened, yet Job remained faithful. He grieved. He cried out, "Why?" He was convinced he would never see good again (Job 7:7).

But he remained faithful.

It's okay to ask God why. It's even okay to complain to and "argue" with him. From Job's story, we see that we can take our hearts to God no matter what's in them as long as in the end, we are faithful to him.

If there is something the Lord could "slay" in this life that would turn us away from him, that thing has mastery over us, and we are making our trust in him dependent upon some earthly circumstance. As long as that's the case, our faith is fickle, because our earthly circumstances are not in our control. Life will always bring things we do not like and would not choose (1 Peter 4:12).

Let us work to defeat the things that hold mastery over our hope and faith in the Lord.

Our hope is firm only when its foundation is Christ himself alone.

"For the Lord sees not as man sees; man looks on the
outward appearance, but the Lord looks on the heart."
—1 Samuel 16:7

This truth is such a comfort because we know the Lord sees our desire
to serve him when it seems the world doesn't notice.

But it's also sobering because we cannot fake a heart for him. What
looks like beautiful service to God to those around us may be flowing
from a heart full of pride or fear of man's opinion. Our motives are
always front and center with the Lord.

Our world is obsessed with how the "outside" things look—
performance, success, appearance, fashion, or the latest décor trends.
But much of the most valuable work can't be seen from the outside,
or perhaps can't be seen from the outside for a very long time.

Our spiritual and emotional growth, our healing from old hurts, and
our integrity in the small things the Lord has given us to do each day
are all largely invisible to those around us. But the Lord sees, and they
are the most important parts of our lives.

Like David—the shepherd boy forgotten in the fields until Samuel
called for him—our lives and work may not be seen or valued by others, but the Lord sees and honors a heart for him.

May we never get so focused on outward appearance that we neglect the heart, and may we be willing to let go of the things that look
impressive to those around us when the pursuit of God requires it.

"For the customs of the peoples are futile; for it is
wood cut from the forest, the work of the hands
of a craftsman with a cutting tool."
—Jeremiah 10:3

We rarely see people building and worshipping actual idols in our culture, but the customs of the world are still futile, and the principles stand. Man crafts an idol with his own hands, then turns around and worships it as if it has some special power. We still do this.

We work hard to build an image of ourselves with wealth, success, or power, then turn around and bow to those things as our protectors, believing they will keep trouble away.

But they won't; they can't. They can be tools and blessings, but they are not gods. They are creations of our own hands and have no power. Our earthly kingdom can crumble at any second regardless of our best efforts at building a safety net; only our relationship with the Lord and our eternal inheritance can be guaranteed. He is our rock and fortress, savior and refuge, our shield and stronghold (Psalm 18:2).

Instead of building a kingdom on the sinking sand of our own handiwork, we can live for things that will not end in futility—building the eternal, unshakeable kingdom by following the Lord's leading, making disciples, and living a life full of the fruit of the Spirit—love, joy, peace, patience, kindness, goodness, faithfulness, gentleness, and self-control.

Following him is the only path to meaning and anything lasting.

"You are the light of the world. A city set on a hill
cannot be hidden; nor do people light a lamp and put it
under a basket, but on the lampstand, and it gives light
to all who are in the house. Your light must shine before
people in such a way that they may see your good works
and glorify your Father who is in heaven."
—Matthew 5:14–16

It's easy to despair as the world grows darker. But have you ever watched a lampstand as a sunny day shifts to dusk and on into night? At first, it's hard to tell whether the light is even on; the brightness of the daylight obscures it and makes it seem unnecessary.

When twilight comes, the lights become noticeable; they no longer blend into the bright background. They might not yet feel crucial; we can still make out enough of the landscape to get by.

But when true darkness comes, the lights become our lifeline. If we're lost in the woods, they lead us home. If we're sailing the seas, they warn us of rocks and land. If we hear a noise, they show us the truth of what's approaching.

When the world is dark, our good works show people the way home to God, warn them when they near danger, and reveal truth when it's hard to tell friend from foe. We reveal the hand of God and shine his hope, protection, and truth out into the world, bringing others to faith in him.

We sometimes despair that no one wants the light, but it's more essential and gleams even brighter when all the world is darkness.

Don't stop shining. When the world is black, people are more aware of their need for the light than ever.

"Is this not the fast that I choose: to release the
bonds of wickedness, to undo the ropes of the yoke,
and to let the oppressed go free, and break every
yoke? Is it not to break your bread with the hungry
and bring the homeless poor into the house; when
you see the naked, to cover him; and not to hide
yourself from your own flesh? Then your light will
break out like the dawn, and your recovery will spring
up quickly; and your righteousness will go before
you; the glory of the Lord will be your rear guard.
Then you will call, and the Lord will answer; you will
cry for help, and he will say, 'Here I am.'"
—Isaiah 58:6–9

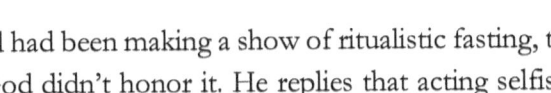

The people of Israel had been making a show of ritualistic fasting, then complaining that God didn't honor it. He replies that acting selfishly, exploiting others, and quarreling with one another is not the way "to make your voice heard on high" (Isaiah 58:3–4).

God doesn't want a religious show. Going to church or reading the Bible doesn't mean anything if we live the rest of our lives treating people with disdain, taking advantage of others, living in anger and un-forgiveness, or ignoring the needs of those around us.

Our prayers fall flat when we—like these people and the Pharisees—follow God's rules without walking in his love and think that is a transaction for which we are owed.

But when his law is written on our hearts and we love him with all our heart, soul, and mind, and love our neighbors as ourselves, the Lord goes before and behind us. He hears and answers.

We find him and his promises as we abide in him.

"But even if I am being poured out as a drink offering
upon the sacrifice and service of your faith,
I rejoice and share my joy with you all."
—Philippians 2:17

If we are to be poured out as a drink offering for the sake of others' faith, we must first be turned into wine.

The grapes must be ripe (mature); they must be crushed, and they must lie alone in the dark until they have fermented.

Have we planted ourselves where we can grow into fruitful vines? Like the psalmist in Psalm 1, are we turning away from walking with sinners and from mocking and insulting others? Do we delight ourselves in and meditate on the law of the Lord day and night? If so, we will be planted securely by the streams, rooted where we can grow ripe and mature. But that's not all.

Then we follow Christ willingly into the winepress to be crushed as he was (Matthew 10:23–25) and to lie dormant in the dark until the appointed time.

Can we be patient in that time in the dark? Can we be glad and rejoice in whatever sacrifice he asks of us, or do we resist his efforts to crush us?

If we allow ourselves to be crushed willingly, we become something that can be poured out for the sake of his kingdom. Being crushed might be painful and our time in the dark may feel hopeless, but as Christians, we know that God is turning us into something more valuable.

Even when we feel helpless and alone, we can rest where he has us and take heart that we are becoming what he intends for the sake of his kingdom and the building up of others' faith.

"Bear one another's burdens,
and thereby fulfill the law of Christ."
—Galatians 6:2

If we're going to bear one another's burdens, we must be in relationship with others so we can see even those burdens that hide in the shadows.

Some may have the burden of sins they have not yet overcome or of difficult relationships. Some have financial burdens or not enough time. Some may be weighed down by the demands of an unreasonable boss, old wounds from those who should've protected them, or grief from loss or unrealized hopes.

How can we help lift these burdens? We can pray and offer our time or money. Cook a meal or mow a yard. Send a message to check in on someone when they come to mind or ask them to coffee or lunch. We can simply look for ways to help, be a listening ear, and be present in their lives. It doesn't have to be complicated. We don't have to have super-strength or special talents to help bear one another's burdens. We just have to be willing, intentional, and available.

Through bearing others' burdens, we enrich our own lives of community and build the body of Christ. But this is also our duty as believers because, "By this all people will know that you are my disciples: if you have love for one another" (John 13:35).

This is the evidence to the world that we are Jesus's disciples and how we fulfill the law of Christ. We live out his purposes in and through us—continuing his work of bringing good news to the poor, proclaiming release to captives, bringing sight to the blind, and setting free those who are oppressed (Luke 4:18).

"Therefore I love your commandments above gold, yes,
above pure gold. Therefore I carefully follow all your
precepts concerning everything, I hate every false way.
Your testimonies are wonderful; therefore my soul
complies with them. The unfolding of your words gives
light; it gives understanding to the simple."
—Psalm 119:127–130

Most of us view God's commandments the way a toddler views broccoli—a necessary unpleasantness if we want to get dessert (heaven).

If we follow them, it's often with half-hearted reluctance.

So it can feel impossible to live the words of this psalm.

It isn't.

The closer we get to the Lord, the more clearly we see his commandments through his heart of love, compassion, provision, and gentle care.

He's not trying to squelch our fun with commandments; he wants to free us from ourselves, give us abundant life, and take our heavy burdens. The broccoli is not only the path to dessert; it gives us the ability to live a full, spiritually healthy life now.

Once we come to see his immeasurable worth, we will not give up his commandments for all the gold in the world. Even the psalmist knows it sounds so unlikely that he repeats it. "Yes! Above pure gold!"

We do begin to "hate every false way" as we recognize their falsehood contrasted with the Lord's truth which we "carefully follow." When we see how wonderful his testimonies are, it becomes far easier for our souls to comply with them.

And no matter how confusing the world may be, unfolding his words lights our path. It gives understanding even to those who shouldn't be able to understand.

His way is truly the best way, and the more we know him, the more we will be able to live that out.

"This is what the Lord says: 'Stand by the ways and see
and ask for the ancient paths, where the good way is, and
walk in it; then you will find a resting place for your souls.
But they said, 'We will not walk in it.'"
—Jeremiah 6:16

Many of us wish God would point us in a direction.

But there's a good way he has already mapped out in his Word, and so often, we say, "I will not walk in it."

"I won't give up this sin. I won't stop building my own kingdom. I will continue to trust in or seek riches. I can't trust you in these circumstances; I must continue trying to pursue my own desires. I will not put you first in my life, Lord."

Often, we resist because we don't believe God will give us what we want. But as we walk his good way, our wants are transformed. We find he gives us the grace and tools to be content in some circumstance we once found unbearable, even if the situation itself is unchanged.

Or perhaps we resist because we want practical steps instead of vague precepts—straightforward answers on what to study, where to work, where to live, or how to parent. As we walk the Lord's path, his direction in even these things becomes increasingly clear as we submit to the Holy Spirit.

The rest for our souls appears when we walk in his good way. When we lose our lives, we find them (Matthew 10:39).

May we, like Abraham, begin to walk where the Lord directs even when we don't know the destination (Hebrews 11:8); God will illumine all the other steps as we go.

"But the Helper, the Holy Spirit whom the Father
will send in my name, he will teach you all things,
and remind you of all that I said to you."
—John 14:26

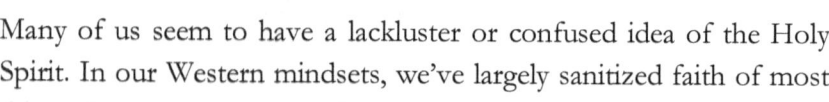

Many of us seem to have a lackluster or confused idea of the Holy Spirit. In our Western mindsets, we've largely sanitized faith of most things that seem supernatural.

Much of this attitude is founded upon fear. Someone could say the Holy Spirit taught them almost anything. But this verse clearly says the Holy Spirit will "teach us all things," in addition to reminding us of things we've learned from the Word.

Of course, we should always test things to see if they align with Scripture. If they are contrary in any way, we can dismiss them immediately, but we should not dismiss them simply because we're afraid they may be false. We are not to "quench the Spirit" nor to "utterly reject prophecies," though we are to examine them closely and only hold on to what will bear good, godly fruit (1 Thessalonians 5:19–21).

Everything has the potential to be misused and misunderstood. Removing our acceptance of the Holy Spirit's interactive presence inside of us has not kept people from misusing the Bible itself, including Jesus's words, over the centuries.

But removing our belief that the Holy Spirit will speak to us has given us a lonely faith, full of head-knowledge but very little relationship. Perhaps it's even one of the failings that has pushed so many people to spiritualism rather than Christianity. People don't want the dry version of faith they see in many churches; they want an interactive, personal God.

They want to know and be known by the God who sees and cares for each of us individually (Genesis 16:13).

"The Lord is near to all who call on him,
to all who call on him in truth."
—Psalm 145:18

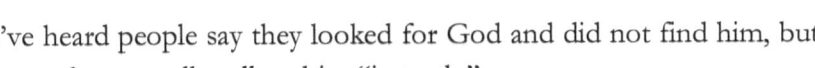

I've heard people say they looked for God and did not find him, but many do not really call on him "in truth."

They call on him searching for something else—comfort or ease in this life or something that makes them feel good but doesn't really require anything of them—and when it doesn't come in the way they want it to, they stop calling and stop seeking.

Many people want a comfortable, impersonal God who won't disturb their lives too much rather than a personal one who is intricately involved in ordering our steps each day and who has a say in what we do or don't do.

When Jesus came, he was rejected by the Jews because he didn't do what people thought he would—give them earthly freedom from their Roman oppressors. He was there to give them something much greater—freedom from their own slavery to self and sin. They couldn't see it and chose not to listen to him, because they weren't calling on him in truth. They were calling for him to take care of their personal agendas and to make their lives what they thought they should be from a human perspective.

They didn't want to be reminded of their personal responsibility; they just wanted the good life.

When we really search and call in truth, we will find God. But if we search and call with our own expectation of what God should be or do, we will find either nothing or—a possibility that's even more alarming—something else.

We must call on God for his own sake.

"And yet Jesus Himself was in the stern, asleep on
the cushion; and they woke him and said to him,
'Teacher, do you not care that we are perishing?'
And he got up and rebuked the wind and said to
the sea, 'Hush, be still.' And the wind died down
and it became perfectly calm. And he said to
them, 'Why are you afraid? Do you still have no
faith?' They became very much afraid and said to
one another, 'Who, then, is this, that even the
wind and the sea obey Him?'"
—Mark 4:38–41

There are many troubles in this life, but the Lord can bring us safely through them all.

Perhaps, like the disciples here, we fear when the storm comes. It looks like God isn't paying attention, and we start to think he doesn't care.

And perhaps, like them, we haven't yet come to understand who this God is, and his power is more frightening than calming. Perhaps we think him untrustworthy. If we can't yet trust him, we need to spend some time getting to know his goodness and faithfulness.

Because once we truly grasp that the infinite, all-knowing, fully loving God who made the universe is in our boat, we can relax.

We don't have to fear. There will be storms, and there will be times when they go on longer and get worse than we'd like, but we can endure in faith knowing that in his time, he will bring us out of our distress, still the storm, hush the waves, and guide us to our desired harbor (Psalm 107:30).

When God is in the boat, our destination is never in doubt.

"Finally then, brothers and sisters, we request and urge
you in the Lord Jesus, that as you received instruction
from us as to how you ought to walk and please God (just
as you actually do walk), that you excel even more."
—1 Thessalonians 4:1

We have this idea that the closer we get to God, the less growth we will need in the way of character and obedience. The truth is that as we walk with the Lord, we will learn there are always ways to do so even more over time.

The closer we get to him, the more we see the sins that are ingrained in our hearts and not only evident in our actions.

Just as we wouldn't notice a speck of dirt at the edge of a mud pile, we often don't see our specks of sin until the most glaring mounds have already been cleared away by Christ's redemptive power and our obedience to him.

Once those are gone, the Holy Spirit shows us things we never realized were rebellion—the different ways we love poorly, the attitudes that do not glorify him, or the things we do only to impress others.

We may find that our selfishness, pride, unforgiveness, resentment, and impatience are more deeply embedded than the things others can see from the outside.

This is not cause for frustration, but a continual reminder guiding us into deeper humility and closer to the heart of God. As Paul says, we have not attained, but we press on (Philippians 4:12–14), confess, and know he will cleanse us from all unrighteousness (1 John 1:9) as we endure for the prize that awaits us (Philippians 3:14).

"But God demonstrates his own love toward us, in that
while we were still sinners, Christ died for us."
—Romans 5:8

As believers, we're not given the option to wait until people are loveable before we start loving them. First John 4:10–11 repeats this idea, "In this is love, not that we loved God, but that he loved us and sent his son to be the propitiation for our sins. Beloved, if God so loved us, we also ought to love one another."

And this is how: we're to love our enemies even when they hate us and are still walking in sin. We're to pray for those who abuse us (Matthew 5:44) and to love as God loves, despite all the reasons people may give us not to.

This displays to the world that we are followers of Christ (Matthew 5:45–48; 1 John 4:20–21). And seeing this Christlike love is often a key to others understanding the love of our Savior and coming to their own salvation in him.

So when we're faced with that person who is still in sin—that unsupportive spouse or parent, the negligent customer service worker, the rebellious child, the unreasonable boss, or the people in power who oppress others or work to thwart justice—may we remember that we can stand for truth in love as Jesus did.

He was not a pushover, nor did he endorse sin and wrong behavior, but he extended an invitation of relationship and peace while speaking truth and living love.

"Then those who sing as well as those who play the flutes
will say, 'All my springs of joy are in you.'"
—Psalm 87:7

As believers in Christ, all of us are to be fountains flowing with rivers
of living water (John 7:37–39), but I love that this verse specifically
speaks of creativity.

God chose to validate the work of the singers and flute players—
some versions say dancers—and this shows us that these are worthy
acts of worship. In our commercialized society, creatives are often made
to feel like their work is tangential to "real life" and isn't important or
meaningful.

This verse reminds us that God is the one who fuels that creativity.

It's also a wonderful reminder that if our creative springs run empty,
he is the only place to go for renewal. All the joy and inspiration comes
from him, and without him, the springs will run dry.

We will become stagnant, and stagnant pools do not produce
beauty. They quickly begin to stink, and algae takes over, eventually
making the water unsafe to drink. They become breeding grounds for
mosquitos, and the fish often become oxygen deprived.

In the same way, a spiritual life not fueled by the Lord will be stagnant and cause us to:

- feel stuck in our lives or creativity.
- see pests begin to take over (unchecked thoughts and feelings of
  doubt, bitterness, etc.).
- be overrun by invasive plants (sin).
- become toxic and life-draining rather than life-giving to those
  around us.
- feel like we can't breathe and have no energy to give.

When this happens, there's only one place to go—back to the springs
of living water which flow through us by the power of the Holy Spirit.

"Behold, now is 'a favorable time,'
behold, now is 'a day of salvation.'"
—2 Corinthians 6:2

"Now" is always the favorable time and the day of salvation, because now is all we ever have. If we will not come now, when? If we will not serve now, when?

Our human nature says we will do so in the future, but that future will be our now when we get there, and we will keep saying the same thing. We can only commit and serve the Lord now.

He is here with us always, ever ready to receive and save; it is not his will that any should perish, but that all should come to repentance (2 Peter 3:9). But we never know when our soul will be required of us (Luke 12:20). This current "now" is the only one we're guaranteed.

If we believe the Lord's salvation is true and that we need to repent and follow, we must believe all else Christ said. We must know that it is worth repenting now and that he is worth following now. Jesus came to save the world (John 3:17), to give us the power to become the children of God (John 1:12), to give us abundant life (John 10:10), and to live in this current world with his overcoming power (1 John 5:4). He wants to give us not only an eternity of salvation, but a life that's worth living now—one full of meaning, hope, and purpose.

Tomorrow is not the day of salvation. Today is. This moment we're living in can be the turning point from which we begin to follow him in every now from here to eternity.

> "This is what the Lord says: 'Make this valley full of trenches.' For the Lord says this: 'You will not see wind, nor will you see rain; yet that valley shall be filled with water, so that you will drink, you, your livestock, and your other animals. And this is an insignificant thing in the sight of the Lord; he will also give the Moabites into your hand."
> —2 Kings 3:16–18

We often can't see how God is going to work. We look for signs, but they don't come. And then he tells us to do something—to take action even in the middle of our need.

Maybe our stream is dry. We're thirsting to death, and we desperately want to believe he's doing something, but we don't see any evidence of him at all.

Then the Holy Spirit prompts us to step out in faith—to expend energy that is already sorely lacking—to forgive out of a broken spirit, to feed someone else from a bare pantry, or to serve someone out of an already overcrowded schedule.

But we step out in obedience and see his promises fulfilled; we dug the trenches, and he filled them, quenching our thirst and sending sustenance.

God himself is the living water, and we don't have to wonder if he's working behind the scenes. His Word tells us that he is. We can count on that and choose to live by faith rather than by sight.

He is a gift-giving, generous God, and he wants to guide, provide for, and protect us.

This is not challenging for him; what seems miraculous to us is an "insignificant thing" to the Lord.

Dry trenches, and even dangerous enemies, cannot overcome his promises, goodness, and provision for those who love him.

"Therefore when Jesus had received the sour wine,
he said, 'It is finished!' And he bowed his head
and gave up his spirit."
—John 19:30

When Jesus died, it felt like everything was over. There was no coming back from that.

But like the seed that falls to the earth and dies in order to bear fruit (John 12:24), Jesus's death was not the end.

If the seed were aware, its falling to the ground would feel like there was no hope. There was no chance to become anything; its life was over. It would feel like it was being buried in death when it was really being planted for life.

Sometimes circumstances in our lives make us feel like everything is over. There's no chance of revival, redemption, or renewal. Hope is dead, and it feels like the end.

But what did Jesus say on the cross? He didn't say, "This is the end," but rather, "It is finished."

We say, "It is finished," not at a hopeless end, but at the completion of a plan.

Perhaps we could learn to say, "It is finished," when we lose the job, lose the loved one, or lose our health. This is the planting. We may not be able to see how life will come of it, but we can trust that just like it seemed too late when Jesus died, it's never too late for him to bring life out of death.

We can bow our heads and say in faith, "It is finished," and know, despite the agony of the moment, that his ways are higher, and his thoughts are higher.

Remember that what feels like an ending might be a completion ushering in something new.

> "'If you can do anything, take pity on us, and help us!' But
> Jesus said to him, "'If you can?" All things are possible for
> the one who believes.' Immediately the boy's father cried
> out and said, 'I do believe; help my unbelief!'"
> —Mark 9:23–24

We often come to the Lord in prayer, desperate for him to work.

But even as we pray, we hear the echoes of that phrase, "...for the one who believes," and we fear that isn't us. We feel the doubt rising, unwanted, in our minds.

That is no cause for despair. The honesty of this man's, "I do believe; help my unbelief!" didn't result in Jesus's reprimand or refusal.

As a good parent rejoices at a toddler's first steps though they are anything but steady, Jesus rejoices at our efforts to trust him. The man's feeble attempt was not a failure, but the first step to building a sturdy and consistent faith.

This shows us what to do with our unwanted thoughts and feelings. We don't ignore or hide them; we take them straight to Jesus and lay them at his feet.

Whether we're dealing with unbelief, unforgiveness, comparison, bitterness, selfishness, or any other thing that may hinder our walk with him, we take it to God and ask for its opposite. "I choose to be joyful; Lord, help my bitterness."

We can act in obedience even where our feelings don't yet follow.

We may take many faltering steps. We often take those wrong things back from God and have to give them to him over and over between our stumblings.

But the quicker and the more often we submit to the Holy Spirit, the more natural it becomes to live in belief, forgiveness, generosity, mercy, and compassion.

> "So Peter, upon seeing him, said to Jesus,
> 'Lord, and what about this man?' Jesus said to
> him, 'If I want him to remain until I come,
> what is that to you? You follow me!'"
> —John 21:21–22

Jesus had just told Peter he was going to be martyred, and Peter's first response was to look back at John and ask, "Well, what about him?"

How often do we look at others and wonder what God has planned for them and how that compares to what he has for us? When we're on a difficult path, we look around to compare other peoples' journeys to ours. We want to see if it's fair or not.

Jesus makes it clear here that everyone's life will be different. What he has for someone else cannot determine what he has for us. The life of faith requires that we follow him in our circumstances, not theirs.

If we keep our eyes on others' journeys, we will destroy ourselves with either envy—believing they have an easier or better road—or pride—thinking our easier or better road is somehow a result of our merit. Both of these will cause us to lose our way.

Our only good path as believers is to keep our eyes on Jesus and to stay in step with where he leads us. That way, whatever it means for us in this life, leads to an eternal inheritance of joy with him.

No matter what anyone else's life looks like, our job is to follow Jesus. The destination will always be worth it.

"Cast all your anxiety on him, because he cares about you. Be
of sober spirit, be on the alert. Your adversary, the devil,
prowls around like a roaring lion, seeking someone to devour."
—1 Peter 5:7–8

Peter tells us to cast our anxiety on the Lord then immediately says something that may incite anxiety—that a violent enemy seeks to devour us.

But God doesn't leave us alone in this. "The eyes of the Lord roam throughout the earth, so that he may strongly support those whose heart is completely his" (2 Chronicles 16:9).

We can cast our cares on God because while Satan is seeking someone to devour, the Lord is seeking the righteous in order to give them strong support. He wants to give aid to his children.

Peter also connects the importance of casting our anxiety on God, because anxiety makes us easier prey. When fear and anxiety steer us, we often:

- react to others and difficulty in harmful ways (Genesis 12:10–20).
- seek to fulfill expectations in our own way when think God is withholding something or not acting on our timeline (Genesis 3:1–7; 1 Samuel 13:10–13).
- refuse to do what God asks instead of being fruitful (Matthew 13:22; Matthew 25:24–30).
- cower before evil instead of standing up to it (Matthew 10:28).

When our hope is placed firmly in the Lord's care, we're much better situated to resist the devil.

God is our protection, and as sheep must follow near their shepherd in order not to be devoured, we also must, "Submit therefore to God. But resist the devil, and he will flee from you" (James 4:7).

Satan can't devour us if we actively resist him and submit to the voice of our Shepherd.

"But when he who had set me apart even from my
mother's womb and called me through his grace was
pleased to reveal his Son in me so that I might preach
him among the Gentiles, I did not immediately consult
with flesh and blood nor did I go up to Jerusalem to
those who were apostles before me; but I went away."
—Galatians 1:15–17

Just as God had work prepared for Paul since before he was born, there
is work specifically designed and prepared for each of us (Ephesians
2:10). These good works might be in the public eye like speaking—
preaching and teaching—or they might be more behind the scenes in
general service—hospitality, bearing one another's burdens, or caring
for the poor and oppressed (1 Peter 4:10–11).

Whatever they are, sometimes our callings look strange to those
around us, but before we consult with flesh and blood, we need to go
away and sit at Christ's feet.

There are those, even in our Christian community, who will prize
what makes sense over devotion to God's call, because the call isn't
theirs. It's ours. People probably told Abraham he was foolish to walk
out when he didn't know where he was going. It didn't make sense for
Peter to try fishing again when he hadn't caught anything all night, nor
to walk on water. Gathering a child's lunch to feed a crowd of five
thousand looks foolish from every angle.

There are certainly times we need to consult others for wisdom, but
there are also times when we know we've received the call of God, and
we need to stop worrying whether it makes sense or not.

We just need to start walking in obedience to that calling despite
what others think.

"I have given them your word; and the world has hated
them because they are not of the world, just as I am not
of the world. I am not asking you to take them out of the
world, but to keep them away from the evil one."
—John 17:14–15

———————◆———————

"I am not of this world." We often look at that verse and think of the
things it keeps us from—our necessary separation from many of the
things the world tells us are good or fun.

But the truth of this verse is that we can look at it and think, "What
a relief!" To not be embroiled in the cares and toils, the scrambling to
get ahead, or the backbiting and selfishness is a supreme gift the Lord
has given us.

We are still in this world, and those things still exist, but we do not
have to become entangled in them. When we walk with the Holy Spirit,
we can allow ourselves to be hated without care or concern, just as
Jesus did. We can live this life without worrying whether we will become successful or achieve the milestones society tells us are necessary.
The cares and toils, the scrambling to get ahead, and the backbiting
and selfishness may be all around us, but we do not have to be "of"
them, because we are not of this world.

May the Lord keep us from the evil one indeed, that we not be
turned away from him by affliction or dragged back into the cares of
this world and the deceitfulness of riches (Matthew 13:18–23). We can
live in rest, peace, and hope no matter the trials or what we lack.

"Who may ascend onto the hill of the Lord?
And who may stand in his holy place? One who has
clean hands and a pure heart, who has not lifted up his
soul to deceit and has not sworn deceitfully."
—Psalm 24:3–4

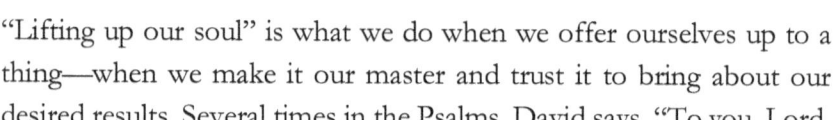

"Lifting up our soul" is what we do when we offer ourselves up to a thing—when we make it our master and trust it to bring about our desired results. Several times in the Psalms, David says, "To you, Lord, I lift up my soul" (Psalm 25:1; Psalm 86:4; Psalm 143:8).

It's easy to lift our souls up to false things, to hope in our own schemes and plans instead of lifting up our souls to the Lord and trusting him. We want to control the outcomes.

But when we trust ourselves and lift up our souls to other things to attempt our purposes and find fulfillment, we guarantee a lesser good and less satisfaction. When we lift up our souls to anything but the Lord, we "labor in vain" (Psalm 127:1).

Psalm 24:7 goes on to say, "Lift up your heads, you gates, and be lifted up, you ancient doors, that the King of glory may come in!"

Lifting up our souls and heads to him is an invitation giving our Lord full access to our lives. And when we invite him, the King of glory will come. He will guide and lead us to his own holy place; our own purposes are guaranteed no such grand outcomes, but in him, we have a sure hope that will not fail.

Let us turn our souls and heads away from the false, deceitful hopes and to the only sure one—God himself.

"Therefore, as you have received Christ Jesus the Lord, so
walk in him, having been firmly rooted and now being
built up in him and established in your faith, just as you
were instructed, and overflowing with gratitude."
—Colossians 2:6–7

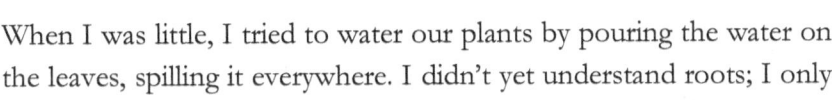

When I was little, I tried to water our plants by pouring the water on the leaves, spilling it everywhere. I didn't yet understand roots; I only understood the plant by what I could see of it with my own eyes.

We often do the same thing in our Christian lives, spending all our time "watering the leaves." We focus on the parts of us that are seen while never actually nourishing our roots. All of that is fruitless, spilling our effort in useless activity.

We'll never grow strong and fruitful except by abiding in the vine (John 15). We must be "rooted and built up" in Jesus—attending to the unseen parts of ourselves by spending time in the Word, praying, studying, praising, living gratefully, taking our thoughts captive, working to heal from past hurts, and being transformed by the renewing of our minds.

When we tend the roots, sometimes the plant itself might look a bit scraggly for a while, and it may be a long time before that plant is able to bear fruit. But the alternative is painting the leaves green and hanging fake fruit on them. This might make us look healthy to other people, but we'll be withering away inside, and we can't keep that up for long.

No one can see our roots, but they make all the difference in our real spiritual health. We need to stop trying to fake the health of our leaves by managing only our outward behavior, and start checking that we're rooted in Christ.

"And he has said to me, 'My grace is sufficient for you,
for power is perfected in weakness.' Most gladly,
therefore, I will rather boast about my weaknesses, so
that the power of Christ may dwell in me."
—2 Corinthians 12:9

When we're confronted with hardship and difficulty, when we come face to face with our enemies, and when we know that our skills are not enough for the Lord's work, we can rest on this verse.

We can practice, learn, and become better at some things, and we can always turn to the Lord for protection and provision, but externally, we'll never have everything the world tells us we need to succeed at God's work or be all the world tells us we should be.

That's okay. Where we lack is where God's power shines. We don't have to be good at that thing; our inabilities don't mean God can't work through us. We don't have to be concerned at the obstacles in our way; God will make a way where there is no way. If it's a task God's given us to do, we can trust that our weakness allows him to work all the more for his kingdom.

We can, in fact, boast in our weaknesses (2 Corinthians 12:9): "Look how God worked despite my ineptitude, lack of knowledge, and all the people coming against his work. Clearly, this work was done through his power!"

So we don't have to dread those things that shine a spotlight on our inabilities or fear those problems that seem insurmountable; we can look forward to them expectantly, trusting that God will work through our weakness.

What we do need is submission and obedience to the tasks God puts in front of us. Everything good comes through his strength.

"For a day in your courtyards is better than a thousand elsewhere. I would rather stand at the threshold of the house of my God than live in the tents of wickedness."
—Psalm 84:10

Can you remember the best day you've ever had or even imagine one better? Now contemplate what it would be like to have a year's worth of similarly amazing days. Three-hundred and sixty-five days of fellowship, fun, accomplishment, and joy sounds incredible. But even that—if it were possible (and it isn't)—wouldn't compare to what awaits us when we reach heaven.

The best day in this life is a mere shadow compared to what we'll experience in eternity, and being a servant in heaven is better than any other existence, no matter what power or fleshly pleasure might come with it.

As believers, we never have to live in the fear of missing out. When we reach eternity, any imaginable joy we did not experience on this earth will seem like a dream.

We will not think, "I wish I'd gotten the chance to do that one thing!" We will see how silly it was that we worried about anything this world could offer when we had all the glories of heaven awaiting us!

The days and years seem long in the middle of our struggle, but one day in heaven will make up for all. If we could fathom that now, we would never be tempted away from the Lord by the things of this life.

Unceasing, unfathomable joy awaits us!

"For where jealousy and selfish ambition exist,
there is disorder and every evil thing."
—James 3:16

We can want things, and we can have ambition, but we have a problem when the wanting things turns to jealousy and comparison, the ambition turns selfish, or either becomes more important to us than the Lord.

Jealousy and selfish ambition create rifts between us and those around us, affecting how we see and relate to them.

They will cause discontentment, insecurity, arguments, and tension in our relationships, jobs, and hearts. They will tempt us to oppress those beneath us, creating "disorder and every evil thing." And if we advance in the world, the problems we can potentially create become bigger and bigger as we gain ability, acclaim, and power.

Jealousy and selfish ambition are steeped in comparison—bringing us satisfaction or dissatisfaction in turn depending on how we measure up to those around us. They make us happy when we prove we're doing better than others—when we have more power, notoriety, talent, intelligence, or money than the majority.

Anywhere we're pleased that someone else has less—whether that is a less impressive house, job, achievement, less interest and attention from others, or any other number of things we may name—we've entered into jealousy and selfish ambition. This is not of God; it's not considering one another as more important than ourselves with humility as Philippians 2:3 commands us.

We shouldn't measure our lives by man's esteem or worldly success. We know these standards are broken and change with the wind. We can rejoice at being last when we follow the Lord, because he says that the last will be first (Matthew 20:16).

MARCH 1

"God is not a man, that he would lie, nor a son of man, that he would change his mind; has he said, and will he not do it? Or has he spoken, and will he not make it good?"
—Numbers 23:19

God will always do what he says, but it's often not on our timeline. It's easy to lose heart, think we misheard, and grow weary.

Our seasons of waiting may grow long. Joseph was in slavery and prison for thirteen years. Abraham and Sarah waited twenty-five empty years for their promised son. Moses was a shepherd for forty years before God brought him back to the task of freeing the Israelites from slavery in Egypt—a task at which Moses had likely long since believed he'd failed.

Our job in the waiting is to follow him faithfully. We don't yet have what we hope for, but we wait for the Lord in patience (Romans 8:24).

I think of godly patience as waiting with trust. We long for the promise, and often we can't see how God could possibly fulfill it. That's why we need hope and faith . . . neither would be necessary if God always acted on our timeline. So we continue our journey, knowing that he is in control, he loves us, wants good for us, and cannot lie.

If we're still waiting, let's not give up or grow bitter. We can remember his promise and rest upon it, living the lives we have faithfully following him even when it feels like slavery, prison, emptiness, or failure.

The fulfillment of the promise is always worth the wait.

> "If possible, so far as it depends on you,
> be at peace with all people."
> —Romans 12:18

It's not always possible to live at peace with everyone, but it is possible to live by the "so far as it depends on us" part.

This doesn't mean we have to keep silent about what is right and wrong, but it does mean we're discerning about when we speak and when we don't. Sometimes the Holy Spirit will prompt us to keep silent and sometimes to speak the truth gently in love.

Many disagreements occur because people—even Christians—show no indication that either party is trying to live peaceably. Sadly, many times, both are simply trying to win an argument or get their way by any means necessary. It's rare to find a sincere debate where people really want to know and learn truth or a sincere discussion where people are showing respect and love, wanting the end to bring understanding, peace, and restoration of relationship.

There are about a thousand ways this verse can play out—in arguments about faith, in marriages, in jobs, or in parenting. In all, the key is being intentional about living peaceably. We do not fall to the level of those who are acting in division, hate, fear, control, or selfishness. We remain loving and kind no matter how we're being treated so all our words and actions continue to honor God and have the potential to draw others to him.

There are probably people in each of our lives with whom we could live more peaceably as far as it concerns us. Let's evaluate ourselves carefully and see how we can take steps in that direction.

"But Mary treasured all these things,
pondering them in her heart."
—Luke 2:19

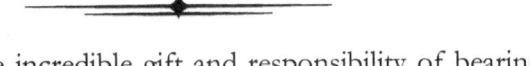

Mary was given the incredible gift and responsibility of bearing and mothering the Son of God.

She could've thought, "God gave me this task; it's my job to get the word out. I've got to give Jesus a good start for his ministry."

If she'd lived in today's society, people would've been pressuring her to create social media accounts, build up a following, get an audience, and make sure everybody knew about this big thing happening in the kingdom of God.

But Mary simply submitted to the Lord's will, treasured the message, and privately pondered the task she'd been given.

God didn't need her publicity; he only needed her obedience.

If the Lord has given us something to do, we may start adding a lot of other tasks he hasn't asked of us. Others may make us feel like we can't fulfill God's calling unless we do all these other things as well.

But maybe those things aren't part of our calling, and they'll simply leave us bogged down, discouraged, and drained.

We can be encouraged that it's enough to simply be obedient, treasure the calling God's given us, ponder what happens in our hearts, and leave the rest to God.

Let's make sure we're attentive to what the Lord has for us and not all the extra tasks the world may pile on top of it. The Lord will complete the work he begins in us.

"Looking only at Jesus, the originator and perfecter of
the faith, who for the joy set before him endured the
cross, despising the shame, and has sat down at the right
hand of the throne of God. For consider him who has
endured such hostility by sinners against himself,
so that you will not grow weary and lose heart."
—Hebrews 12:2–3

Jesus is both the foundation of our initial faith, and the one who makes it possible to move forward.

We look to him so that we can continue this life of faith in a troubled world without giving up or giving in. He can sympathize with every pain and every temptation (Hebrews 4:15).

We see in his life the pain, hostility, and shame he endured, and we can follow his example when we experience the same, because we know that both the joy and the purpose set before us are worth the battle.

Jesus did not let that pain, hostility, and shame make him question the path God put him on. He looked to the joy set before him and did not falter or hesitate no matter the difficult road. His example shows us victory not in spite of but through and because of that difficult road. His cross was his victory.

If you're enduring suffering and disgrace right now, hold fast to the Word of God. Endure to the end, for, as Christians, all our difficulty will be turned into triumph, and the victory gained through that suffering is worth everything that comes along the way. There is joy coming.

"The Lord's bond-servant must not be quarrelsome, but be kind
to all, skillful in teaching, patient when wronged, with gentleness
correcting those who are in opposition, if perhaps God may
grant them repentance leading to the knowledge of the truth,
and they may come to their senses and escape from the snare of
the devil, having been held captive by him to do his will."
—2 Timothy 2:24–26

Our human nature is to see enemies in those who don't live according
to biblical principles, but this verse tells us how we should and should
not treat them.

We should be kind, skillful in teaching, patient when wronged, and
gentle in correction. We should not be quarrelsome.

Why? So perhaps those people who are captive to the devil will
come to the same repentance and saving knowledge of Jesus Christ we
did. We were just like them before salvation (1 Corinthians 6:11).

God knows that argumentative, confrontational behavior doesn't
persuade hearts. Skilled teaching presented with kindness, patience,
and gentleness does.

The phrase "skillful in teaching" implies that we have studied and
practiced. This isn't something we leave to chance. We study to ensure
that our words are true (2 Timothy 2:15). We grow in grace—which
will help with the kindness, patience, and gentleness part—and in
knowledge—which will help with the skilled teaching (2 Peter 3:18).

With these verses in mind, next time we encounter someone who
is living unbiblically or even opposing biblical truth, let us respond with:

- kindness instead of hate.
- skilled teaching instead of hasty words.
- patience instead of irritation, even if we've been mocked or insulted.
- gentleness instead of harshness, even if someone is wrong.

This is how to free people from the lies of the devil and draw them to
Christ.

"But as for me, my feet came close to stumbling,
my steps had almost slipped. For I was envious of the
arrogant as I saw the prosperity of the wicked."
—Psalm 73:2–3

It's easy to stumble and slip when we look around at people who aren't serving God yet seem like they're doing so well.

"Where are my blessings?" we think. "Why am I even trying if it's all in vain and my reward looks more like punishment?" (Psalm 73:12–13).

The answer comes later in the chapter, and the author finds it by spending time with the Lord: "It was troublesome in my sight until I entered the sanctuary of God" (Psalm 73:16–17).

Those people may prosper in this life, but their end is eternal destruction (Psalm 73:17–29). But as faithful believers, no matter what difficulties we face here, our eternal destination is joy in the presence of the Lord (Psalm 73:23–28).

When we look around, start to wonder where God is, and become tempted to follow the way of the wicked, may we take those fears and thoughts to the Lord. It's in his presence that we'll be reminded of truth and his goodness.

This world is not our home. All the rewards of this earth will be meaningless once we hit heaven and useless if we're not part of God's family.

If we believe our rewards should be earthly, we're in danger of stumbling and slipping. The Lord is our strength to resist that temptation, and he is our incorruptible portion (Psalm 73:26), both in this life and the next.

"I urge you, brothers and sisters, by the mercies
of God, to present your bodies as a living and
holy sacrifice, acceptable to God, which is
your spiritual service of worship."
—Romans 12:1

———————◆———————

We often make a distinction between the spiritual and the physical, separating the things we do in the service of the kingdom of God from the things we must do in the day-to-day. This is just one of the verses that reminds us they are inextricably connected.

What we do in and with our bodies every day either glorifies God as spiritual worship . . . or it doesn't. Everything we do from the moment we wake up till the moment we fall asleep can be worship.

And we aren't talking about over-spiritualizing the mundane. We don't have to over-spiritualize it, because we can glorify God by working hard (Colossians 3:23–24), by showing integrity in the small, daily tasks before us (Luke 16:10), by helping others without grumbling (1 Peter 4:9), and by abstaining from the things that do not glorify God (1 Thessalonians 5:22–23).

It's easy to think of our verse only in the context of making sure we don't displease God in what we do in our bodies, and that matters, but there is also the beauty of the Lord giving purpose and value to the ordinary tasks we do every day. Those things are living sacrifice and spiritual worship.

Many of us feel we aren't doing anything important with our lives, but this is God telling us it's all important.

So let's go about our days joyfully, knowing that everything from the dishes to going to work to reading our kids a bed-time story can be an act of worship.

"The wind blows where it wishes, and you hear
the sound of it, but you do not know where it is
coming from and where it is going; so is everyone
who has been born of the Spirit."
—John 3:8

The world prescribes a formula for our lives. It's the commonsense equation that everyone thinks "works." If you do "A" and then "B," you will get "C."

And "C" usually equals (we hope) a predictable, comfortable existence in this life.

But is that what we're called to as Christians? To follow the world's formula and hope it works?

This verse reminds us that God has more for us than a worldly plan and a predictable life.

He wants us to follow him, and like Abraham, that sometimes means we will go out with no idea where we're headed (Hebrews 11:8).

If God has been calling us in a direction that seems scary or risky, and we've been hedging, it's time to listen. If we're impulsive by nature, we need to spend enough time in prayer to know this is not just our own next harebrained schemes. We run it by some trusted Christian advisors. But we test even their advice to determine whether they are operating under worldly mindsets, simply telling us what we want to hear, or could be influenced by their own fear of the unknown rather than helping us hear the Holy Spirit.

We operate our lives based on obedience to Christ rather than worldly wisdom.

God's path might have us living a life that is not predictable or comfortable, but it will be more full of kingdom purpose than we ever could've dreamed.

"Jesus answered, 'My kingdom is not of this world. If my
kingdom were of this world, my servants would be
fighting so that I would not be handed over to the Jews;
but as it is, my kingdom is not of this realm.'"
—John 18:36

◆

Many people—both in Jesus's time and now—reject Jesus because they want his kingdom to be of this world. It's human nature.

We want victory over all the broken systems, the injustice, and the suffering now. We want to see the cruel governments, the wicked leaders, and the oppressive organizations fall.

We would be happy to pick up our swords and defeat our enemies rather than loving them.

But God's kingdom is not of this realm. That's why we still have tribulation though he has overcome this world (John 16:33).

Through the Holy Spirit, our inner man is free from the fear of death and this world's trappings and temptations (Romans 6:18; Romans 8:2; Hebrews 2:14–15), though our outer man is still subject to the powers of this world (Matthew 22:21; Romans 13:1), wicked though they may be.

Our kingdom is not here, and our hope is not here.

Our Lord is preparing a place for us (John 14:2), and once we arrive there, we will recognize that this world's kingdoms were always as ephemeral as our childhood imaginings.

When we've built our foundation of hope on him (Luke 6:46–49), anything of this world can be shaken and our faith will remain intact, because our hope is in the eternal, invisible kingdom not made by human hands (Acts 7:48).

May we never turn away or lose hope because our kingdom in this world is crumbling.

"Therefore I urge you, brothers and sisters, by the
mercies of God, to present your bodies as a living and
holy sacrifice, acceptable to God, which is your spiritual
service of worship. And do not be conformed to this
world, but be transformed by the renewing of your
mind, so that you may prove what the will of God is,
that which is good and acceptable and perfect."
—Romans 12:1–2

We often try to be transformed only by changing our actions but forget about the renewing of our minds.

It's true that the more we live our lives in obedience to God's Word, the more clearly we'll be able to discern what is good, acceptable, and perfect in our lives (John 7:17). But our thoughts, feelings, and subconscious beliefs drive our actions (Luke 6:45).

So we must work and will to obey him in our bodies, but we must also actively and intentionally retrain our thoughts, feelings, and beliefs. To do this, we must examine our inner selves; we can't take our thoughts captive if we don't know what they are (2 Corinthians 10:5). We may find out that we say we believe one thing but live as if we believe something else.

Where we discover that our inner lives don't line up with the Word of God, we can identify the lies we're living, find Bible verses that speak truth into those lies, and have them at the ready when our thoughts, feelings, and reactions reflect the world instead of the Lord.

As we present our bodies to the Lord in obedience and renew our minds to align with his truth, we will no longer live according to the desires, fears, and false expectations of this world. We will be renewed and transformed into Christ's image.

> "But I tell you the truth: it is to your advantage that I am
> leaving; for if I do not leave, the Helper will not come to
> you; but if I go, I will send him to you."
> —John 16:7

It seems strange to us that it could be better to have the Holy Spirit than to have Jesus standing right beside us. We often think of the Holy Spirit as a mere figurehead—a nice thought, but not very practical.

But the Bible says that the Holy Spirit will:

- give us wisdom, skill, and gifts for his work (Exodus 31:2–6; Deuteronomy 34:9; 1 Corinthians 12:7–12).
- speak through us (2 Samuel 23:2; Mark 13:11; 1 Corinthians 2:13).
- direct our steps (1 Kings 18:12; Psalm 143:10; Acts 13:4; Acts 16:6).
- always be with us (Psalm 139:7).
- convict of us of sin, righteousness, and judgment (John 16:8).
- guide us into all truth (John 14:26; John 15:26; John 16:13; 1 John 2:27).
- reveal the will of God (John 16:13).
- intercede when we don't know how to pray (Romans 6:26–27).
- give us power to resist sin and be transformed into a new man (Romans 7:6; Romans 8:2; 2 Corinthians 3:18; Galatians 5:16–26).
- bring us life (eternal) and peace (Romans 8:6).

But we can also quench the Spirit (1 Thessalonians 5:19). We lessen his power in our lives and give the devil a foothold by:

- not obeying the Word (John 15:10,14; Acts 7:51).
- holding on to anger (Ephesians 4:26–27), bitterness, and unforgiveness (Ephesians 4:30–32).
- continuing in willful sin (Isaiah 63:10; Galatians 5:16–26).
- neglecting spiritual service and gifts (1 Corinthians 14:12; 2 Timothy 1:6).

The Holy Spirit will become more and more real and powerful to us as we wholly submit our lives to him in obedience.

> "Ask, and it will be given to you; seek, and you will find;
> knock, and it will be opened to you. For everyone who
> asks receives, and the one who seeks finds, and to the
> one who knocks it will be opened."
> —Matthew 7:7–8

We all know that God doesn't give us everything we ask for, so what does this verse mean?

I think the answer lies here: "you will seek me and find me when you search for me with all your heart" (Jeremiah 29:13).

If we ask and seek for things other than him, we will often be disappointed. He continually shows himself, yet we keep rejecting him because we're so focused on whatever condition we've given:

- "I'll be content in you when you give me a spouse."
- "I'll rejoice in you when you resolve my financial difficulties."
- "I'll love you when you heal me."
- "I'll trust you when you make me successful."

These may not be conscious thoughts, but it's easy to fall into asking and seeking for a thing from God instead of for God himself.

We've asked for a stone, but he is handing us bread; we've asked for a snake, but he's given us a fish (Matthew 7:9–11)—he will give us the gift that nourishes.

The progression of "ask, seek, knock" also indicates a sort of mounting persistence. Asking is less active than seeking. Seeking is less forceful than knocking. Knocking implies we've hit a barrier, but we don't give up.

Sometimes people ask God to show himself and stop there, but our persistence in continually seeking him in all things will be rewarded with the gift of God himself.

It's through seeking him and his righteousness first that everything else we truly need will be provided (Matthew 6:33).

"There are different kinds of gifts, but the same Spirit
distributes them. There are different kinds of service, but
the same Lord. There are different kinds of working, but in
all of them and in everyone it is the same God at work."
—1 Corinthians 12:4–6

We have a very narrow idea of what serving means, and we often look around at others, trying to figure out how we should serve by imitating them.

For years, I served God in the ways society and the church made me feel I should, but I always felt burnt out and like nothing I was doing made any difference. I wasn't considering what the Lord wanted me to do—only trying to serve the way I saw others serving.

I read about a woman who watched all her neighbors grow beautiful gardens, but she just couldn't do it. Everything kept dying, and she couldn't figure out what she was doing wrong. She prayed in frustration, "Why does my garden keep dying, Lord?"

"I never told you to plant a garden," he said.

She had decided to follow the path she saw others on rather than asking what the Lord had for her.

It's not wrong to plant a garden or to try different ways of serving God, but if we serve out of the overflow the Spirit is producing in us (John 7:37–38) rather than imitating others, we will likely prevent many fruitless endeavors and our own exhaustion, overwhelm, and frustration.

There are different kinds of gifts, service, and working, but all are led by the same God. Walking closely with him is the surest way of using our gifts in ways that make a meaningful, eternal impact and leave us feeling refreshed rather than drained.

"But the greatest of you shall be your servant."
—Matthew 23:11

If we took this verse to heart day in and day out, how different would our lives be?

Most of us resent the menial tasks, the humble jobs—we feel like we're above the lowly things and think they get in the way of what really matters. We often want to do what we consider to be the important things and not be bothered with the stuff of mere mortals.

But what does the Bible say the mark of greatness is?

Servanthood. Humility.

"With humility consider one another as more important than yourselves" (Philippians 2:3). "Give preference to one another in honor" (Romans 12:10).

Even if we're leaders, we're to lead as servants rather than looking to be served, not seeking our own honor or advancement, but rather seeking how to build others up.

Greatness considers no task too lowly and is willing to do the things to which many of us would respond, "That's not my job."

Sometimes the Lord must humble us externally because we haven't learned this lesson. Our humbling is then a blessing because "pride goes before destruction, and a haughty spirit before stumbling" (Proverbs 16:18).

This humbling may keep us in lowly positions to preserve our souls and his honor; he wants to keep us from that prideful fall. If our hearts have not learned servanthood and humility, achieving worldly greatness would only launch us into a life of useless pursuits and leave us empty in the end.

May our hearts be humbled and glad to serve, looking outward to the good of others rather than focused inward on our own desires. That is what makes greatness.

"Now the seventy-two returned with joy, saying,
'Lord, even the demons are subject to us in your
name!' And he said to them, '. . . do not rejoice in
this, that the spirits are subject to you, but rejoice
that your names are recorded in heaven.'"
—Luke 10:17–20

Our human disposition is to get excited about visible success and power. It impresses others, and it makes us feel good about ourselves.

But Jesus says this isn't where were to place our joy. As he does everywhere else in the Bible, he reminds us to focus on the things that can't be seen (2 Corinthians 4:18)—our assurance of salvation and our relationship with God.

Rejoicing in anything else will always tempt us away from God. We may be tempted to pride which feels good in the moment, but that pride will turn to feelings of shame and inadequacy if the same type of success does not come again. Or perhaps if we don't see the same kinds of outcomes in the future, we'll begin to doubt our own faith or—even worse—the faithfulness of God.

Jesus says to focus on our secure eternity with him and to let that be the source of our joy.

It's easy to get excited and caught up in outward validation and evidence, but our concentration should be on maintaining our own inward relationship with Christ. That can never be distorted by earthly motives, and without it, everything that looks like power and success in the world will actually be wood, hay, and stubble (1 Corinthians 3:12).

"Put out into the deep water
and let down your nets for a catch."
—Luke 5:4

Jesus told Simon Peter—a fisherman—how to fish. Peter had been fishing all night and come up empty, but when Jesus told him to do it again, he obeyed.

Perhaps we've been doing something—even a thing we're educated in and know we are doing the "right" way—without getting the return we'd hoped for.

But sometimes we're doing what we do all in our own strength. Sometimes it's not until we've given up and called it a night that we get to see God work.

Maybe we've given up but then heard the Lord say, "Not yet; go out one more time . . . out into the deep."

It takes effort and time to go out into the deep. We're often tired. We've been "fishing" for a long time with no results.

It is all too easy to say, "I've done my duty, Lord. I'm calling it quits."

But if Jesus calls us to go back out, we should never hesitate, but rather answer like Peter does, "Master, we worked hard all night and caught nothing, but I will do as you say and let down the nets" (Luke 5:5).

"OK, Lord . . . I don't understand, but I'll do it because you said so." He gives us his Word for a purpose, and it will not return void (Isaiah 55:11).

Going out into the deep requires pushing through our own failure, exhaustion, and disappointment, but it's always worth it when the Lord calls us there.

"So for one who knows the right thing to do
and does not do it, for him it is sin."
—James 4:17

In this world, it's common not to face up to something we've done until we're found out. Many people only seem to regret the fact that they got caught, not the thing itself.

But this verse moves into our thoughts, motives, knowledge, and actions. We can avoid what God has asked of us on the outside without anyone else ever knowing about it, but that doesn't absolve us if we're neglecting the Lord's direction.

Sometimes we hide from what he asks us to do. Like Gideon, we're afraid to stand up to the enemies of God. Like Saul, we don't want to face our sin. Like Jonah, we run from God's command to witness to evil people.

But we're never really hiding.

God doesn't have to catch us in the act of doing something wrong or avoiding what he's called us to do. He sees it all from the beginning. If there's something we refuse to give up at his leading, a particular sin we won't let go of, or something we avoid doing though the Lord's clearly directed us to do it, it's just as sinful now as it ever will be, whether another human ever knows about it or not.

Gideon eventually conquered his fears through the Lord's gentle assurance. Saul endured the consequences of his sin, though we never see him take responsibility or repent for it. Jonah obeyed the Lord's direction after enduring discipline.

There's no reason to wait to follow the Lord's leading; obeying him always leads to a deeper relationship with him and a purposeful, blameless life that we will never regret.

"For the Lord has rejected those in whom you trust,
and you will not prosper with them."
—Jeremiah 2:37

In whom—or what—do we trust?

That person might solve a problem in the moment, and that thing might temporarily satisfy a craving, but we will not prosper with them in the end.

Satan will tempt us to put our trust in the things of this world, whether in institutions (Psalm 146:3–4), other people (Psalm 118:8–9), ourselves (Proverbs 3:5–6), or things (Psalm 20:7). He tries to convince us that God isn't really going to take care of us, so we must find someone or something who will.

The enemy promised Eve knowledge, and she got it, but it was not the knowledge that prospers. The devil may promise us pleasure or wealth or success, and we may get it for a season (Hebrews 11:25), but it will always be knowledge, pleasure, wealth, or success that destroys rather than prospers.

Trusting in the Lord isn't always easy, and it doesn't necessarily lead to ease or comfort in this life, but he is the only trustworthy object that will always, always prosper and not harm us in all the ways that matter (Jeremiah 29:11).

May we see Satan's deception for what it is: an attempt to destroy each of us and our identity as sons and daughters.

God has given us beauty, freedom, and purpose forever. Forever begins now as we trust in him instead of our own ways, other people, or other things.

"When he began his ministry,
Jesus himself was about thirty years old."
—Luke 3:23

Don't you wonder if Mary and the others who knew Jesus was the Messiah were puzzled by the fact he hadn't yet begun doing things they assumed the Messiah would do?

If we haven't hit certain milestones or accomplished something notable by thirty, society often makes us feel we're behind, failing, and running out of time.

But God's timing is always perfect, and he's in charge of every season of our lives (Ecclesiastes 3:11; Psalm 31:15).

His greatest purposes for us are that we become like him (2 Corinthians 5:17), exhibit the fruit of the Spirit (Galatians 5:22–23), love him and love others (Matthew 22:36–40; 1 Corinthians 13), and make disciples, teaching them to follow him (Matthew 28:19–29).

Those things may not look like visible accomplishments in this world, and even if they do, it may not come for many years.

Many of the great heroes of the Bible had long seasons of waiting when they must've felt they weren't doing anything significant. Moses tended sheep in the desert for forty years; Joseph was in slavery and prison for thirteen years; and Abraham and Sarah waited about twenty-five years for their promised son.

If three years of public ministry was enough for Jesus's great purpose to be accomplished, there's no reason we should expect to have forty or fifty years of prominent, public, continual success, even in the good works he's prepared for us to do (Ephesians 2:10).

Often, there is some work he needs to do in us or in the world before the time is right.

But when we're following him, we can trust that he will bring his great purpose to fruition in our lives (Philippians 1:6).

"For we walk by faith, not by sight."
—2 Corinthians 5:7

If we follow the idea of walking by faith instead of by sight to its natural conclusion, it reveals that some of the things we do by faith won't look like good decisions according to "sight."

And if we're supposed to trust the Lord rather than lean on our own understanding (Proverbs 3:5), we can conclude that our understanding might often lead us astray.

We spend a lot of time doing what our sight and understanding would tell us is the "smart" thing. But the smart thing is not always the wise thing, and the wise thing may look foolish to the rest of the world (1 Corinthians 1:27–29).

When we look to the world to find out if we're doing the right things, we're inevitably going to get the wrong answer.

We may be walking further and further from God's will while the world cheers us on and tells us how wonderful we're doing. And when we're following the path the Lord has for us, the world may call us failures.

The only true direction and peace we will find on this life's journey is to walk by faith and not be distracted by what our sight and understanding says based on our own limited knowledge.

We only have to look at the people in the Bible to see that much of what God asked of them didn't make sense in the natural world.

We shouldn't be surprised if God calls us outside the realm of the ordinary. We can follow him confidently, knowing he will lead every step of the way.

"The Lord is the portion of my inheritance and
my cup; you support my lot. The measuring lines
have fallen for me in pleasant places; indeed,
my inheritance is beautiful to me."
—Psalm 16:5–6

We must choose our portion, the thing that sustains us day-by-day and moment-by-moment.

When we choose the Lord as our sustenance, the omniscient, unchangeable God who loves us infinitely holds our future and all that comes with it. With that future, our inheritance is sure.

When we choose other things, we attempt to take our provision out of the Lord's hands and put it into our own; yet we are finite, fickle creatures who can't see the big picture and usually don't know what's best. The sustenance the world provides changes at every whim of man or breath of circumstance; it brings no guarantees and any inheritance we do get will certainly not be eternal.

Only when we choose the Lord will our portion, our lot, and our inheritance be beautiful, pleasant, and certain. Only this inheritance cannot be stolen, destroyed, or damaged (Matthew 6:19).

Our hope is not the blind hope of shallow optimism that believes everything along the way will be fine. It's the eternal hope assured by knowing someone trustworthy has prepared something better for us (Hebrews 11:16) and is guiding us home. The journey may be tough, but as we follow our Lord, we can know the destination is sure, and the inheritance will all be worth it.

"But seek first his kingdom and his righteousness,
and all these things will be provided to you."
—Matthew 6:33

What does seeking God's kingdom mean?

It's prioritizing the eternal kingdom of God rather than our temporary kingdom in this world. It's choosing to focus on building up and encouraging others in faith and through discipleship. It's living out the fruit of the Spirit and caring for those around us.

We will not be anxious about our earthly kingdom's success or failure, but rather on the building up of God's eternal kingdom. We'll be more concerned about all of that than we will be on whether we have enough provision for this life, as it's just finished discussing in Matthew 6:25–32.

What does seeking his righteousness mean?

It's the righteousness of faith in justification, cleansing us through Christ's sacrifice so we can be in full relationship with God (Romans 3:25; Romans 4:5; Romans 5:1).

It's also the righteousness of self-control and obedience in sanctification, becoming holy as he is holy through the power of the Spirit (Romans 6:19; 1 Peter 1:14–16; John 14:21).

We come to Christ in faith and repentance (1 John 1:9), then continue in faith and repentance, no longer obeying our fleshly desires (Romans 6:12) and no longer presenting our bodies as slaves to impurity and lawlessness (Romans 6:19). We flee youthful lusts (2 Timothy 2:22) and live by the Spirit, putting to death the deeds of our bodies (Romans 8:13). Jesus was fully righteous, and as we practice that righteousness and avoid sin, we show we are of him (1 John 2:29; 1 John 3:7–10).

In total, this means we put eternity, our faith in Christ, and our pursuit of following him above every other goal in our lives.

MARCH 23

"Will the clay say to the potter, 'What are you doing?' Or
the thing you are making say, 'He has no hands'?"
—Isaiah 45:9

God is always working on us, forming us into a vessel fit for the works he's prepared for us. That process never ends. Sometimes we look at ourselves and can't tell what he's making. It looks formless and even useless.

Like a jar without handles, we think we are missing some important component. How could we be of use when we're lacking in this way?

Or we may think we know what God has designed us for, and decide, based on that, that he has made a mistake . . . or several. This misshapen vessel we've become with its strange divots and cracked edges isn't fit for the role we imagined.

But we don't know the purpose for which God is crafting us. Perhaps we need to fit somewhere handles would only get in the way. Perhaps the very thing we think we need is something that would take us further away from the Lord and make us unsuited to the work he has for us to do.

When we can't see the good in the vessel God has created, our job is to continue living faithfully and waiting for the revelation that reveals our function in the body of Christ and the kingdom of God.

We can trust that he is molding us into the exact vessel needed for a purpose crafted specifically for each of us. He will reveal that purpose in time, and it will take into account all of the things we are and all of the things we are not.

"As having nothing and yet possessing all things."
—2 Corinthians 6:10

This is the beauty of the Christian life. Anything wonderful we have in this earthly life is a bonus, but not a necessity, to our joy.

As Christians, we have everything that matters: a redeemed soul, an eternal and certain hope, the Holy Spirit as comforter and guide, and eternal truths in the Word about how to live now in fulfillment, joy, peace, purpose, and to the glory of God.

He's given us all our soul needs in this life, and that can't be taken away (Luke 10:41–42). Any good things we gain in this physical world should be held loosely; they can all be taken away, and our hearts should not be dependent upon them.

We can possess those temporary things, but our souls can live in the same peace and hope whether we do or not.

We can live in contentment even in our lack because we know that eternity has more and better things than we could ever imagine (1 Corinthians 2:9).

We don't have to live like the world does—scrabbling and clawing to gain and hold what we have here. We can lose our earthly possessions yet continue living at rest in the confidence of our eternal inheritance, looking forward to a better land (Hebrews 11:16) and knowing our real life begins when this one ends.

Whatever we do or don't have in this world, we can live as if we possess all things because all that truly matters can't be taken away from us, and all the trials we have on this earth will not even be a blip in our infinite joy.

> "But the Lord answered and said to her, 'Martha, Martha,
> you are worried and distracted by many things; but only
> one thing is necessary; for Mary has chosen the good part,
> which shall not be taken away from her.'"
> —Luke 10:41–42

Are we living worried and distracted by many things? We often bustle around thinking we're serving the Lord while doing things he never asked of us, missing out on the richness of relationship with him.

There's so much on our to-do lists, but only one thing is necessary—to sit at the Jesus's feet.

All other efforts may crumble, and all other goals may lay beyond our ability, but this one thing is necessary.

If we choose it, it will not be taken from us; its benefit is guaranteed and eternal.

We neglect it because it's invisible. We can't quantify it, and we feel the need to prove our worth with accomplishment, so instead of resting with him, we busy ourselves in ways others can see.

But Mary didn't worry about what Martha thought of her; she was simply hungry for Jesus's words.

When we look around our homes, our lives, and the world, let's take a deep breath and stop scurrying around overwhelmed, frustrated, and overworked.

If we make only one resolution in this New Year, let it be to sit at Jesus's feet and allow his words to fuel our souls. In the short-term, the worth of our private devotion may be hidden to others, but the long-term benefit is the fruit of the Spirit overflowing in our lives—peace, love, and joy that no one can take from us.

Let us rest and choose the good part—the only thing that is necessary.

"How long, Lord? Will you forget me forever? How long
will you hide your face from me? How long am I to feel
anxious in my soul, with grief in my heart all the day?
How long will my enemy be exalted over me?"
—Psalm 13:1–2

This psalm is a comfort to us . . . a reminder that everyone feels forgotten sometimes. The key there is "feels." Sometimes it feels like God is distant and like all we can do is try to figure things out for ourselves. Sometimes it feels like no good deed goes unpunished.

But it isn't true. David knew it too. His psalm ends with this, "But I have trusted in your faithfulness; my heart shall rejoice in your salvation. I will sing to the Lord, because he has looked after me" (Psalm 13:5–6).

He didn't feel like the Lord was looking after him at that moment; nevertheless, he says that the Lord has *already* looked after him. He knew that whatever his current circumstance, God had already intervened for him and would be with him in the end.

Even when David's feelings told him he was alone and forgotten by God, he chose to continue in faith, trusting in God's ultimate purpose, love, and salvation.

When we feel like God is distant, it's all right to talk about it, to pray about it, and to ask him about it. But if our faith is real, it must go on believing and trusting that God is faithful even when there is every earthly reason to doubt. Faith that falters at the shifting sands of this world is not built on the firm foundation of Jesus Christ, and we build that kind of faith by doing what he says (Luke 6:46–49).

"If you love those who love you, what credit is that to you? For even sinners love those who love them. And if you do good to those who are good to you, what credit is that to you? For even sinners do the same. And if you lend to those from whom you expect to receive, what credit is that to you? Even sinners lend to sinners in order to receive back the same amount. But love your enemies and do good, and lend, expecting nothing in return, and your reward will be great, and you will be sons of the Most High; for he himself is kind to ungrateful and evil people."
—Luke 6:32–35

What would the world look like if we actually did this? When we look out into the world—even the Christian community—we see far more hating, insulting, and reviling of our enemies.

What if, when something terrible happened to our enemies—or even to people we simply don't like—we not only refrained from gloating (which I see too often even amongst Christians), but we reached out, offered aid, and gave to those who undoubtedly consider us enemies as well?

Could we help that man who wronged us if he were in trouble? Could we loan something to the people who failed us with no promise of getting it back?

There is no special virtue in treating only those who love us with kindness and love. That is only human nature.

Jesus freely gave everything both for those who loved him and those who hated him.

When we learn to do this as well, we live out the love of Christ.

"For if you keep silent at this time, liberation and rescue
will arise for the Jews from another place, and you and
your father's house will perish. And who knows whether
you have not attained royalty for such a time as this?"
—Esther 4:14

Mordecai knew the Jews wouldn't be destroyed; they had God's promise for this. So he knew that even if Esther did not step up, some other avenue of help would come.

But Esther was there, placed in a unique position to have an audience with the king, though at great danger to herself.

Nothing about this situation was ideal. Esther was probably a teenager when she was forced into the king's harem, and this was after she'd been orphaned and put in her uncle's care.

An orphaned child bride with no choice in her life path, yet, "Who knows?" Mordecai said. "Maybe you were placed here for this purpose, for this time."

Some of us had a terrible start and no advantages in life. Some of us have never been able to make our own choices, and we've landed in hard situations we never would've picked given the chance.

Let's consider that, perhaps, the Lord is still in charge—that maybe each of us have been put here just at this time for a purpose we can't yet see.

The tapestry of the world is full of terrible things the Lord used for good. As Joseph said in Genesis 50:20, what man means for evil, God means for good. God is always working, and we can be a part of what he is doing. If not us, he will raise up someone else. We can be faithful where we're placed even when we can't understand and would never have chosen it.

"One who loves discipline loves knowledge,
but one who hates rebuke is stupid."
—Proverbs 12:1

None of us like it when someone brings attention to our mistakes, faults, or bad behavior. It doesn't feel good to know we've done something wrong or hurt someone.

But if we're wise, we will listen to correction humbly and with the purpose of trying to learn and grow. When correction comes our way, it's easy to react emotionally because it hurts our pride, but as we mature, the less defensive we will become when our faults and flaws are pointed out.

Our focus on feeling or looking right decreases while our focus on truly acting and being right according to God's Word increases.

However, it's also good to remember that not all correction is founded on truth, and not everyone who corrects is speaking in love even if they are speaking truth. We need to be discerning in order to determine if the correction is valid. If it's coming from a wise friend or mentor who loves us, we need to be able to hear and accept the true correction without taking offense in our hearts.

Taking some time to process correction from others before responding can help us learn to react calmly and wisely instead of responding out of hurt feelings or shame. That can even mean saying we need some time to think and stepping away from the conversation in the moment. It may mean taking those words to another godly, trusted friend and asking for insight.

As iron sharpens iron (Proverbs 27:17), the process of being shaped is difficult and painful, but without it, we will not become what God has intended us to be.

"For you were called to freedom, brothers and sisters;
only do not turn your freedom into an opportunity for
the flesh, but serve one another through love."
—Galatians 5:13

We often take freedom to mean we get to do whatever we want—no constraints, no responsibilities, and no one telling us what to do—and we frequently speak of freedom in Christ in order to staunchly defend a behavior other Christians may not agree with. While Paul certainly makes it clear that there are different convictions, and that some may not be necessary (1 Corinthians 8), he primarily speaks of freedom in the sense of not being controlled by our flesh.

Christ's freedom gives us the ability to lay down our own selfishness, worldly desires, fear of man's opinion, (John 5:41), and the cares of this world and deceitfulness of riches (Matthew 13:22).

His freedom is not so we can do anything we like regardless of what people think, but so we can live in loving service of others.

Only after the Spirit rules the flesh (Galatians 5:16) are we willing, prepared, and even happy to pour out our lives in the service of others. The freedom is from our own slavery to sin, ourselves, and the trappings of this world.

It isn't given so we can indulge our earthly, fleshly desires, but so we have the power to overcome them.

Are we using our freedom in Christ to give ourselves allowances to do certain things or for the purpose of serving and loving those around us?

"Your sun will no longer set, nor will your moon wane;
for you will have the Lord as an everlasting light, and the
days of your mourning will be over. Then all your
people will be righteous; they will possess the land
forever, the branch of my planting, the work of my
hands, that I may be glorified. The smallest one will
become a thousand, and the least one a mighty nation. I,
the Lord, will bring it about quickly in its time."
—Isaiah 60:20–22

What a beautiful prophecy about our forever future as believers with God in heaven.

The Lord will be our eternal light. There will be no short days of winter nor long nights of summer, only the Light of the World illuminating everything.

All our mourning will come to an end—no more crying, sorrow, pain, or death (Revelation 21:4).

Everyone there will be fully righteous; we will no longer battle this world of sin and heartache, broken relationships, temptation, and discord. We will rest in perfect harmony. Just as the wolf will lie down with the lamb and the lion with the calf (Isaiah 11:5–6), all humankind will live peaceably together.

And while we may feel like we're the smallest or least in our lifetime, that's not an issue in heaven. There, the least one will be like a mighty nation. We can't fathom what this might entail, but it will be glorious!

And the Lord will do all this in its proper time. He's not slow, though it may seem like he is to us, but patient, ensuring all have the chance to come to him (2 Peter 3:9).

These promises are our inheritance and the hope that will carry us through the current darkness, sorrow, and discouragement.

"The men who were blind came up to him, and Jesus said to them, 'Do you believe that I am able to do this?' They said to him, 'Yes, Lord.' Then he touched their eyes, saying, 'It shall be done for you according to your faith.'"
—Matthew 9:28–29

Many would take this verse to mean if we have enough faith, we will definitely be healed, and God will remove any difficulty in our lives.

But this mindset doesn't consider the "yet not my will but yours" spoken as Jesus prayed that his cup of suffering be removed (Luke 22:42).

And we can't forget the "thorn in the flesh" (2 Corinthians 12:7–10) God left in Paul's life for the good of his character.

There's a tension between believing but not expecting, between trusting without demanding, between confidence in God's goodness yet knowing that goodness may not fix every problem in this life.

In his all-knowing wisdom, God ordains which of our sufferings remain for our own good, as Paul's thorn, or the good of others, as Jesus's death.

The Word makes it clear we will struggle (1 Peter 4:12); every illness won't be healed, nor every difficulty removed.

We must, like Shadrach, Meshach, and Abednego, know that God "is able to rescue us," but also that "even if he does not," we will not turn away from him (Daniel 3:17–18).

We must, like Esther, say, "If I perish, I perish" (Esther 4:16).

We must, like Job, say, "Though he slay me, I will hope in him" (Job 13:15).

Our faith is faith in him and him alone that will result in our eternal healing. It trusts that he can heal us but is not dependent upon him doing so.

"And now says the Lord, who formed me from the womb
to be his servant, to bring Jacob back to him, so that Israel
might be gathered to him (for I am honored in the sight
of the Lord and my God is my strength). He says, 'It is
too small a thing that you should be my servant to raise
up the tribes of Jacob and to restore the protected ones of
Israel; I will also make you a light of the nations so that
my salvation may reach to the end of the earth.'"
—Isaiah 49:5–6

In this prophetic passage about Jesus, God says that reconciling only Israel to himself is "too small." He's going to make a way for all nations to come to him. His true purpose is bigger.

Don't we sometimes look at what God has called us to do and think, "That's too big for me"? We may try to back out like Moses (Exodus 4:10–13) or ask for multiple reassurances like Gideon (Judges 6:36–40). The task already seems impossible. And then God says, "Oh, not only that. Think bigger."

God sent Jesus not only for the Israelites, but for all mankind. God had Moses not only lead the Israelites out of Egypt, but straight through the Red Sea on dry land. God not only defeated the Midianites with the already out-numbered Israelite army; he had Gideon whittle that army down, creating humanly insurmountable odds.

When we submit to living in his service, the Lord will use us mightily in ways we could never have foreseen.

All of these are small things to him.

"This is my commandment, that you love one another,
just as I have loved you. Greater love has no one than
this, that a person will lay down his life for his friends."
—John 15:12–13

We normally see this second verse in reference to Jesus's sacrificial death on the cross, and that's certainly part of its meaning.

But when we see it in context, we realize that Jesus was speaking not only of the way he would die for others, but of the way he lived for them—the way he had loved them throughout his life.

That makes this verse much more difficult to live up to. There are many people for whom we might die if it came to saving them from a fire, but with whom we cannot bring ourselves to spend a civil evening.

We must not only be willing to die for that prisoner, stranger, homeless person, grumpy neighbor, or demanding family member; we must also be willing to live for them. We must be ready to do not only the grand gestures that might gain fanfare, but to continue in loving-kindness that may never be noticed despite the constant pressure of an unappreciative spouse, a rebellious child, or a spiteful coworker.

This looks like laying down our day-by-day wants, our selfishness, our irritation, and our pride in order to love them well.

Whether we would die for someone is rarely tested; whether we will live for them is a daily practice of self-control, humility, and love.

"This is what the Lord says: 'Let no wise man boast
of his wisdom, nor let the mighty man boast of his
might, nor a rich man boast of his riches; but let the
one who boasts boast of this, that he understands
and knows me, that I am the Lord who exercises
mercy, justice, and righteousness on the earth; for I
delight in these things,' declares the Lord."
—Jeremiah 9:23–24

All of us live and work to build something we can be proud of. Whether we open our mouths to boast or not, how we live reveals what we long to boast about.

Do our actions reveal that our pride and value are placed on our intellect, worldly wisdom, our abilities, our physical strength, our position in society or the workplace, or our worldly goods and wealth?

Do we bask in the approval garnered by these things? Are they what we hope people see when they look at us?

If so, we're missing the point.

Second Corinthians 4:18 says, "For the things which are seen are temporal, but the things which are not seen are eternal."

Our knowledge of God leads us to live in the eternal unseen. It means that whether we eat or drink or work or raise children or cut lawns or clean toilets, we do all to the glory of God (1 Corinthians 10:31).

Our earthly advantages or disadvantages do not affect our self-worth either for good or for bad because we boast only in whether we know the Lord and he knows us.

"He will not cry out nor raise his voice,
nor make his voice heard in the street."
—Isaiah 42:2

The loudest people seem to get the most attention. Those who yell and argue are taken to be the most passionate and maybe even the smartest or most well-equipped.

But that isn't the case. This prophetic passage about Jesus reminds us that he didn't think it necessary to share truth by being the loudest or the most aggressive.

He shared it quietly, patiently, and intimately. He shared it humbly.

It's human nature to gather around hype, but Jesus didn't aim for hype; he aimed for love, truth, and relationship.

When hype is the main tool, we need to listen to the message behind it carefully. Is it trying to win us over with simple excitement? Is it reflecting truth, hope, and love? Is it calling us to things that will grow us in healthy ways, or is it asking something worldly of us? Is the messenger making disciples or peddling a product? Is it biblical? Does it carry within it the fruit of the Spirit, or is it fueling earthly desire, impatience, fear, or quick action?

We live in a world susceptible to excitement, and we like quick-fixes and short-term rewards—two things hype is often good at promising.

The Lord is often the still, small voice that says to wait, hope, and rest. Let's be certain our ears are open so we can hear his voice above the noise of the world that yells, "Act now!" and "Don't miss out!" and makes promises it cannot keep.

"Do not be deceived, God is not mocked; for whatever a
person sows, this he will also reap. For the one who sows
to his own flesh will reap destruction from the flesh, but
the one who sows to the Spirit will reap eternal life from
the Spirit. Let's not become discouraged in doing good,
for in due time we will reap, if we do not become weary."
—Galatians 6:7–9

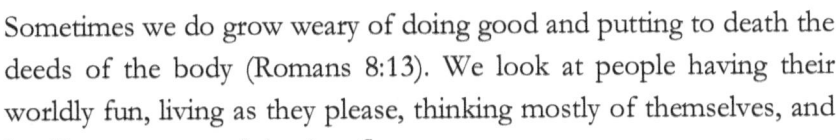

Sometimes we do grow weary of doing good and putting to death the
deeds of the body (Romans 8:13). We look at people having their
worldly fun, living as they please, thinking mostly of themselves, and
by all appearances, doing just fine.

So we wonder . . . is it worth it?

Dying to self (Romans 6:6), choosing others over ourselves (Philippians 2:3), carrying a cross to follow Jesus (Luke 9:23), being self-disciplined and choosing not to satisfy the many lusts of the flesh (anything that has us wanting it *now*) (1 Peter 4:2), and loving our enemies
(Matthew 5:44) is not easy.

But neither is the path of self-indulgence. That road leads to hardship,
ill health, ruin, broken relationships, and ultimately, eternal destruction.

Doing good and living righteously are hard, but they reap immeasurable long-term rewards and pleasure. Sin reaps short-term pleasure
(Hebrews 11:25) but ends with much harder and more destructive consequences.

We can see this even in our earthly lives. Exercising is hard, but so
is being unhealthy. Sacrifice in marriage is hard, but so is divorce. Disciplining our kids with consistency is hard, but so is watching them go
down a harmful path.

Following God is the ultimate long-term decision; the rewards are
eternal, and we will reap them in the end if we do not give up.

> "'Futility of futilities,' says the Preacher, 'Futility of
> futilities! All is futility.' What advantage does a person
> have in all his work which he does under the sun?"
> —Ecclesiastes 1:2–3

Most of us have lived the idea that once we achieve some goal, we'll have it made. We could never be unhappy then! But it's not true. We learn this over and over in life but always seem to forget—the Christmas present we begged for becomes commonplace after a couple of weeks, that relationship we pined over becomes strife-filled in ways we didn't expect, the job we worked so hard for is now empty and unfulfilling, the wealth we earned bought a lot of stuff, but we're still unsatisfied. It's never enough.

Solomon is renowned as the wealthiest and wisest man who ever lived, and he conducted this happiness experiment for himself. He tried wisdom (learning/intellect), pleasure (women/possessions/drink/parties/luxury), work (effort/skill/success), and he tells us it was all vanity. He denied himself nothing, and he found it all empty.

If Solomon tells us he tried everything, and that wasn't the answer, we should be listening. All the learning, intellect, pleasure (wholesome or not), luxury, relationships (healthy or not), skill, and success in the world won't make us happy if that is where we're seeking our happiness.

Solomon's conclusion? "For who can eat and who can have enjoyment without [God]? For to a person who is good in his sight, he has given wisdom and knowledge and joy" (Ecclesiastes 2:25–26).

Only in the Lord do we have true joy. We don't have to wait for the next stage, accomplishment, or experience in life to make us happy. It won't work. We find our happiness now—right where we are—in seeking the Lord.

"This is what the Lord says: 'Cursed is the man who trusts
in mankind and makes flesh his strength and whose heart
turns away from the Lord. For he will be like a bush in the
desert, and will not see when prosperity comes, but will
live in stony wastes in the wilderness, a land of salt that is
not inhabited. Blessed is the man who trusts in the Lord,
and whose trust is the Lord. For he will be like a tree
planted by the water that extends its roots by a stream,
and does not fear when the heat comes; but its leaves will
be green, and it will not be anxious in a year of drought,
nor cease to yield fruit.'"
—Jeremiah 17:5–8

The beginning of this passage sounds like doom and gloom. But as we read further, we see the Lord is actually warning us in love: "Don't trust in man or in your own strength; don't turn away from me. If you do that, you're placing yourself in a desert wilderness where nothing can grow and where you will not be satisfied. Trusting in me roots you deeply, where even if circumstances, other people, or your strength fails, you will remain peaceful, secure, confident in the face of hardship, and fruitful."

The things of this world will leave us empty; only trusting in him will keep us nourished.

If we follow our own way, a drought will leave us withered and fruitless because we have wandered away from the source that waters our soul.

With the Lord's direction, the trials and troubles that come along will not shake us, because we will be rooted in God himself—the only source that sustains us.

"And now, behold, bound by the Spirit, I am on my
way to Jerusalem, not knowing what will happen to me
there, except that the Holy Spirit solemnly testifies to
me in every city, saying that chains and afflictions await
me. But I do not consider my life of any account as
dear to myself, so that I may finish my course and the
ministry which I received from the Lord Jesus, to
testify solemnly of the gospel of God's grace."
—Acts 20:22–24

Paul knew he was walking into more difficulty by going to Jerusalem, but he also knew it was worth it. He didn't consider even his life to be more important than doing the work the Lord had given him.

Do we take God's call so seriously? We often walk into difficulty without knowing it's coming, but what if we knew that chains and affliction awaited? Would we walk forward willingly for the sake of the Gospel and the kingdom of God?

Do we consider our lives, possessions, and reputations as dear to us, or do we persevere in the Lord's work, valuing it over and above even those?

This attitude doesn't mean we can't mourn difficulty and loss; we may serve the Lord "with tears" as Paul says in verse 19. But if we can't give all for the sake of service to God or in keeping with obedience to him, then those things we will not let go of hold too much of our devotion.

If we understand the Gospel, we will "count all things to be loss in view of the surpassing value of knowing Christ Jesus my Lord" (Philippians 3:8), and we will be willing to lose all to gain eternity with him (Matthew 3:44–45).

"A man's steps are ordained by the Lord;
how then can a person understand his way?"
—Proverbs 20:24

How can we plan or make sense of our journey through life? The answer is that we can't. Without the Word guiding us like a lamp (Psalm 119:105) and the Holy Spirit telling us whether to turn to the right or to the left (Isaiah 30:21), we're all just aimlessly meandering through this life.

But when we follow his direction, we can be certain of the steps we take—certain they are not meaningless, certain they will accomplish good for his kingdom, and certain they are taking us to true joy, peace, and eternal hope. We can be confident that what man means for evil, God means for good even when we can't fathom what good purpose could come of our experience (Genesis 50:20).

We cannot understand the purpose of our path in life. If I'd been in charge of where my steps had taken me, I would've led a very different life, yet I can look back and see God's hand at every turn. He was guiding even when I was resistant.

As Christians, we may not understand our way as we're on it, but we can understand and trust the infallible goodness and faithfulness of our Guide.

In *Not Knowing Whither*, Oswald Chambers says, "When I am going on with God in his path, I do not understand, but God does; therefore, I understand God, not his path."

Let us seek not to understand our path, but to understand our God. Our growing confidence and belief in his goodness and love for us will give us the peace to take each step along a path we do not understand.

"For the sorrow that is according to the will of God
produces a repentance without regret, leading to salvation,
but the sorrow of the world produces death."
—2 Corinthians 7:10

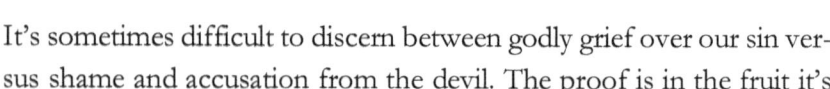

It's sometimes difficult to discern between godly grief over our sin versus shame and accusation from the devil. The proof is in the fruit it's producing.

Does it have us paralyzed in shame or turning away from our sin in repentance? Does it have us wallowing over past regrets or diving further into Christ because we recognize the depth of our need for him? Does it keep us from stepping out in God's plan for us because we're not worthy, or does it have us so grateful for God's forgiveness and grace that we step out because we know his strength is made perfect in our weakness (2 Corinthians 12:9)? Does it have us constantly thinking about ourselves, or does it have us turning our eyes to Christ?

For years, I felt most disillusioned with God when I failed at following him well. He finally revealed that if my own failures led me to doubt him, I wasn't really trusting him to begin with; I was trusting myself.

Our sin should frustrate us, but it should not send us away from God or turn us toward obsessing over our own failure.

If it pushes us into despair over sins we have turned away from, it's accusation. If it pushes us toward righteousness, repentance, and Christ, it's godly grief and conviction.

Jesus knew Peter would fail and told him, "When you have turned back, strengthen your brothers" (Luke 22:31–32).

Our first step after we fail is to turn back to Christ. Our second step is to encourage those around us who might be wallowing in their own failure.

"But Jesus was saying, 'Father, forgive them;
for they do not know what they are doing.'"
—Luke 23:34

Even while being sinned against by unrepentant people, Jesus carried no grudge.

While on the cross, he:

- forgave and asked mercy for his tormentors while still suffering in the middle of pain, torture, and injustice.
- made sure his mother had a caretaker, both providing for her and honoring John with a calling (John 19:26–27).
- ministered and witnessed to the thief on the cross next to him (Luke 23:39–43).

This is a picture of how we're to act while suffering, even terribly and unfairly, at the hands of evil. We're to pray for our enemies, to forgive, to care for our brothers and sisters, and to minister to unbelievers.

It's so easy to let bitterness take root, unforgiveness win, and resentful anger take over. These are so often our dominating sins, but if they're allowed to smolder in the background, every new hurt will be like gasoline on a fire, inflaming those attitudes all over again. This will not only prevent us from doing the good we could do in the lives of those around us, but will do both us and others harm (Hebrews 12:15).

However, if we smother the cinders of offense by constantly turning from those attitudes in ourselves, by forgiving how Jesus forgave (Ephesians 4:31–32), by being willing to lay down our lives for others (John 15:13), and by trusting that the last shall be first (Mark 10:31), the gasoline of pain will find no spark to ignite.

When suffering, we must continually give our own hurt to the Lord so these things don't overtake us and we can be a gift to others even in the midst of our own pain.

> "'And when did we see you as a stranger, and invite you in, or naked, and clothe you? And when did we see you sick, or in prison, and come to you?' And the King will answer and say to them, 'Truly I say to you, to the extent that you did it for one of the least of these brothers or sisters of mine, you did it for me.'"
> —Matthew 25:38–40

Many people feel they are unqualified for the work of the Lord; they have no special talents.

But the Bible never says we need special talents to do great work for the kingdom of God. It says, "But the greatest of you shall be your servant. Whoever exalts himself shall be humbled, and whoever humbles himself shall be exalted." (Matthew 23:11–12). It says to wash one another's feet (John 13:14–17) and to be hospitable and to serve each other (1 Peter 4:9–10). It says to care for the orphan and the widow and keep ourselves unstained by the world (James 1:27). It says to welcome the stranger, clothe the naked, feed the hungry, and visit the sick and those in prison.

This is not only being the hands and feet of Jesus; the Bible says it is as if we are actually serving Jesus himself.

All of us can do these things, but there are few earthly honors in them. They are not flashy or impressive.

The truth is that the flashy and impressive gifts often get in the way of serving God by inflating egos and tempting us to seek earthly glory for ourselves rather than the glory of God.

Knowing this to be true, we can live lives of humble service without doubting our worth or purpose.

"Love does no wrong to a neighbor;
therefore love is the fulfillment of the Law."
—Romans 13:10

We tend to think our secret sins harm no one but ourselves, but everything that doesn't fulfill the law harms other humans in one way or another.

Secret sins prevent us from becoming who God created us to be (Psalm 139:13–18; Jeremiah 1:5) and from doing the good works he set out for us before we were ever born (Ephesians 2:10).

Maybe our laziness, procrastination, or fear of failure is keeping us from pressing into the purpose God has for us. Even this is harming others because it means we're not investing what God has given us into his kingdom (Matthew 25:14–30). When we bury what he's given us to do instead of acting on it, we're withholding not only our service for him, but what he's given us to help others along in their faith.

Doing no wrong to a neighbor requires not only inaction, but action.

We must spend our time and our words wisely rather than frivolously, representing Christ in actions fueled by the Holy Spirit. We walk each morning with Christ anew, allowing him to guide our steps.

It is no easy thing to live a life where we do no wrong, but love is our calling, and that's what it requires.

What steps can we take today to cease doing harm and begin walking in the good works the Lord has called us to?

"For no one can lay a foundation other than the
one which is laid, which is Jesus Christ. Now if
anyone builds on the foundation with gold, silver,
precious stones, wood, hay, or straw, each one's
work will become evident; for the day will show it
because it is to be revealed with fire, and the fire
itself will test the quality of each one's work."
—1 Corinthians 3:11–13

Jesus is the only foundation beneath our lives that will result in anything that has eternal meaning and value.

If we try to work according to the world's wisdom, societal norms, or what other people think we should do, if we try to copy some other person's life, or if we attempt work according to our own personal talents without consulting the Lord, all of that work will have no lasting impact. It will be destroyed.

Only where we build on Jesus and abide in him will our work have any meaningful, lasting effect. "And if I give away all my possessions to charity, and if I surrender my body so that I may glory [in martyrdom], but do not have love, it does me no good" (1 Corinthians 13:3). Grand actions like giving away all our possessions to the poor or being willing to die for Christ would look wonderfully sacrificial to others and may bring lots of human praise, but if the love of Jesus is not in them, they are nothing.

It's comforting that the opposite is also true. All things we build on the foundation of Christ and do in service to him will pass the test of fire in eternity no matter how small or menial—all our chores, duties, jobs, and hobbies can be built on him.

"But we were hoping that it was he who was going to redeem Israel. Indeed, besides all this, it is now the third day since these things happened."
—Luke 24:21

This was said by the men on the road to Emmaus after Jesus's resurrection, but before it was publicly known.

These men were disheartened. Jesus had said he would rise after three days, but here they were, three days later. They had believed in Jesus, but it looked like they were wrong.

It was too late. God hadn't come through.

So many notable stories in the Bible had an "it's too late" moment— Abraham and Sarah, Moses, Joseph, Ruth, Zechariah and Elizabeth.

"Is anything too difficult for the Lord?" God asks of Abraham in Genesis 18:14. He says it again in Jeremiah 32:27, "Behold, I am the Lord, the God of all flesh; is anything too difficult for me?"

And Jesus says in Matthew 19:26, "With people this is impossible, but with God all things are possible."

Even Job says, "I know that you can do all things, and that no plan is impossible for you" (Job 42:2).

When we feel like it's too late for something in our lives, this teaches us to hold on to God, his goodness, his power, and his sovereignty. If it's in his will and purpose and we are following him, he will make it happen, even if it's beyond the realm of all human possibility.

The "it's too late" is where our faith either becomes real or fades away into disappointment and bitterness. Faith that only believes it's possible when we can see the way ourselves is faith in a small god.

We serve a big God whose plans will not be thwarted. Nothing is too difficult for him.

"For this is the love of God,
that we keep his commandments;
and his commandments are not burdensome."
—1 John 5:3

The more we practice the Lord's commandments, the more we come to realize that they are not burdensome . . . they are freeing.

The command to "consider others more important than ourselves" (Philippians 2:3) is freeing because we no longer have to worry about whether we're getting ahead or someone else is getting something we think we deserve. We can trust God that whether we get any reward in this life or not, we will reap a good reward in God's timing if we don't give up (Galatians 6:9).

The command to forgive others is freeing, because we no longer have to hold on to anger or seek justice. God will handle that.

The command not to fear, not to be anxious, and not to fret are all freeing because they assure us that God is in control even when we know we're not.

And the more we understand who God is, the more freeing his commandments feel, because we come to see his love, trustworthiness, and sovereignty in them.

It's when we try to follow the Lord's guidelines without having a relationship with him that they feel burdensome; they all feel like arbitrary rules for him to exercise control.

We learn from the relationship that his commandments are set because he loves us, wants the best for us, and wants to protect us from false hopes and painful consequences. When we believe someone wants good for us, we trust their advice.

When we truly learn who God is, his commandments set us free.

"And in the early morning, while it was still dark, Jesus
got up, left the house, and went away to a secluded place,
and prayed there for a time. Simon and his companions
eagerly searched for him; and they found him and said to
him, 'Everyone is looking for you.'"
—Mark 1:35–37

Serving others well doesn't mean we're at the mercy of what they want from us.

It means we're at the total mercy of what God wants, and that might be disappointing to those around us.

Jesus often withdrew when people were waiting and even looking for him. He didn't allow the expectations of others to dictate his actions. He did exactly what the Lord had for him in that moment, and he did it in the Lord's strength.

If we're serving as God directs, those around us may not always be pleased with our decisions.

There might be some people who think, "Hey, she just left, and we needed more from her," or "It was rude not to come when so many people were expecting him."

Only by taking this example from Jesus and making the time to withdraw and be with the Father can we know where we can best spend our time. If we're serving without his direction, our natural tendency is to feel that peoples' needs dictate our actions.

They do not.

We are always to be led by the direction of the Holy Spirit, which will come as we are purposefully abiding in the vine of Jesus Christ through prayer, submitting to his will, and learning from the Word.

"You will know them by their fruits. Grapes are not
gathered from thorn bushes, nor figs from thistles, are
they? So every good tree bears good fruit, but the bad
tree bears bad fruit. A good tree cannot bear bad fruit,
nor can a bad tree bear good fruit."
—Matthew 7:16–18

The truth of our Christianity is made evident by bearing good fruit, and the Bible defines that fruit as love, joy, peace, patience, kindness, goodness, faithfulness, gentleness, and self-control (Galatians 5:22–23).

Many self-righteous people are proud of their version of Christianity because of all the things they don't do. You won't catch them drinking, smoking, or cursing, and they show disdain for anyone who does.

But we can follow a list of rules perfectly without exhibiting most of those fruits of the Spirit. The Pharisees were the embodiment of this problem, and Christ called them "blind guides," "hypocrites," and "white-washed tombs" (Matthew 23:13–36).

Christianity cannot be boiled down to only a list of dos or don'ts. I know many proudly self-righteous people who primarily bear strife, anger, selfishness, bitterness, scorn, comparison, and discontentment, also influencing others to believe this is acceptable to God (Matthew 15:14; Matthew 23:13,15).

Their rule-following is not bearing good fruit; they have missed the Lord's heart.

We are absolutely supposed to be obedient to God's commands, but doing so in the manner God intended will grow the fruit of the Spirit rather than inhibit them.

We can test our fruit by watching what it produces both in our own lives and in the lives of those around us. Are we producing love or selfishness? Patience or discontentment? Gentleness or harsh criticism?

It's easy to see the fruit when we're honest with ourselves.

"The one who is faithful in a very little thing is also
faithful in much; and the one who is unrighteous
in a very little thing is also unrighteous in much."
—Luke 16:10

Sometimes it feels like everything gets in the way of doing the big, important things. But this passage in Luke 16 makes it clear that our diligence even in the menial, invisible duties we've been given shows our faithfulness.

Jesus performed miracles, but he also washed the disciples' feet. He preached, but he also spent much time in prayer.

Our priorities and character show in every small thing we do with integrity . . . the dishes, our jobs, raising children, stewarding our money, and anything else we could put there.

We might be placed where it doesn't seem like anything we do could possibly matter to the Lord, but when we look at the stories in the Bible, we see that was true of many of the most notable people we find there.

God's purpose for Moses didn't become clear until after he'd spent forty years as a shepherd. David was tending his father's sheep when Samuel came to anoint a king, and his father believed him so unlikely to be chosen that he wasn't even called in from the fields. Joseph had no idea he would save nations from starvation as he lived the life of a faithful and industrious slave and prisoner. Jesus was a carpenter until he was thirty.

Wherever God has placed us, that is where we're to be faithful. In each of the small tasks that seem like they couldn't possibly impact the kingdom of God, we work as if we are doing them for God (Colossians 3:23–24). They all matter to him.

"I know, Lord, that a person's way is not in himself,
nor is it in a person who walks to direct his steps."
—Jeremiah 10:23

What pressure we put on ourselves to know each next step! But knowing God means we can trust him to lead us through each moment, each day, and each decision.

That's good, because when we look to ourselves, we're often tempted to take only steps that are comfortable, safe, pleasurable, and make sense to our limited understanding.

But God can see the whole of time from the beginning to the end; he will always lead us down purposeful paths that yield spiritual fruit with eternal value.

When we're confused by life, uncertain of our direction, or tired of taking steps that have led only to emptiness, this is the answer: "Trust in the Lord with all your heart, and do not lean on your own understanding. In all your ways acknowledge him, and he will make your paths straight" (Proverbs 3:5–6).

And the Word lights that path for us (Psalm 119:105) by showing us how to live, beginning with the greatest commandment: to love the Lord your God with all your heart soul and mind. Everything else flows from this (Matthew 22:36–40).

And how do we love him? By keeping his commandments (John 14:15), which are designed to direct our steps toward the best way—though we know the best is not always the easiest.

So if there are areas we've been holding back from the Lord, unwilling to trust and follow, that's where we start.

As we acknowledge and obey him more and more in our ways, the path will become more distinct and straight before us. This is the beginning of allowing the Lord to direct our steps.

"But from those who were of considerable repute
(what they were makes no difference to me; God
shows no favoritism)—well, those who were of
repute contributed nothing to me."
—Galatians 2:6

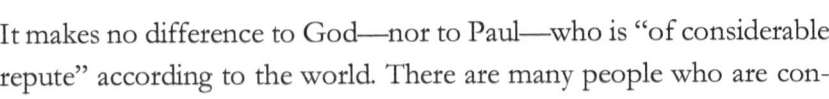

It makes no difference to God—nor to Paul—who is "of considerable repute" according to the world. There are many people who are considered influential, especially in our world of "influencers."

But whether people are "influencers" or not should make no difference to us. They might influence the world, but the simple fact of their fame and reputation should not mean we listen to them more than to God.

Worldly influencers who do not speak or live truth can contribute nothing meaningful or lasting to our lives—whether they be famous politicians, popular false teachers, the latest sports celebrities, or the most recognized movie stars.

Popularity or power alone should never make us believe one person deserves more attention, respect, or authority in our lives than another. Many will use that popularity and power as a pretext as the men Paul was referring to did—to manipulate truth to achieve their desired ends and to increase their influence.

God shows no partiality. He does not look at the outward appearance or position, but at the heart (1 Samuel 16:7).

May we never attempt to win favor from those who have status simply because they hold power or position. May we treat every person as an equal and hold fast to godly standards even if it puts us in opposition to those the world applauds.

"For God is not a God of confusion but of peace."
—1 Corinthians 14:33

If we're confused, we can be certain that's not what the Lord wants for us. He gives the "peace that surpasses all comprehension" (Philippians 4:7). The fact that it passes comprehension means we can have it no matter the circumstances in our lives or in the world. Those around us will wonder how we can still have peace in difficult, confusing, or agonizing circumstances.

Even when we don't know what to do or why terrible things are happening, we can have peace because we place our trust in the loving God who declared the end from the beginning and whose plans will be established (Isaiah 46:10).

Confusion is almost always wrapped up in worry about the future, which means it has at least a few drops of mistrust mixed in with it. We're doubting that God has declared the end, doubting that he will come through, or doubting whether he truly loves us and means us good.

And though we don't know our futures and we don't have to pretend to like everything that happens in our lives, we do know we can trust God to be with us and uphold us whatever comes because we know the end of the story.

With that knowledge, we don't have to let our confusion reign. We can sit in our not-knowing without our hearts hammering in fear. We don't have to know every answer because we're guided by the one who does. The one who established the universe leads his children step-by-step in our path to eternity with him.

The anxiety of confusion is not resolved by knowing the answers but by trusting the one who does.

> "Jesus answered, 'Where I am going, you cannot
> follow me now; but you will follow later.' Peter said
> to him, 'Lord, why can I not follow you right now?
> I will lay down my life for you.'"
> —John 13:36–37

———◆———

Peter said this right before Jesus's arrest, and I'm sure he was sincere . . . he just didn't quite understand what following Jesus would mean.

The next day, Peter took out his sword and cut off the ear of the high priest's servant in defense of Jesus. Had others taken up weapons, I think Peter would've gladly fought to the death.

He was willing to fight but not to surrender.

He was willing to die in body but not to die to self.

He was willing to go out in a blaze of glory but not to humbly surrender without fanfare.

He was willing to die for Christ but not yet willing to live for him.

Dying for Christ looks noble and sacrificial, but it only takes a few moments of courage. Living for him requires laying down our lives over and over in all the drudgery of daily life.

It requires turning the other cheek, loving our enemies (Matthew 5:38–48), and being willing to be hated as Christ was hated (Matthew 10:24–25). It requires living in humility (Philippians 2:3–4), not seeking our own desires but focusing on the eternal destiny of others (1 Corinthians 10:33), being a servant (Matthew 20:26), and battling our flesh and all the worldly and spiritual forces that come against us (Galatians 5:17; Ephesians 6:12).

Let us lay down our swords and self-important ideas of a glory-seeking battle and die daily (1 Corinthians 15:31) in order to take up our crosses and truly follow Jesus (Luke 9:23).

"But a natural person does not accept the things
of the Spirit of God, for they are foolishness
to him; and he cannot understand them,
because they are spiritually discerned."
—1 Corinthians 2:14

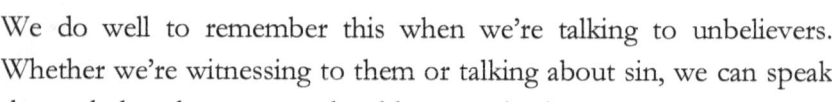

We do well to remember this when we're talking to unbelievers. Whether we're witnessing to them or talking about sin, we can speak the truth, but they may not be able to receive it.

Raising our voices in anger won't help. Calling them names won't help. Acting in an un-Christlike manner won't help.

We look to Jesus for our example. He spoke truth and gave evidence from the Word, but he didn't try to convince or persuade. He didn't engage in pointless debates when people asked trick questions designed to expose some flaw in his teaching.

To those who could not hear, he simply told the truth and moved on. He planted a seed with love.

This verse also helps us with those people we love who we long to see come to Christ. It reminds us that their souls are not our burden to carry. We do what we can—love them, tell the truth, be examples, and pray for them—but the battle for their soul is the Lord's. They may not yet be in a spiritual place to hear that truth.

We tell it to them as many times as the Lord prompts, but it isn't in our power to make them hear it. We may speak the truth eloquently and perfectly, and they may still not come to the Lord.

Many people couldn't hear truth from the mouth of Jesus himself. Some will certainly reject it from us.

We tell the truth in love and move on, leaving the rest to the Holy Spirit.

"Now may the God of hope fill you with all joy and
peace in believing, so that you will abound in hope by
the power of the Holy Spirit."
—Romans 15:13

Paul is saying we can live in all—not some—of the fullness of joy and peace Christ offers right now.

How? In believing.

And what is belief? It's acting on what God's Word tells us is true.

If our friend builds a boat and we say we're sure he's done a great job, but we won't get in the boat, we don't really believe. It's only words.

To believe means we will live as Christ tells us we should and do what he says even when we don't like it and when the world and our feelings tell us something else is better.

If we never act on our faith, then our belief is never proven, and our lives never show us or others that God is trustworthy and what he says is true. For our belief to become real and grow, we must continually step further out into God's depths (Luke 5:4).

Obedience is the path to walking in the power of the Holy Spirit. If we're still seeking to build our own kingdom instead of the Lord's, if we're sowing to the flesh rather than the Spirit by choosing sin and self over his Word, then we're quenching the Spirit (1 Thessalonians 5:19). But if we're believing—obeying—we will hear his guidance more and more clearly as we go on.

And the result is all joy, all peace, and an abundance of hope!

And who doesn't want that?

Obedience to the one true, good God doesn't lead to constriction but to freedom and rest.

"Behold, God is my helper;
the Lord is the sustainer of my soul."
—Psalm 54:4

The omniscient, omnipotent God who never sleeps (Psalm 121:4–5) and cannot lie (Numbers 23:19) is our helper.

The Lord who endured undeserved torture, sacrificed himself for us out of his great love, and overcame death by resurrecting after three days is the one who sustains us.

The Creator of all who set the boundaries of the sea (Psalm 33:6–7) cares about everything in our lives from the steps we take (Psalm 37:23–26) to the number of hairs on our head (Luke 12:7).

The Lord whose streams of living water never fail even in the scorched places (Isaiah 58:11) and who owns all the beasts of the field and the cattle on a thousand hills (Psalm 50:9–10) is our portion and the provider of our daily bread.

Nothing is too hard for him (Genesis 18:14); there is no greater help. When all seems against us and there's no human way out, we don't have to despair. All our battles are the Lord's (1 Samuel 17:47). He commands armies we cannot see (2 Kings 6:15–17). We do not need to have the most "horses and chariots" on our side (Psalm 20:7).

We can rest in the palm of his hand (Isaiah 49:16) and be gathered under his wings (Psalm 91:4). We can be strong and courageous even in insurmountable odds, knowing that he'll never leave nor forsake us (Deuteronomy 31:6).

When we're hopeless and worn, tired and ready to give up, we can continue to walk faithfully forward and trust the Lord to fight for us (Exodus 14:14).

"The thief comes only to steal and kill and destroy."
—John 10:10

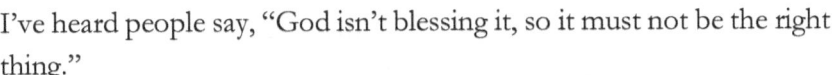

I've heard people say, "God isn't blessing it, so it must not be the right thing."

What they usually mean is, "This is hard, and I've hit a lot of obstacles, so it must not be God's plan."

But when I look at the stories in the Bible, I don't see evidence that the right path is always easy.

The Bible is full of people directly following God's instruction and being met with hardship, rejection, pain, and even death. Doing the right thing while following God often leads to direct opposition from those doing the wrong thing while enslaved to the devil.

The path is hard because there is an enemy trying to thwart God's plan and turn people away from faith, but God uses what is meant for evil and works it to good for those who love him (Genesis 50:20; Romans 8:28).

There will be battles, but there's a difference in how we carry the difficulty when we're walking with the Lord; we lay it on him. We don't have to carry it alone. We choose to deny ourselves and serve him faithfully through it even when we have no power over the circumstances. We can trust him with the outcome.

That marriage, career, or calling isn't necessarily wrong just because it's hard. They may be fraught with frustration and difficulty, but the Bible makes it clear that we will struggle in this life and that our faith will be tested.

God doesn't promise us easy, but he does promise to be with us, and we know he has the ultimate victory as we follow him into eternity.

"But whoever has worldly goods and sees his brother
or sister in need, and closes his heart against him, how
does the love of God remain in him? Little children,
let's not love with word or with tongue, but in deed
and truth. We will know by this that we are of the truth
and will set our heart at ease before him."
—1 John 3:17–19

If the world's cry against us is that we speak words of love but never act on it, they are right to reprimand. If we say we love but no one around us can point to anything loving in us, we are lying to ourselves and to others (1 John 4:20).

"By this," it says, we will know if our own hearts are of the truth.

If we never actively love those around us by laying down our own lives (1 John 3:16), let's come before the Lord in prayer and confession and ask him to change our hearts as we begin to work with intention to change our deeds.

Laying down our lives means giving something up that is our own (John 15:12–13)—if it's worldly goods we can bless others with, we will give there. But we could fill in that blank with other things as well. "But whoever has . . ." time, a listening ear, a day to watch someone's children, the skills to repair a car, kind words instead of harsh ones, or anything else ". . . and sees his brother or sister in need, and closes his heart, how does the love of God remain in him?"

Are our hearts at ease before the Lord, knowing that we are loving not only in word, but in deed and in truth?

"But their minds were hardened; for until this very
day at the reading of the old covenant the same veil
remains unlifted, because it is removed in Christ. But
to this day whenever Moses is read, a veil lies over
their hearts; but whenever someone turns to the
Lord, the veil is taken away."
—2 Corinthians 3:14–16

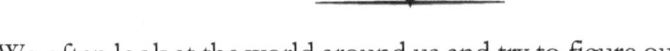

We often look at the world around us and try to figure out how to "lift the veil" that divides unbelievers from salvation.

Too often, I'm afraid we settle on something other than Christ. We try to lift the veil using exciting worship services or cultural relevance. We think it depends on our enticing words, our brilliant presentation, and our masterful debate tactics about the currently trending topics.

But Paul says, "I determined to know nothing among you, except Jesus Christ, and him crucified" (1 Corinthians 2:2). He says his speech and preaching was not with enticing words of man's wisdom lest the hearers' faith should stand in the wisdom of men rather than in the power of God (1 Corinthians 2:4–5).

It's not wrong to craft our words or to speak well—indeed, we're instructed to grow in knowledge (Colossians 1:9–10) and teach skillfully (2 Timothy 2:24)—but if our foundation relies on our worldly tactics and wisdom rather than on knowing and speaking of Jesus Christ and his salvation, we may as well stay silent. All other considerations are secondary.

The veil is lifted only in Christ when the hearers turn to him. No appeal, however winsome, will enact true change if it is not infused with Christ.

MAY 1

"But the vessel that he was making of clay was spoiled in
the hand of the potter; so he remade it into another
vessel, as it pleased the potter to make."
—Jeremiah 18:4

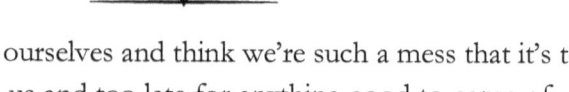

Many of us look at ourselves and think we're such a mess that it's too late for God to use us and too late for anything good to come of our lives. We've been wounded too many times, made too many mistakes, and haven't lived up to our potential.

But nothing is too late for God. Our lives might be a mess with seemingly no purpose, but we can come to him broken and cracked.

He is the potter who formed us with intention and abilities we were designed for (Isaiah 49:5; Ephesians 2:10; Matthew 25:15; Psalm 139). If we're broken, our designer and maker can repair us and reshape us back into another vessel that is once again whole and purposeful.

It might hurt. Our lives might look worse before they look better. The process may feel like destruction rather than healing. It will take time to put us back together, mend our cracks, and fire us in the kiln to transform us into a whole vessel once again.

Afterward, we may not look the same on the outside, but we will be complete and purposeful.

If we put ourselves in the Potter's hand and submit to his care, he is faithful to complete any work he begins in us (Philippians 1:6). He knows the exact length of time and temperature we must stay in the fire in order to come out whole.

There's no such thing as too late. The sooner we allow ourselves to be remade, the sooner our purpose is restored.

"What is the source of quarrels and conflicts
among you? Is the source not your pleasures
that wage war in your body's parts?"
—James 4:1

Wanting something and not getting it—or even simply fearing that we won't get it—is the source not only of quarrels and tensions with those around us but also of many of our inner struggles and temptations.

It's good to perform a self-check when we're feeling out of sorts, dissatisfied, and fearful.

- "What am I wanting that's causing me to lash out at others?"
- "Is attempting to attain this desire pushing me toward sinful behavior?"
- "Can I trust God with this? Is he obligated to provide it, or am I expecting and demanding something he hasn't promised me?"
- "Is it right for me to put this expectation on other people in a way that stirs up strife in my relationships, or am I trying to get people to fulfill a desire that isn't their responsibility?"

There are some "wants" we should fight for—justice, respect, love, etc. But even this fighting should have Christ overlayed. It should never be from selfishness, fear, or fleshly pleasure but always trusting God and pursuing truth.

Instead of reacting angrily or manipulating circumstances to get what we want, let's hold our desires loosely and offer them up to God, setting our minds on things above rather than things on this earth (Colossians 3:2).

Keeping the desires of our flesh from ruling over us and trusting God with them should be part of our behavior as Christians.

This will put us at peace within ourselves and with other people as far as it depends on us (Romans 12:18), and it will leave us ready to receive God's guidance, even when that guidance goes against our desires.

"Therefore, whether you eat or drink, or whatever you do,
do all things for the glory of God."
—1 Corinthians 10:31

Eating and drinking are two of the most basic human activities, so if we can eat or drink to the glory of God then everything we put our hands to every second of every day can be to his glory.

This helps us look at our daily tasks in a new light and infuses even the most menial tasks with purpose.

Whether it's doing the dishes, drafting a report for work, calling a friend back, paying bills, or whittling down that to-do list, all our actions can be infused with great purpose and done to the glory of God . . . or not.

This stems from the position of our hearts, attitudes, motives, and desires. Most of us—if we're paying attention and being honest—can clearly see if we're doing a task to God's glory.

If we aren't, it's not necessarily a simple thing to correct. We have a lifetime of habits formed around how we feel about paperwork, vacuuming, or mowing the lawn—any task that seems unimportant or unenjoyable. But we can begin to change those attitudes by:

- intentionally asking how we can do them to God's glory.
- considering why they might be important to the kingdom of God.
- thinking about the consequences of leaving those tasks undone.

Chances are that by doing things that seem bothersome and insignificant, we're loving others, showing people the integrity and work ethic formed by our relationship with God, and performing chores that provide for and improve our lives and the lives of those who depend on us.

The day-to-day things are not holding us back from the things of God.

They are all things of God.

"'I also swore an oath to you and entered into a
covenant with you so that you became mine,'
declares the Lord God."
—Ezekiel 16:8

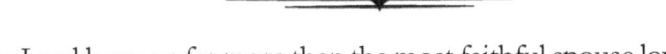

The Lord loves us far more than the most faithful spouse loves his wife or her husband. We are his, and he loves us perfectly.

Have you ever seen the sorrow brought about when the love of one spouse grows cold and they've begun seeking satisfaction elsewhere? Whether it's to infidelity, hobbies, work, friends, or children, the committed spouse feels the sharp knife of sadness and betrayal at the wedge now between them.

They may even become angry and jealous toward the thing that's taken their place. The Lord is the same. When our love strays and we begin seeking satisfaction elsewhere, he is jealous for us, angry at the thing that has stolen our affection, and he mourns the distance between us.

Later in this chapter, it says, "But you trusted in your beauty" (Ezekiel 16:15). Instead of trusting the Lord with our lives and remaining faithful to him, we too often begin trusting in our own innate abilities—the very things he gave us—to gain short-term fulfillment. We stray from the real love, intimate relationship, and foundation we have in him to the false love of this world and the sinking sand of our own abilities.

This grieves him, as it would grieve a person whose spouse prefers the fake, selfish satisfaction of pornography to the act of real, mutually selfless love with them.

Where are we trading the true love of God for the false love of this world? Let us put the temporary pleasure aside and build the lasting satisfaction that comes in a relationship built on the continual commitment that we are his.

"Therefore we do not lose heart, but though our
outer person is decaying, yet our inner person is
being renewed day by day."
—2 Corinthians 4:16

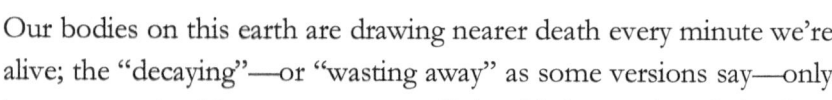

Our bodies on this earth are drawing nearer death every minute we're alive; the "decaying"—or "wasting away" as some versions say—only becomes noticeable as we age or get ill, but it's happening all the time.

But the minute we become a Christian, our inner person begins to be renewed spiritually.

We must choose to accept that the outer, bodily man is wasting away and change our focus from flesh to spirit. Otherwise, the fear of that change and the fear of death may take away the peace that Christ gave to believers when he conquered death; it will take our focus away from the things above and put them back on things below (Colossians 3:2).

As believers, our goals should constantly become less about this temporary outer tent of a body and more about the eternal inner self.

The worldly man is always growing further away from the possibility of attaining new earthly goals, becoming more infirm with the passing years. His time grows shorter every minute he's alive.

But the faithful Christian is growing nearer his highest goal of perfect union with Christ every minute until the very moment of his death.

We are never without purpose despite the growing limitations that come with age.

If our outer person is wasting away in failing health or unmet desires and goals, we can take heart, knowing that the inner person is being renewed day by day. We are forever growing closer and closer to our ultimate aim of Christ and his kingdom.

"I in them and you in me, that they may be perfected in
unity, so that the world may know that you sent me, and
you loved them, just as you loved me."
—John 17:23

Jesus prayed for unity for his followers. Why? "So that the world may know that you sent me, and you loved them, just as you loved me."

When we are living together in unity as the body of Christ, it's evidence to the world that Jesus is the Savior and proof of God's love for the world.

And when we're not living and working together in unity, people aren't seeing the love of Christ; it doesn't look like we're working for the Lord.

I met a woman who said she believes in God, but she doesn't like church people. She'd known a family who'd been active in a church their whole lives. Their little boy got cancer, and the church did almost nothing, but a local bar raised enough to cover his entire treatment. The bottom line: she didn't see Christians loving each other.

Learning how to live and work together as one body matters more than we can know. As it says in 1 Corinthians 12:26, "If one part of the body suffers, all the parts suffer with it; if a part is honored, all the parts rejoice with it."

We need each other, and the world notices if their Christian friends are surrounded by love from other believers or if they're left to fend for themselves, isolated and lonely.

Living as one body doesn't happen by accident. It's something we have to work at. We have to look for needs and ways to fill them. Who in our local church body is hurting today? How can we help?

"So Jesus answered them and said, 'My teaching is not my own, but his who sent me. If anyone is willing to do his will, he will know about the teaching, whether it is of God, or I am speaking from myself.'"
—John 7:16–17

Obedience breeds understanding. There are times in our Christian walk when we don't understand something in the Word or something the Lord prompts us to do. Either it feels too hard, too scary, or it just plain doesn't make sense to our worldly minds.

This verse and my own personal experience both show me that when we are "willing to do his will" simply because we trust him, we begin knowing about the teaching. What looked like a foggy barricade before us begins to clear, revealing the path God has put us on.

So many of his teachings seem difficult and inscrutable. They feel like things no one would ever want to do.

- "Love your enemies" (Matthew 5:44).
- "Consider one another as more important than yourselves" (Philippians 2:3).
- Crucify the passions and desires of the flesh (Galatians 5:24).

It's in the obedience that those hard things begin to feel life-giving rather than soul-crushing and freeing rather than confining.

Suddenly, we're no longer slaves to our hate, our selfishness, and our desires; we're slaves to Christ's goodness, love, and peace (Romans 6:16–18). It's here, after we release all the things we thought we wanted, that we begin finding the easy yoke and light burden he promises.

Our knowledge and understanding follow the obedience. We should never wait till following the Lord's commands makes sense to us because when we follow, the revelation comes. It's when we lose our life for Christ that we find it (Matthew 10:39).

"If the dead are not raised, let's eat and drink,
for tomorrow we die."
—1 Corinthians 15:32

We sometimes wonder at the fact that the world doesn't live right-eously according to God's Word, but from their perspective, doing whatever feels good in this life makes sense. They might as well enjoy all the earthly things they can because they believe the good this world offers is the only good they will ever get.

If there's nothing to come after death, why wouldn't they pour all their efforts into attaining riches, pleasure, and happiness right now? Their chances to achieve these things and enjoy life decrease the longer they live. There's no reason to do otherwise.

But as Christians, we know we will have eternal delight in the pres-ence of the Lord with no more pain, tears, or sorrow (Revelation 21:4). We know that following the Lord, even where it means denying our earthly desires, brings us closer and closer to eternal happiness.

Instead of judging people for the lack of understanding that leads them to walk in the flesh, we should have compassion for their eternal souls and strive to show them truth so they can learn to seek the true, lasting pleasure of being in Christ.

One way we can do this is by living our lives in a way that shows our hope is not dependent on this world's successes or pleasures. We can enjoy those things if we have them, but because of our eternal hope, we can live in contentment even if we don't.

"'Not by might nor by power, but by my Spirit,'
says the Lord of armies."
—Zechariah 4:6

We go through much of our time thinking, "How will I ever get the stuff done, achieve success, figure out what I should do, pay the bill, or navigate this relationship?"

This is the answer to all of it—not by might, nor by power, but by his Spirit. We learn and work hard, we practice and grow, we live responsibly and act in wisdom, but, ultimately, all our human effort can only go so far. We're blind to so much behind the veil of time, knowledge, and experience. None of us have enough strength or know-how to navigate all the uncertain waters of this world.

As long as we lean on and trust in our own intelligence, understanding, talents, skills, abilities, or our own financial and time resources without taking things to the Lord, we will continue asking, "How will I ever . . . ?"

We don't know enough or have enough. But the Lord does.

So next time we think, "There's not enough time or money; I'm too tired, confused, and hopeless," let's remind ourselves, "It's not by how much time or money I have or by my own strength; it's only by his Spirit."

Then we can take it to the Lord in prayer before we've worn ourselves out with human effort. We don't have to come to God with things as a last-ditch effort after we've proven that our might and power are not enough. We can do it from the start, asking him for wisdom, and moving forward with the confidence he's guiding us all along the way and growing us in grace and knowledge (2 Peter 3:18).

"But now God has arranged the parts,
each one of them in the body, just as he desired."
—1 Corinthians 12:18

This verse calms one of our greatest fears—the fear that we have no purpose and God cannot use us.

It reminds us that he created each of us just the way he meant to, and he is not going to abandon the work of his hands (Psalm 138:8).

Sometimes we don't seem to be accomplishing much at all, and it feels like maybe he has forgotten his work. But when we remember what the Word says—that he is never-changing and cannot lie—we are assured that he is faithful to complete his good work in us (Philippians 1:6).

The Lord knows the path each life needs to take. He knows all our weaknesses and failures. He doesn't need us to be talented enough, skilled enough, or knowledgeable enough.

Moses wasn't a good speaker (Exodus 4:10). Gideon wasn't a natural leader (Judges 6:15). David committed adultery and murder (2 Samuel 11). Peter denied him (Luke 22:54–62).

The Lord is going to fulfill a good purpose in and through us despite our lack of innate ability and even despite our sin as we repent and turn back to him in obedience.

The most purposeful thing we can do when don't feel capable or when we fail is to run straight to God with our weaknesses. The creator knows what he made each of us for, and as we submit, he will accomplish it.

> "For whoever wants to save his life will lose it; but
> whoever loses his life for my sake will find it."
> —Matthew 16:25

We often look at the first part of this verse and think how hard it is. Rarely do we look at the second part of the verse and rejoice. We're so focused on the difficulty of dying to self, we forget about the joy of what we're guaranteed in its place.

When we're still encumbered with trying to "save our lives" on this earth, we're beset with all sorts of concerns, desires, and anxieties.

Can I do it?

Will it work out?

This isn't fair!

Needing this life to fit our expectations straps us to the circumstances around us. We're dependent upon them meeting our desires and fulfilling our expectations. And if they're not what we want or think they should be, we drift into anger, anxiety, bitterness, or disappointment. We're at the whims of this uncertain world.

But when we're willing to lose our lives for Christ's sake, our ability to be full of love, joy, hope, and all the other fruits of the Spirit is no longer dependent on the ever-changing conditions and situations we find ourselves in.

When we can't succeed, when things aren't fair, and when things don't work out, we can still go on with hope. We are free from our wants and expectations.

When we give up our lives intentionally for Christ's sake, we cannot be shaken. We become fixed on the only unchanging, sure foundation, so when the world around us crumbles, we don't fall apart with it.

> "And he said, 'Come!' And Peter got out of the boat and
> walked on the water, and came toward Jesus. But seeing
> the wind, he became frightened, and when he began to
> sink, he cried out, saying, 'Lord, save me!'"
> —Matthew 14:29–30

Not all the disciples asked to get out of the boat . . . but look what happened when Peter did ask! Because his confidence was in the Lord, he walked on the water.

Even though it was storming, his faith in Christ was stronger than his fear of the storm . . . until it wasn't.

The wind didn't bring him down. The waves didn't bring him down. His fear and doubt did. He looked around at the wind and started thinking about how strong the storm was instead of how strong Jesus was.

If we keep our eyes on Christ and we're doing something he has called us to do, we will go on without being tossed about or sinking even when life is stormy.

But if we start focusing on the overwhelming circumstances and believing that maybe Jesus really doesn't have the situation in hand, we will start to sink.

Let's ask the Lord if we can get out of the boat and watch what he will do in and through us. If we feel the circumstances start to overwhelm us, we put our eyes back on him and remember he is the same God who calms the wind and waves, the same God who raised Jesus from the dead, and the same God who has gotten us through so many things and provided for us in so many ways before.

The miracles come when we don't look at the circumstances, however overwhelming they seem, but instead look at him.

> "There is a way which seems right to a person,
> but its end is the way of death."
> —Proverbs 14:12

◆

We can make sensible decisions at every turn in life yet end up far away from the Lord or any good purpose he has for us. This is why asking the Lord for wisdom (James 1) is so important. Worldly wisdom—what makes sense to us if we are treating this world as our home—is rarely going to lead us down the narrow road to Christ.

We often get worried when we're taking a path others question; their disapproval makes us insecure. We wonder if we're doing the right thing or going off on a foolish quest.

But the Lord's path will often look like a foolish quest to people who are worldly-wise (1 Corinthians 1:27). And sometimes the Lord gives us a path we can't explain, just like he sent Abraham out without telling him where he was going.

Many would say, "The Lord wouldn't just tell you to 'Go,' without any further direction. You need to wait for more instruction." But often, the Lord is waiting for our obedience in order to show us the next step.

Others' questioning shouldn't cause us insecurity about our choices unless we know them to be godly people who are also walking with the Lord. And even then, God puts us all on unique paths, so ultimately, our decisions can only be made by being obedient to and meditating on God's Word, constantly walking in the Spirit (John 3:8; Galatians 5:16–17), and praying without ceasing.

> "A time to weep and a time to laugh;
> a time to mourn and a time to dance."
> —Ecclesiastes 3:4

Our world would have us believe we should never have to weep and never have to mourn—that our supreme goal is happiness and fun, and that we should be exempt from sadness and pain.

But this is a recipe for disillusionment and denial. We will all face pain and sorrow in this life.

Our efforts to ignore, bury, or run from it will not change that.

When it's time to weep, don't be afraid to weep. When it's time to mourn, don't be afraid to mourn. We don't have to hide or ignore it. We don't have to act like we enjoy our suffering. The Lord never says to pretend everything is fine.

He says, "In the world you have tribulation, but take courage; I have overcome the world" (John 16:33).

We can have courage even while we weep and mourn, because we know the overcoming is already accomplished.

But we should also not be afraid to laugh and dance. Christianity is not meant to keep us from enjoying the good things the Lord has given us in this life. Joy is one of the fruits of the Spirit, and solemnity is not a mark of righteousness.

If we're in a time of weeping and mourning, we don't have to lose hope. And if we're in a time of laughing and dancing, it shouldn't become the source of our hope.

The seasons of this life will always shift unsteadily, but we have a God who never changes, cannot lie, and who has promised the life to come is free from weeping, pain, and sorrow. All of heaven will be a time for joy.

> "But the tax collector, standing some distance
> away, was even unwilling to raise his eyes toward
> heaven, but was beating his chest, saying,
> 'God, be merciful to me, the sinner!'"
> —Luke 18:13

This tax collector was so aware of his sins he would not even lift his eyes to the heavens while praying.

The Pharisee, in the meantime, prayed to thank God they were not like these other sinful men, but that they were good and righteous, boasting in the middle of their prayers by listing all the good things they did.

Jesus tells us that the tax collector went away justified in the sight of the Lord while the Pharisee did not (Luke 18:14).

This story strikes home when we consider the times we've seen someone else's sin and thought something like, "Well, at least I don't struggle with THAT."

We may not be putting those words in our prayers, but if the attitude exists in us at all, we're missing a trait that's essential for followers of Jesus—humility.

There will never be a time in our Christian walk when superiority and disdain for other peoples' struggles will be acceptable. There will never be a time we don't need to pray, "God, be merciful to me, a sinner!" just as much as we ever did.

We are always to come to the Lord and walk through life in humility.

"For everyone who exalts himself will be humbled, but the one who humbles himself will be exalted" (Luke 18:14).

> "We are of good courage and prefer rather to be
> absent from the body and to be at home with the
> Lord. Therefore we also have as our ambition,
> whether at home or absent, to be pleasing to him."
> —2 Corinthians 5:8–9

Sometimes this life is hard, and as faithful followers who have a sure eternal inheritance, we might wish to skip the current difficulty and go ahead and start that existence that has no tears, pain, or sorrow (Revelation 21:4).

There's nothing wrong with that wish. To be with the Lord fully should be our greatest desire as believers.

But we don't get to choose when we get there. It's the Lord's will and wisdom that ushers us into heaven at the right time, but it's by living his will and pleasing him now that we make our lives here most like what they will be in the eternal kingdom.

Our whole ambition is to be set on pleasing our Lord.

Matthew 6:10 says, "Your kingdom come. Your will be done, on earth as it is in heaven."

Though the world around us may not help build the kingdom, we can. With every simple act of obedience, we grow nearer to our Lord, and our lives become more and more like they will be once we reach the kingdom of God, revealing more of the nature of God and his kingdom to others. Through this, our joy is made full even now (John 15:11).

Let us press on, longing for our Lord and eager to please him now just as we will in eternity, even while we still live in the troubles of this world.

"He who said to them, 'This is the place of quiet, give rest
to the weary,' and, 'This is the resting place,' but they
would not listen. So the word of the Lord to them will be,
'Order on order, order on order, line on line, line on line,
a little here, a little there,' that they may go and stumble
backward, be broken, snared, and taken captive."
—Isaiah 28:12–13

The Lord wants to teach us the truth that leads to a place of quiet and
gives rest in Jesus.

But in our stubbornness, we often only see his rules—"order on
order, line on line." Like toddlers, we haven't proceeded beyond the
"milk" of understanding (Isaiah 28:9), so we see these rules as arbitrary,
not believing there are greater purposes behind them.

And we remain spiritual toddlers for far too long, feeling like God
is restricting us unfairly or trying to prove our "goodness' by following
them.

But there is only one work that will not perish: "that you believe in
him whom he has sent" (John 6:29). This means we can believe all he
says and follow it even when we don't understand the objective reasons
behind his rules.

Viewing God's commandments as "orders upon orders" (instead
of simply believing Jesus and all he taught) will only ever lead to pride
if we're really good at keeping them (like the Pharisees) or despair if
we aren't.

Only the obedience that comes from love (John 14:15) leads us to
quiet, freedom, and rest, because it comes from trust that all he says is
good and truly best for us. It doesn't require the straining and striving
we normally put into obedience when we truly believe it will also bring
about the best good for our lives.

"Now the serpent was more cunning than any animal
of the field which the Lord God had made. And he
said to the woman, 'Has God really said, "You shall
not eat from any tree of the garden"?'"
—Genesis 3:1

Eve had the entire world at her disposal . . . all except one tree. Satan wanted to keep her focused on that one thing God had kept from her; he also confused and exaggerated the difficulty of God's restriction so it seemed excessive and unreasonable.

The devil still uses these same tactics; he continually draws our attention away from all the wonderful things the Lord gives us so we will focus anywhere God has said no. We start thinking more and more about the things we can't or don't have and how God must not love us because he's keeping those things from us.

Satan wants us to believe we're not walking in freedom and that the Lord's rules are unfair.

But only God's freedom is truly free. It's like a fence . . . yes, it keeps us from going beyond it, but everything good is within. It exists because everything outside of it will hurt us in the end.

Satan's "freedom" would have us climbing the fence and running out into traffic. His main goal is to "steal, kill, and destroy" (John 10:10). He wants us injured, wounded, angry, defeated, trapped, bitter, and divided from God.

When Satan tempts us to look at what God has not allowed us, our defense is to turn our eyes back to all the good God does give and remember that anything our loving Father restricts or withholds is because he knows dangers we cannot see; he would protect us from the pain of discovering them the hard way.

"Then the Lord said, 'Behold, there is a place by me,
and you shall stand there on the rock.'"
—Exodus 33:21

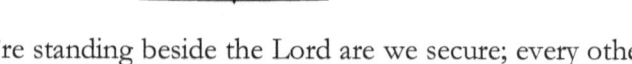

Only when we're standing beside the Lord are we secure; every other place we could stand will lead to shifting sand and a faulty foundation.

There are days when we don't place ourselves beside the Lord—when we choose to walk in ways contrary to what he tells us in his Word or what we know he's called us to. Instead of standing beside him, we stand by our sin—whether from fear or selfishness—and that puts us on shaky ground.

It's easy to think, "I'll just trust this today and go back to trusting God tomorrow," but that "today" often turns into several days or weeks or months. It's always that much harder to go back to standing beside him when we've gotten into the habit of standing by our flesh.

When we're tempted to choose something we know is opposed to the Lord's will, a good question to ask ourselves is, "Do I really believe his Word is true? Do I believe following him will result in better things than giving in to my desires or feelings in this moment?"

As believers, if the answer to that question is no, we need to dig into our beliefs about the Lord!

But if we answer those questions with a yes, then choose ourselves anyway, we know we're not only walking away from the Lord's will and in danger of giving the devil a foothold, we're also acting in opposition to our core beliefs, which always leads to inner turmoil and dissatisfaction.

Let's remember that it's always worth following him, even when it means denying ourselves or walking into difficult situations.

Beside him is always best.

"Now in the same way the Spirit also helps our
weakness; for we do not know what to pray for as we
should, but the Spirit himself intercedes for us with
groanings too deep for words; and he who searches the
hearts knows what the mind of the Spirit is, because he
intercedes for the saints according to the will of God.
And we know that God causes all things to work
together for good to those who love God, to those
who are called according to his purpose."
—Romans 8:26–28

We often hear the first and the last of these three verses independently but rarely in context with one another.

It's quite comforting that the Spirit intercedes when my groanings are unintelligible and I don't know what or how to pray.

But this passage also calms the fear that we're praying things outside of God's will. For when "we do not know what to pray for as we should," the Holy Spirit intercedes for us "according to the will of God."

Many of our prayers are about removing suffering, and that's okay. Even Jesus prayed this way in the garden: "My Father, if it is possible, let this cup pass from me" (Matthew 26:39).

But just as Jesus's prayer was not granted, what we hope and pray for may not be what would lead to the greatest eternal good.

But when our hearts join Jesus in adding his, "yet not as I will, but as you will," we can be sure the Holy Spirit makes all our prayers right, and that God will work all things—our misguided prayers, all of our suffering, the good in our lives, and the things we don't understand—to good for those who follow him (Romans 8:28).

"Put on the Lord Jesus Christ, and make no
provision for the flesh in regard to its lusts."
—Romans 13:14

The word "lust" is also translated "desires." It can mean anything from anger, bitterness, and sexual sin to greed, alcohol, or man's approval—any worldly desire we give a place in our lives.

This "putting on" of Christ literally means to "clothe yourself with," "to sink into," or to "invest in clothing."

"Putting on" is ongoing. We do not clothe ourselves once; we clothe ourselves every day with fresh clothing. Counting on our Sunday service or on a spiritual experience we had years ago to guard us from the desires of the flesh isn't enough. Our spirits need to put Christ on anew every day.

And we only "sink into" something substantial. You can't sink into a linen shirt, but you can sink into a down jacket. Putting on Jesus each day protects us from the elements—our fleshly desires and the darts of the enemy. Without Christ, we are exposed.

And investment means this garment isn't cheap. We may have to sacrifice to acquire it. Jesus is that pearl of great price so valuable that paying absolutely everything we have would be worth it to have him . . . even unto death. In daily life, this looks like "investing" our finances, time, service, and our whole lives as the Lord leads—all our heart, soul, mind, and strength (Mark 12:30).

Caring for our flesh in healthy ways is responsible, but when it comes to its lusts, we're to "make no provision." We do not plan out how we can satisfy our unhealthy desires.

We clothe ourselves with Jesus so those fleshly desires get no say in our decisions, our time, or our activities.

"For your sake we are killed all day long; we were
regarded as sheep to be slaughtered. But in all these things
we overwhelmingly conquer through Him who loved us."
—Romans 8:36–37

We all love the idea of overwhelmingly conquering, but we often forget the context in which that phrase is placed. According to the Word, we "overwhelmingly conquer" even when we're being "killed all day long" in persecution.

Many times, this verse is taken to mean we will succeed at our worldly pursuits, that we cannot lose, and that we will triumph over our enemies.

We think of it like a conquering king coming in to rule a nation; he's taking charge and having things done his own way.

But that's not what this verse is talking about. It's telling us that even when we lose the battle on this earth according to worldly standards, we're still conquerors—and not just conquerors, but overwhelmingly so. Nothing can take our triumph because no enemy can snatch us from God's hand. Even when believers are murdered for our faith, the victory we have in our heavenly reward puts us on the winning side.

That victory is not dependent upon earthly wins and losses; it's only dependent upon our faith in Christ and our enduring through trials for the joy set before us just as Jesus did (Hebrews 12:2).

When we don't seem to be winning in our circumstances, we are still overwhelming conquerors as we trust him just as Christ was a conqueror when he hung, dying, on the cross. It did not look like victory, but it was. He endured for the joy set before him, and so can we.

"I will give thanks to you, because I am awesomely
and wonderfully made; wonderful are your works,
and my soul knows it very well."
—Psalm 139:14

We often look at ourselves and see only the things we don't like about our bodies, our abilities (or inabilities), our insecurities, our personalities, and our struggles.

We all have things that aren't considered ideal according to this world's judgment—things that, by our standards, hold us back in success or relationships.

But God made each of us unique reflections of himself, capable of serving and reflecting his image out into the world in different ways.

Some of us struggle with anxiety or mental illness, some from physical illness or disability, and some of us can't seem to manage in social situations no matter how hard we try.

We're each still fearfully and wonderfully made. God knows our best and highest purpose in life. Just like the blindness in John 9:1–3 was not a punishment, there is always something in our difficulty that God can and will use to show his love and glory to others.

Our service is to offer that struggle up to the Lord. Sometimes our prayers may be, "God, I don't have anything good or strong or perfect to offer you. I only have this sadness, this anxious heart, this grief, this struggle, this weakness."

We are fearfully and wonderfully made. Just like that man born blind, it may take years of struggle to see what the Lord is going to do with that difficulty, but even while we're weak in body, we can grow strong in the Spirit (2 Corinthians 4:16).

God made each of us, and wonderful are his works. Do our souls know it well?

"If I speak with the tongues of mankind and of angels,
but do not have love, I have become
a noisy gong or a clanging cymbal."
—1 Corinthians 13:1

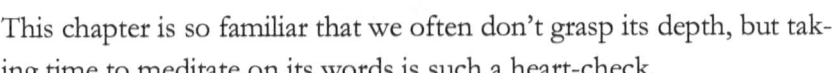

This chapter is so familiar that we often don't grasp its depth, but taking time to meditate on its words is such a heart-check.

What is motivating our words? Do we speak just because we can? So people will think we're smart or wise? So we can win arguments? Or is it out of love?

All reasons except the last render our words, at best, pointless, and at worst, harmful.

Our most eloquent speech is no more meaningful than a toddler banging kitchen pots and pans together if that speech has no love in it.

Love is the essential ingredient that gives our words power and makes them fruitful. How many times do we speak truth and try to correct others without seasoning our words with love? It's a pointless endeavor.

The Lord gives no caveats here. He does not say, "It's okay to speak without love if the people are really evil, have really hurt you, or have been speaking without love to you." Even when speaking difficult truths to evil people, it should be done with love for the hearers.

This is a question to ask ourselves regularly: "Why do I want to speak into this circumstance or discussion? Is it because of love?"

Words of love can change lives. If we cannot look at the people in front of us and love them, we may as well remain silent and pray until what we want to say is truly motivated by love.

"And the redeemed of the Lord will return and come to
Zion with joyful shouting, and everlasting joy will be on
their heads. They will obtain gladness and joy, and
sorrow and sighing will flee away."
—Isaiah 35:10

As Christians, we are the redeemed of the Lord. We deserved an everlasting punishment for our crimes, but he paid a debt he did not owe, and now, we are promised an everlasting joy!

While sometimes the "everlasting" part feels too far away as we struggle through life on this earth, once it's gained, we will realize how brief all our troubles here really were, and all our sorrow and sighing will flee. There's no question about that.

We will not resent the troubles we had here; we will not regret the things we never got the chance to do or have. We won't care about any of that.

Whatever troubles we're living through now, we can rest on this everlasting promise and trust that they will be a mere blink of an eye to us once we reach eternity, where we shall have no more tears or pain (Revelation 21:4).

Each of our lives can tell the story of a steadfast faith as we take one step after the other in divine hope of that everlasting joy. Even when enemies plague us, friends are fickle, injuries abound, and the weather of circumstance makes our journey hard, we can go on with confidence.

In our eternal Zion, the pain will be forgotten, and joy and gladness will be our inheritance.

"For the body is not one part, but many. If the foot
says, 'Because I am not a hand, I am not a part of
the body,' it is not for this reason any less a part of
the body. And if the ear says, 'Because I am not an
eye, I am not a part of the body,' it is not for this
reason any less a part of the body."
—1 Corinthians 12:14–16

Many of us believe that because we're not an "eye," we're not of the body. We have nothing to offer. We may not say that out loud, but we live it when we think things like, "Because I'm not a teacher, singer, preacher, or because I'm not outgoing or smart, etc., I have nothing to offer the body."

But verse 18 says, "Now God has arranged the parts, each one of them in the body, just as he desired."

God has designed and placed each of us into the body of Christ just how he intended.

Believing we have nothing to offer is like us telling God, "You did it wrong. You made me the wrong part. I'm useless."

But God doesn't do things wrong. He designed each of us just as he intended and created work for us to do according to that design (Ephesians 2:10).

Even the Christian community seems to value some parts of the body of Christ more than others, but God makes it clear that we are all needed.

Let's not waste time wishing we were some other part of the body. Let's believe that God designed us as we are on purpose and that he will guide us in how to serve the body there.

"Or who enclosed the sea with doors when it went out
from the womb, bursting forth; when I made a cloud its
garment, and thick darkness its swaddling bands, and I
placed boundaries on it and set a bolt and doors, and I
said, 'As far as this point you shall come, but no farther;
and here your proud waves shall stop'?"
—Job 38:8–11

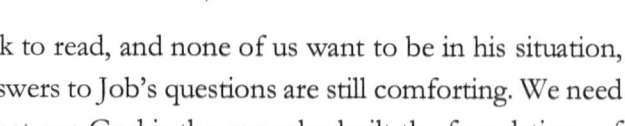

Job is a hard book to read, and none of us want to be in his situation, but the Lord's answers to Job's questions are still comforting. We need to be reminded that our God is the one who built the foundations of the earth, the one who arranged the seas, and the one who holds them in their place.

When we consider his power, knowledge, and goodness in these mighty things, it's so much easier to rest in his sovereignty.

We no longer have to understand what's happening when we trust the one who's in control.

It doesn't mean we must enjoy the difficulties in this life. It simply means we see that the great God of the universe is not unaware of or unable to redeem those difficult things and that the wonder of our eternal lives to come will far overshadow this suffering.

As the Lord says to the sea, "this far and no farther," so he says to the suffering of Job. And so he says to Satan of our difficulties: "You can only seek to steal, kill, and destroy my people in this life. In eternity, they will be fully healed and fully mine—safe forever. No more tears, pain, or sorrow."

Rest in the forever that comes after "this far and no farther."

"All things are permitted for me, but I will not
be mastered by anything."
—1 Corinthians 6:12

If there is something in our lives that tells us where to go and what to do, if we place our identity in it, if we cannot imagine being content without it, or aren't sure we could give it up if the Lord asked, we're in danger of that thing becoming our master.

There are a few obvious things people are dominated by—addictions, lusts, unforgiveness, and anger. But there are many more socially acceptable things that can dominate us as well—relationships, food, health, jobs, position, or money.

If any of those things are given priority over following God, we're attempting to have two masters—a thing the Word tells us is impossible (Matthew 6:24).

There are many good, permissible things we hope for in this world that make life easier and more enjoyable—safety, health, security, a wonderful community, and so forth. But if doing without them would turn us away from God, they hold too much sway in our hearts, and it's time to dethrone an idol.

As with the rich young ruler, God will always show us the choice, but he will not force us to make it. May we not go away from Christ sad as that young man did, overtaken by a worldly master and unwilling to give it up.

The greatest commandment is to "love the Lord your God with all your heart, and with all your soul, and with all your mind, and with all your strength" (Mark 12:30).

As believers, no one and nothing should take a higher place in our desires, will, thoughts, or efforts over following Christ.

Nothing else should drive us or our decisions.

"God is light, and in him there is no darkness at all. If we say that we have fellowship with him and yet walk in the darkness, we lie and do not practice the truth; but if we walk in the light as he himself is in the light, we have fellowship with one another, and the blood of Jesus his son cleanses us from all sin."
—1 John 1:5–7

Walking in the light, for us, means we walk with Jesus—we strive to walk as he walked (1 John 2:6). We will not do it perfectly, but where our imperfection shows through, we repent and have confidence we are forgiven through his sacrifice (1 John 1:9).

And the result of this walking in the light? Fellowship with one another. We don't often connect in our minds that walking closely with Christ results in closeness with others, but this tells us that fellowship is dependent upon walking in the light.

I wonder how many of our relationships are broken because one or the other of us has decided we "have no sin" (verse 8) or we have not confessed and repented of our sin (verse 9).

Confession and humility before the Lord and each other are key to walking in fellowship. When we think, "If only they would . . .", we're ignoring our own part in the rift. When we look within and confess our part, we're walking in the light.

And that's worth it even if the relationship remains broken, which it may. It takes both parties walking in the light and in confession, repentance, and humility for true fellowship to exist.

"Woe to you, scribes and Pharisees, hypocrites! For you tithe mint and dill and cumin, and have neglected the weightier provisions of the law: justice and mercy and faithfulness; but these are the things you should have done without neglecting the others. You blind guides, who strain out a gnat and swallow a camel!"
—Matthew 23:23–24

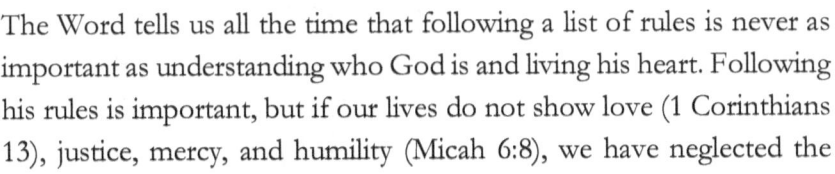

The Word tells us all the time that following a list of rules is never as important as understanding who God is and living his heart. Following his rules is important, but if our lives do not show love (1 Corinthians 13), justice, mercy, and humility (Micah 6:8), we have neglected the weightier things.

Are we trying to obey him with a formulaic list of duties like the Pharisees, or are we giving our whole hearts to him by submitting to the Spirit, serving and loving others, humbling ourselves to walk in his ways, sharing his Word and his kingdom with others, surrendering to him, and defending the weak? Are we only obeying outwardly for self-serving reasons, or are we denying ourselves, taking up our cross, and following him?

The Pharisees made rules more important than people. Jesus showed that the rules were made for the good of the people. If we're using them to hurt others, we're using them wrongly.

If we are scrupulously tithing and appearing at church every time the doors are open, prideful of our "goodness" and holding all others to our external standard of perfection, but not walking in and sharing his steadfast love, we have strained out a gnat and swallowed a camel. We are like a noisy gong or a clanging cymbal. We have missed the beauty of the Father's heart.

"Do all things without complaining or arguments; so that
you will prove yourselves to be blameless and innocent,
children of God above reproach in the midst of a crooked
and perverse generation, among whom you appear as
lights in the world, holding firmly the word of life, so that
on the day of Christ I can take pride because I did not run
in vain nor labor in vain."
—Philippians 2:14–16

Doing all things without complaining or arguments is not the way of the world; there are many duties we would prefer not to do, both at work and at home. It's easy to grumble and gripe, and it often feels impossible not to. So let's look at the reasons these verses say to live this way and try to find our motivation there.

- So we can be blameless and innocent before the world. How refreshing it would be to work and live with people who do all things without grumbling? It would be hard for others to find fault with that cheerful heart.

- So we can shine the light of Christ in the darkness of a crooked and twisted world. If we live like this, people see it and wonder why. It will draw people to Christ because it's how he lived his own life.

- So when we stand before the Lord, we can be confident we didn't live our lives chasing things that don't matter in the end but doing his work.

When we're tempted to complain and argue, let's reflect on these words instead and honor Christ with our attitude in all things. This is one way we practice prioritizing the things of the Spirit over the things of the flesh (Galatians 5:16–17).

It will ensure we have not labored in vain.

JUNE 1

"For the Lord God is a sun and shield; the Lord gives
grace and glory; he withholds no good thing from
those who walk with integrity."
—Psalm 84:11

Sometimes it feels like God is withholding something good from us. It's the oldest lie—the one the devil used on Eve in the Garden of Eden. He convinced her that God was withholding something good from her even though there was only one tree from which she could not eat. The devil put her attention on that one thing and had her questioning God's goodness and intentions toward her.

I can look back and see things I desperately wanted but did not receive . . . things that seemed good. But I can see that getting those things at those times would've done me harm. I didn't really know what was "good" for me, and I'm grateful now that God withheld things from me.

He wasn't withholding good things; he was withholding dangerous things that seemed good on the surface. But God—knowing our inmost heart—knows what is actually good for us.

Adam and Eve had the perfect existence—complete provision and perfect fellowship with one another and the Lord—only that one tree wasn't available to them. Yet by focusing on what they couldn't have, they ran outside of God's plan. They chased the one thing not allowed to them, and they caught it, to their detriment.

May we always live in the broad freedom God has granted us (Psalm 18:19) and trust that if it feels like he is withholding something, that thing would not actually be good for us in the long run.

"For my thoughts are not your thoughts, nor are your
ways my ways,' declares the Lord. 'For as the heavens are
higher than the earth, so are my ways higher than your
ways and my thoughts than your thoughts.'"
—Isaiah 55:8–9

It's comforting to remind ourselves that the Lord knows far more and far better than we do when things don't work out the way we hoped or prayed. The Lord sees and knows all the tiny steps each of our lives need to take in order to create the tapestry of the world from the beginning of time until the end.

It's a tapestry that takes all the bad and brokenness our sin created—the dark threads of sickness, sorrow, evil, pain, and death—and weaves them into a beautiful picture of hope and redemption.

For those of us inside of time, it's like seeing the tapestry from the back. It's all knots and tangles and in pieces that don't look like anything; we can't see the pattern. But God, on the other side, omniscient and outside of time, takes those dark threads and turns them into triumphant depth and outlines of the people he is shaping us to be.

Because sin entered the world, the world is broken, and evil is possible (Romans 5:12). In that brokenness, we hurt one another. But because God is good and loves us, he's promised that he can and will reshape all of those hurts and transform them into good for those who love him (Romans 8:28).

The ultimate healing is coming in our forever life, but in the meantime, we can trust that our sufferings are worked to good purpose. His thoughts are higher than our thoughts, and his ways are higher than our ways.

"Do not trust in noblemen, in mortal man, in whom there
is no salvation. His spirit departs, he returns to the earth;
on that very day his plans perish. Blessed is he whose help
is the God of Jacob, whose hope is in the Lord his God."
—Psalm 146:3–5

Many of our hurts come from trusting in mortal mankind.

Maybe we trusted in parents who failed us, a spouse who left, or
friends who betrayed us. Maybe we put our trust in a church leader
who fell into sin, a church that abandoned us when we needed it most,
or a government that didn't support the cause of justice.

These are soul-crushing failures, but they aren't surprising, and they
shouldn't shake our faith.

A person's badness cannot invalidate the truth of Christ, because
it's for people's badness that Christ came (Luke 19:10; Mark 2:17). This
is why we need him. Our faith is not in humans, but in Christ himself.

When those things happen (and they will), we often become lost
and disillusioned with faith in general. But if our faith can be broken
by the deeds of people (even our own), institutions, or the failure of
our own hopes and plans, then that's where we've placed our trust.

But blessed is he whose hope and help is in the Lord.

Hope placed in him keeps us on solid ground where we cannot be
swayed by the storms of this life and the disappointments of men who
cannot save us.

Let's take our eyes off ourselves, other men, institutions, and our
own plans and put them back on the steady ground of hope in the Lord
alone.

"Your word is a lamp to my feet and a light to my path."
—Psalm 119:105

Sometimes we don't know what to do, and we go round and round trying to figure it out.

But the best decision-making strategy is to stop and spend time in the Word and in prayer, then wait. God's guidance is the only sure guidance.

Sometimes the answer isn't a direction; it's simply peace in the not-knowing, which is an answer in itself.

When we walk with the Lord, we can have the peace that passes all understanding even when we don't know what to do, because we are certain that he does. If we're paying attention and being obedient, he will always reveal the steps to us as we need them.

A lamp does not show us the end of our journey—only the next few steps.

Sometimes we think we've let him direct our steps but realize on the way that we're actually only letting him lead as long as we approve of the destination. We start going our own way and ignoring his guidance, the Word, and the Holy Spirit if we start thinking it might be leading us somewhere we don't like.

But God is not like GPS. We don't punch in the destination then ask him for directions.

If we want to know where to go, we must follow Christ, and the act of following someone else inherently implies we don't know where we're going.

If we choose our own path, we will be walking blind in a world of pitfalls and misdirection.

Christ and the Bible are our Word (John 1:1)—the light that reveals our direction on the good path he has for us (John 8:12).

"A disciple is not above his teacher, nor a slave above his master. It is enough for the disciple that he may become like his teacher, and the slave like his master. If they have called the head of the house Beelzebul, how much more will they insult the members of his household!"
—Matthew 10:24–25

Our human nature wants to believe that serving God will have us living our best life (in worldly terms) in the here and now.

But God's plans don't always—or even often—look like earthly success. Trusting him will often mean walking a lonely road off the beaten path . . . a road that the world may not appreciate or recognize as valuable. We can look at nearly any Bible character to find that theme. Joseph was sold into slavery by his family. Moses was in exile from Egypt, losing all his earthly connections and power. Most of the Old Testament prophets were unappreciated and even hated. John the Baptist was beheaded. Most of the disciples were martyred. Jesus was murdered.

Jesus was perfect, and he still didn't get his earthly due. They even said he was working with Satan. So if we feel like people aren't paying attention or are even hostile toward what we're doing when we're following the Lord, we're in good company, and we shouldn't be surprised.

Others' approval or disapproval cannot tell us if we're walking in the Lord's will. Our only aim should be obedience to him, and we shouldn't be shocked when that obedience leads to unpopularity or persecution.

"I am not able to carry all this people by myself,
because it is too burdensome for me."
—Numbers 11:14

Moses was tired . . . tired of being responsible for everything and tired of the peoples' complaints. In the surrounding verses, he basically says, "Why did you give me this job, God? I didn't ask for it; I don't want it, and if this is how things are going to continue, just kill me!"

It sounds dramatic, but I think we all feel this way to some extent at some point. And the truth is, the burden often *is* too heavy for us. We need to roll it over on God and stop trying to control everything. And sometimes, we need the help of the community around us.

In this case, God tells Moses to gather other leaders—seventy of them—and divide up the work. If it was going to take seventy people to do the work Moses had been trying to do on his own, no wonder he was distraught!

When we're feeling overworked, overwhelmed, and overwrought, we need to ask ourselves if there are some folks we can divide the load with. There's no shame in asking for help; it's the posture of humility. And sometimes, we've taken on burdens that are not our own, stealing the good works prepared for others (Ephesians 2:10) and keeping them from entering into the service God has given them to do.

When the burden is too heavy, we first take it to the Lord and see if he gives us permission to retreat from some obligations or to hand some of the work to others who can help carry the load.

"For the moment, all discipline seems not to be pleasant,
but painful; yet to those who have been trained by it,
afterward it yields the peaceful fruit of righteousness."
—Hebrews 12:11

A child rarely enjoys discipline, but we all know that if it's not given, the child will be poorly equipped for life and a terror to those around him.

Parents give discipline to prepare children for the responsibilities and difficulties that will inevitably come in life, but kids don't understand that in the moment. They only know it's unpleasant. It often takes years before a child is old enough to understand and to be grateful for that discipline.

The same is true of us and the way the Lord disciplines. There are things in us that will not serve us or the kingdom of God well in the long-term.

Today, the discipline only feels like painful punishment. We don't understand all that is coming in our lives and how we need to grow to face those things in a godly way that brings glory to God and does not destroy us. In actuality, that painful discipline is training.

"My son, do not reject the discipline of the Lord or loathe his rebuke, for whom the Lord loves he disciplines, just as a father disciplines the son in whom he delights" (Hebrews 12:5–9; Proverbs 3:11–12).

The Lord will not leave us with attitudes unbefitting of a child of the king or that render us unable to complete the work laid out for us. He will keep training the bad out and the good in until we take in the lessons.

"I will say to God my rock, 'Why have you forgotten
me? Why do I go about mourning because of the
oppression of the enemy?' As a shattering of my
bones, my adversaries taunt me, while they say to me
all day long, 'Where is your God?' Why are you in
despair, my soul? And why are you restless within
me? Wait for God, for I will again praise him
for the help of his presence, my God."
—Psalm 42:9–10

This is a reminder that it's okay to ask why and cry out to God in our heartbreak and disappointment. Feeling like he's abandoned us is neither proof that he has nor an indication that our faith has somehow failed. It's normal to have times we feel forgotten, when enemies mock us, and when evil seems to have the upper hand.

However, even when we feel forsaken, we can continue speaking truth to ourselves about who God is and reminding ourselves of the help of his presence. When we wait and keep our hope in him even in the middle of darkness and difficulty, we can know we will praise him again because he has promised to be our salvation, and we will be in his presence forever.

Our circumstances do not determine whether his eye is on us or not. We can run to him with those feelings of forsakenness and remind ourselves that he cannot lie and that all he has spoken will come to pass.

"But those who want to get rich fall into temptation and
a trap, and many foolish and harmful desires which
plunge people into ruin and destruction. For the love of
money is a root of all sorts of evil, and some by longing
for it have wandered away from the faith and pierced
themselves with many griefs."
—1 Timothy 6:9–10

We usually think this passage only applies to those who already have wealth, but the poorest man might desire to be rich.

Longing for money, even if we don't get it, can lead us into many types of evil. It may cause us to resist a call of God that doesn't seem lucrative, to fear standing up for truth, to pursue wealth above the things of God, to envy those who have more than us, to use our wealth to feed sinful desires, to oppress others to line our own pockets, or to be selfish with what the Lord's provided.

The rich young ruler wanted Christ and eternal life, but at Jesus's instruction to sell all his possessions, he went away sad (Mark 10:17–27). He couldn't bring himself to prioritize eternal life over his earthly comfort.

A believer can be wealthy; they're just not to depend on that wealth (1 Timothy 6:17; Proverbs 11:28; James 5:1–3), be arrogant about it (James 4:13–17), oppress others (James 5:4–6), or hold it greedily (Luke 12:16–21).

We must hold everything loosely and be willing to release it if Christ tells us it's coming between us and our faith in him.

When worldly riches are our goal, we will find our end in grief, evil, and emptiness, but aiming for the Lord will lead us to righteousness, hope, joy, and an eternity without pain and sorrow.

"And not only this, but we also celebrate in our
tribulations, knowing that tribulation brings about
perseverance; and perseverance, proven character; and
proven character, hope; and hope does not disappoint,
because the love of God has been poured out within our
hearts through the Holy Spirit who was given to us."
—Romans 5:3–5

This passage teaches us that hope has the most unexpected origins. Upon seeing suffering, our human reaction is almost never, "Ahh, there is hope being born."

In this world, we will likely endure things that, by all earthly standards, should shake our hope and faith. But the true measure of our hope will come clear through these situations.

Where others see only a useless valley of dry bones in our lives, the one who hopes believes the Lord will raise those "bones" from the dead, and, in the process, make us warriors for him (Ezekiel 37).

Where others see only ravenous lions, the one who hopes believes the Lord's angels can close the lions' mouths (Daniel 6).

Where others see only the evil of men, the one who hopes believes that God is working it all for good (Genesis 50:20).

Hope cannot exist if there is no valley, no lions, or no evil. It lives in defiance of the sorrow of this world and goes on, even when its outcome is not realized in this life (Hebrews 11:13). It's about believing that God will make a way where there is no way . . . where we could never make a way with every ounce of skill and effort and willpower we have (Isaiah 43:19).

Living in hope is not living in the absence of suffering but living by the power of the Holy Spirit in spite of suffering.

"Then Jesus said to his disciples, 'If anyone
wants to come after me, he must deny himself,
take up his cross, and follow me.'"
—Matthew 16:24

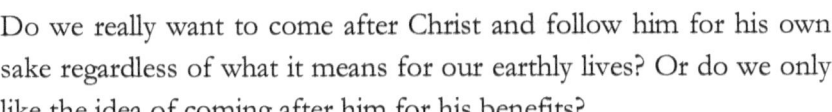

Do we really want to come after Christ and follow him for his own sake regardless of what it means for our earthly lives? Or do we only like the idea of coming after him for his benefits?

Following him means denying ourselves and taking up a cross.

Many of us believe we can carry that cross without ever denying ourselves, but we will never be able to bear it if we're still setting our minds on the flesh, not the Spirit (Romans 8:6–9, Galatians 5:16–17).

We will pick it up and find it too heavy. We cannot carry its weight along with our desires and this world; we must let go of one or the other, and we too often lay the cross back down (Matthew 6:24), go back to following ourselves or the world, and end up with nothing. Losing our lives is the way to finding them (Matthew 10:39).

As Abraham was willing to sacrifice Isaac, we must be willing to offer all our earthly hopes to God. This doesn't mean we will never have any of them, but we must never rely on them, grip them tightly, or prioritize them above going after Christ himself.

If we hope to bear the weight of the cross, we must be willing to say no to ourselves in order to say yes to the Lord, and we will never do so if we don't truly love him and want to follow him (John 14:21).

"I will raise my eyes to the mountains; from where
will my help come? My help comes from the Lord,
who made heaven and earth."
—Psalm 121:1–2

I love how David so often poses a question to himself then answers it with the truth he knows.

Instead of sitting around thinking about all the what-ifs and straining to find the answer by his own efforts, David stops and puts the situation in the Lord's hands.

He recognizes his own limitations but doesn't let that spiral him into fear. He makes sure, instead, that those limitations send him to God.

The Lord tells us not to worry about tomorrow (Matthew 6:34). This is how we can do that. Instead of pretending we can control all the variables, make all the provisions, and ensure nothing is left to chance, we accept that our own efforts can only go so far toward guaranteeing our safety, our desires, or our fulfillment.

As believers, our confidence is not based on pretending that nothing can go wrong, but on the fact that the Lord holds all things in his hands even when they do. We know that all our earthly trials and sufferings will not matter to us one bit when we reach heaven (2 Corinthians 4:17–18); they will seem like a long-ago dream. Our only security is in the Lord's salvation and the lasting things of eternity.

What a difference in our attitudes if, at each problem, we take a step back and acknowledge that whatever we may face, the all-powerful, all-knowing Lord is on our side and has already overcome the worst this life can do to us.

"By this we know that we are in him: the one who
says that he remains in him ought, himself also,
walk just as he walked."

—1 John 2:5–6

Jesus walked in love, caring for those who didn't deserve it—those who lived in shame and pain and sought something better.

He walked in peace, constantly trusting the guidance from his Father—our own heavenly Father—in where he should go and what he should do, never concerning himself with what man thought of it.

He walked in compassion, healing the sick and lame and providing for the poor.

He walked in truth, speaking it even when it caused division or difficulty.

He walked in selflessness, never asking what was in it for him, but faithfully completing the work given to him by God.

There are too many characteristics of Christ to list here, but I hope we all strive to see how he walked and follow his example. This is proof—both to ourselves and to the world—that we are in him.

Our lives may not look successful in an earthly sense, we may stumble along the way, and everyone may not like us—they hated Jesus to the point of having him executed—but as we walk through life this way, we will impact others in meaningful ways that we never could have planned or predicted.

People may be brought into Christ as they see us walking as he walked, in his goodness, faith, mercy, and love.

"As each one has received a special gift, employ it in
serving one another as good stewards of the multifaceted grace of God. Whoever speaks is to do so as one
who is speaking actual words of God; whoever serves is
to do so as one who is serving by the strength which
God supplies; so that in all things God may be glorified
through Jesus Christ, to whom belongs the glory and
dominion forever and ever. Amen."
—1 Peter 4:10–11

God encompasses all gifts, but we, as individuals, cannot. His grace is
multifaceted like the light passing through a diamond; each of us re-
flects different aspects of him out into the world.

He's made each of us unique—some to speak and some to serve. I
love how broad that is, because there are innumerable situations in
which one can speak and innumerable ways in which one can serve.

The key is that whatever we do, we do it "by the strength which
God supplies." We can spend years trying to serve without considering
how God is leading, strengthening, and equipping us as individuals.
When we do this, we aren't serving out of his strength but attempting
to serve out of our own.

Even good works can be works of the flesh if they're not God-led.

Though we may not see the earthly outcomes we hope even when
serving faithfully, if our service also leaves us drained and hopeless,
let's step out of the bustle and back into the stream of Christ's living
water where he will guide our steps into serving through his strength
in the ways he has called us.

"See that no one repays another with evil for
evil, but always seek what is good for one
another and for all people."
—1 Thessalonians 5:15

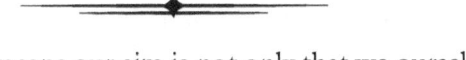

"See that . . ." This means our aim is not only that we ourselves do not repay evil for evil, but that we work to ensure our Christian brothers and sisters do not repay evil for evil as well.

More and more in the world, we see the opposite—people, even Christians, seeking revenge and wishing to enact harm on those who have hurt, oppressed, or mistreated them.

We're to oppose oppression, but we're not to give it back to those who caused it. We're to seek the good that may bring others into repentance and fellowship with God, and that goodness includes discipline and truth, but never evil, hatred, or vengeance. All we do should be with love and good for that person in mind.

God assures us that there is justice. Whatever it looks like to us, the wicked will not get away with their wrongs. "Vengeance is mine," God says. It's not ours to seek, and if we truly understand the awful eternal judgment the wicked will face, we will always hope for their redemption.

We can never know when repaying an evildoer with good instead of what they deserve will reveal the love of God to them and save them from the worst fate imaginable.

By seeking their good, we follow the example and show the love of Christ, who, in the midst of his death on the cross, sought forgiveness for those who caused his suffering: "Father, forgive them; for they do not know what they are doing" (Luke 23:34).

"Do not be grieved, for the
joy of the Lord is your refuge."
—Nehemiah 8:10

Nehemiah said this after Ezra read from the law to the people as they wept and mourned, realizing they had abandoned God's ways.

This is a wonderful reminder that when we are grieved and fearful because of our sin, ruminating in guilt or shame is not where we will find safety. We find it in our joy in him and his continual faithfulness to forgive when we confess and turn away from our sins (1 John 1:9).

2 Corinthians 7:10 says, "For the sorrow that is according to the will of God produces a repentance without regret, leading to salvation, but the sorrow of the world produces death."

Godly grief and fear will lead to repentance and refuge, not despair and regret.

If we dwell on the guilt and shame, we're still focusing on ourselves rather than on Christ.

The goal is to take our eyes off ourselves and our weakness altogether and put them on Christ and his salvation—the only true place we will find joy, healing, and redemption.

We need the joy of the Lord in order to remain obedient; we must understand his steadfast love and great mercy and believe that he wants what is good for us.

Jesus said, "If you love me, you will keep my commandments" (John 14:15), but if we doubt his heart and goodness toward us, we won't trust him or his commandments or his love, and we will stray from his ways once more.

Let's replace our guilt and shame with joy in the Lord; that is where we find our refuge and strength.

"Sir, I have no man to put me into the pool when
the water is stirred up, but while I am coming,
another steps down before me."
—John 5:7

This man had been ill for thirty-eight years, and he thought there was no hope. He had decided that the healing pool was his only answer and that he would never be able to get in it because he had no one to help him.

This miracle reveals that when Jesus shows up in our lives, he fills the lack left by others. It is right and Christlike for others to bear our burdens, come alongside us in our hurts, and work to right the wrongs they might've done to us, but that's never guaranteed in this broken world.

Parents, spouses, children, and friends may fail us, but ultimately, we can be made whole even if everyone else is letting us down.

We're not guaranteed all physical healing in these mortal bodies, but God is all we need for complete spiritual healing; no other person's action or inaction can keep us from that. We don't need a pool stirred by an angel or a man to put us in it. We need only follow Jesus's instruction after he asks, "Do you want to get well?" (John 5:6).

Sadly, there are often areas in which we don't want to be made well and are unwilling to obey—small sins and grievances, great sins and hurts, holding on to anger and unforgiveness, addictions, and the cares and pleasures of this world that so easily distract us from him.

May we desire to be made whole in all things, and may we trust the Lord to do it.

"Do nothing from selfishness or empty conceit,
but with humility consider one another
as more important than yourselves."
—Philippians 2:3

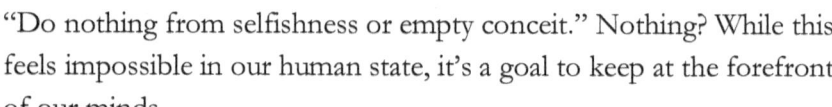

"Do nothing from selfishness or empty conceit." Nothing? While this feels impossible in our human state, it's a goal to keep at the forefront of our minds.

It's difficult, but it's also freeing.

How many things do we do because we want to achieve something that will impress others? Because we want to feel successful? Or because we're worried about keeping up with others?

Those things are all empty conceit and often come with a side of selfishness and pride. They're primarily about our ego.

And we don't have to do them. We feel so much pressure to live up to the world's expectations. This is permission to stop.

There's nothing we have to achieve to prove our worth to others. There's nothing we have to achieve to prove our worth to ourselves.

When we check our motives for an activity, we can ask:

- Is it selfish, discounting the needs of others?
- Is it for empty conceit, only concerned with looking good in front of others or for the sake of our own egos?
- Does pursuing it cause us to consider others less important than ourselves?

Jesus was never concerned with what others thought of him or making a name for himself, and we shouldn't be either. Living like he did might not look successful to the world, but when we reach heaven, we want to be able to say, "My only ambition was not for myself but for you and your kingdom, Lord. I sought nothing for my reputation."

As believers, living lives of humility in service to the kingdom of God is the greatest success.

"Woe to you, scribes and Pharisees, hypocrites! For you
are like whitewashed tombs which on the outside appear
beautiful, but inside they are full of dead men's bones
and all uncleanness. So you too, outwardly appear
righteous to people, but inwardly you are full of
hypocrisy and lawlessness."
—Matthew 23:27–28

According to the law, the Pharisees were the height of moral goodness. They never stuck a toe out of line.

But Jesus came along and told us that someone can do all the right things and act all the right ways but be completely morally bankrupt.

The Bible says God looks at the heart (1 Samuel 16:7), and Jesus says we recognize true believers by their fruit (Matthew 7:15–20).

It's clear the scribes and Pharisees did not display the fruit of the Spirit: love, joy, peace, patience, kindness, goodness, faithfulness, or gentleness. They did seem to have self-control, but that came primarily from self-serving ego and the position of power it gave them.

Cleaning the outside without the help of the Holy Spirit will never make the inside clean. Real goodness includes outward righteousness, but the focus is on the transformation of our hearts and minds as the source of that outward righteousness (Romans 12:2). It's not simply a list of dos and don'ts we rigorously apply to ourselves and others; it comes from the power of Jesus's sacrifice, the Holy Spirit's indwelling, and our total submission to God.

If we're only concerned with the outside, we're really only interested in how we look rather than who we are. Jesus isn't satisfied with the outside only; he wants the whole person—heart, soul, and mind (Matthew 22:37).

"Are you seeking great things for yourself?
Do not seek them."
—Jeremiah 45:5

Jeremiah's scribe Baruch was feeling sorry for himself, like God hadn't honored him for his faithfulness. He didn't trust that his eternal reward was worth it; he wanted earthly rewards now.

Don't we all do this to some extent when life gets hard? "But I've been doing my best to follow you, Lord. Why did you let this happen? Why do I continue to struggle?"

This often reveals our motives and where we've put our heart's desire. We were hoping for an earthly reward—seeking great things for ourselves rather than seeking God and his righteousness.

God isn't being harsh by pointing out the misguided motives; he goes on to remind Baruch that judgment is coming on all this world, so it's not the place Baruch should put his hopes.

Our earthly ambitions are based on fleeting things that are passing away—all flesh is like grass and withers away (Isaiah 40:6–8). The great things we generally seek for ourselves are vain attempts to get something that will not last, but God wants us to receive real, lasting rewards.

When we begin to feel resentful of the path God's put us on, may we ask ourselves, "Whose kingdom am I building?"

His kingdom is the only one that will last, and only he knows what steps we should take to help build it. We only know what we desire, but he knows what truly matters and will show us how to walk in the good works he's prepared for us (Ephesians 2:10).

May we seek to be faithful rather than great and to receive the often unseen eternal rewards of the Lord.

"God is our refuge and strength, a very ready help in
trouble. Therefore we will not fear, though the earth
shakes and the mountains slip into the heart of the sea;
though its waters roar and foam, though the
mountains quake at its swelling pride."
—Psalm 46:1–3

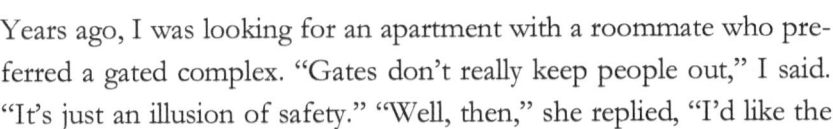

Years ago, I was looking for an apartment with a roommate who preferred a gated complex. "Gates don't really keep people out," I said.
"It's just an illusion of safety." "Well, then," she replied, "I'd like the
highest illusion of safety possible."

The world is not a safe place. Even when we think we're in control
and protected, things can change in the blink of an eye.

We're never actually in control. God is, and has always been, our
only sure refuge.

When things are going smoothly and it seems like everything is under control, it's easy to trust in our environment and circumstances
instead of in him; we begin to trust that illusion of safety.

We should invest in our lives—we're instructed to be hard workers
and to build relationships—but we shouldn't begin to trust in security,
wealth, or relationships more than we trust our God. We must hold all
of this world loosely, willing to give it up at the Lord's prompting. He
may call us to leave everything familiar behind, as Abraham did (Genesis 12:1; Hebrews 11:8).

When God is our refuge and strength, our faith will remain even if
we lose earthly security, wealth, or relationships. It will remain even
when the earth gives way, the mountains move, and the waters roar.

> "Then these men said, 'We will not find any ground
> of accusation against this Daniel unless we find it
> against him regarding the law of his God.'"
> —Daniel 6:5

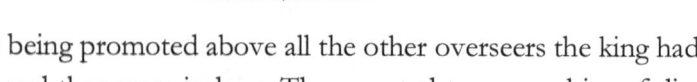

Daniel was being promoted above all the other overseers the king had appointed, and they were jealous. They wanted to accuse him of disloyalty to the king, but they could find nothing.

When we consider the fact that Daniel was a foreign captive taken into the king's service and likely made a eunuch, this is saying something. By all earthly rights, he should've hated the king and the kingdom he was serving. We would hardly blame him if he'd been planning sedition and murder.

But Daniel served with such integrity that no fault could be found in him. Those men knew, however, that his devotion to God was unfailing, and they found a way to use that against him.

If we were forced into servanthood in an evil household, would we do our job so faithfully that our master would trust us above all others? If others tried to find a way to bring us down, would there be evidence that would convict us and bring shame to God's name? Would our dedication to God be enough to incriminate us if that were the criteria?

Like Daniel, we live in an evil world, often in difficult circumstances we did not choose. How do we perform our duties to those in authority over us? They're often not godly people, and it would be easy to say they're not worthy of our effort, but our service is to God (Colossians 3:23–24). Our integrity is to him, and our only fault should be that we will not disobey God's law to follow man's, no matter what power that man has.

"All bitterness, wrath, anger, clamor, and slander must
be removed from you, along with all malice. Be kind to
one another, compassionate, forgiving each other,
just as God in Christ also has forgiven you."
—Ephesians 4:31–32

We can probably look at this list and determine which direction we trend.

It's easy to be bitter, wrathful, angry, and slanderous. Those things arise from our desires, our ideas of what is right and fair, and what we believe we deserve.

But kindness, compassion, and forgiveness can only be achieved by abiding in Jesus Christ. They don't come naturally and will not happen without us putting firm intention into living them out.

This requires thoughtful response rather than impulsive reaction. It requires dealing with hurts by loving our enemies rather than simply expecting not to be wronged.

Many situations in this world could make us bitter and angry, but we're called to live in kindness and forgiveness regardless. If we're living this way when nothing happens to be bothering us, there is no reward (Matthew 5:46). We're to do it in the midst of chaos, injustice, and pain, just as Jesus did.

"Father, forgive them; for they do not know what they are doing" (Luke 23:34). Jesus said this while still in the throes of a torturous death.

To us, it looks very much like those people knew what they were doing, but Jesus knew they were deceived.

We wrestle not against flesh and blood but against principalities and powers (Ephesians 6:12); those who we feel deserve our bitterness and wrath are blinded by those powers.

We're to be kind and forgiving and not let our hearts be hardened. Our compassionate forgiveness can show others the power and love of Christ.

"Finally, brothers and sisters, whatever is true,
whatever is honorable, whatever is right, whatever is
pure, whatever is lovely, whatever is commendable, if
there is any excellence and if anything worthy
of praise, think about these things."
—Philippians 4:8

This verse is sandwiched between two others about having the peace of God, and I'm pretty sure that's not an accident.

Even secular studies have revealed that focusing on the things we're grateful for is beneficial for long-term mental health, while focusing on the negative things in our lives only brings inner turmoil.

It's human nature for the bad to outweigh the good in our minds. We let ten bad minutes ruin our whole day or one negative comment outweigh seven good ones. This is called "negativity bias," and it's not good for us. It gives the bad more power over us than the good and gives Satan a place to sow anger and bitterness in our hearts (Ephesians 4:27; Hebrews 12:15).

God knows that it's better for us to spend our time considering the good things and to let them overshadow the bad in our hearts and minds, bringing his peace. This doesn't mean we pretend the bad doesn't happen or that it doesn't affect us, but it does mean we don't let it control us or our faith in the Lord.

When our negative thoughts are taking control in our minds, it's good to ask ourselves, "What is true in my life today? What is honorable? What is right, pure, lovely, and commendable?"

If we're going to have anything on repeat in our minds, it needs to be these things.

We focus on them and let the peace of God rule in our hearts.

"I can do all things through him who strengthens me."
—Philippians 4:13

This is one of the most known, loved, and shared verses in the Bible, but it's almost always taken to mean something that it doesn't mean.

We say it when we have that job interview, that ball game, that cancer treatment.

"I can do all things!"

"I can get the job."

"I can win the game."

"I can beat the cancer."

And that may be the Lord's will for us. But that's not what this verse means.

The previous verses are, "For I have learned to be content in whatever circumstances I am. I know how to get along with little, and I also know how to live in prosperity; in any and every circumstance I have learned the secret of being filled and going hungry, both of having abundance and suffering need" (Philippians 4:11–12).

These are the things Paul is saying we can do. We can be content even when we don't get the job, win the game, or beat the cancer, because our hope lies in something that will matter long after all that is over.

Christ has overcome this world not by saying we will always win or be successful or have it easy right now but by giving us a way to live with him forever beyond the here and now. This world is not our home, and nothing that can happen in this world is the end of hope for believers.

We can suffer failure, loss, and hunger yet still have hope, knowing Christ has already accomplished the ultimate overcoming.

> "The people who survived the sword found grace in the
> wilderness—Israel, when it went to find its rest."
> —Jeremiah 31:2

We have survived the sword—the slavery of our own sin and unrighteousness—through Christ's sacrifice.

We have headed into his grace, but perhaps it hasn't yet taken us where we hoped to be.

We went out of Egypt thinking we would find rest, and so far, we only see emptiness in every direction. We're wandering in the wilderness without any apparent means of survival.

We mistakenly believed that as soon as we left Egypt, we would have everything we ever wanted, but while we're in this world, we live in the wilderness between slavery and rest.

It's not comfortable. It's not home. It's not easy.

Our rest isn't complete until we reach eternity, but we are headed there. The Lord has promised it, and only by relying on and following him will we reach our destination.

In forty years of wandering, neither the clothing nor the sandals of the Israelites wore out (Deuteronomy 29:5). When there was no food and no water, he provided manna from heaven every day and water from the rock (Nehemiah 9:15). His provision was not the fanciest new clothes nor the finest foods and wine, but they had what they needed, and most importantly, they had HIM.

He led them as a pillar of cloud by day and a pillar of fire by night; he never left them (Exodus 13:21–22).

When the wilderness looks, to the human eye, devoid of all we need, may we remember that, for now, we're still traveling in the wilderness on the way to our rest, but we have a heavenly Father who knows the way and has made full provision for our journey.

"But flee from these things, you man of God, and pursue
righteousness, godliness, faith, love, perseverance, and
gentleness. Fight the good fight of faith; take hold of the
eternal life to which you were called, and for which you
made the good confession in the presence of many
witnesses."
—1 Timothy 6:11–12

Following Christ is active. It requires fleeing the love of money, the cravings of this world (1 Timothy 6:9–10), the lust of the eyes, the lust of the flesh, and the pride of life (1 John 2:16). It requires resisting the devil and submitting to God (James 4:7). It requires pursuing righteousness, godliness, faith, love, steadfastness, gentleness, and all other fruits of the Spirit.

It requires putting on the armor of God so when temptation comes, we're ready to resist with the truth (Ephesians 6:10–18) and fight the fight of faith despite an enemy who wants to knock our confidence in God out of us at every turn.

None of this is mere accident. Just as none of us will become proficient at the piano by looking over a piano score each morning, we will not build a strong faith by reading a few verses. We must put our hands to the keys over and over—be in the Word, spend time in prayer, and intentionally implement that Word in our lives, thoughts, and actions—before it will become fruitful, consistent, and natural in our actions and everyday lives.

Our spirit is often willing, but our flesh is weak, just as many wish they could play the piano but never put in the effort and discipline.

Following Christ requires we discipline our flesh in order to become strong in practicing our faith. Running the race with endurance requires training (1 Corinthians 9:24–27).

"Elijah was a man with a nature like ours, and he
prayed earnestly that it would not rain, and it did not
rain on the earth for three years and six months."
—James 5:17

We think Elijah was somehow supernaturally spiritual, but this verse says he had "a nature like ours."

In 1 Kings 19:3–4, Elijah runs away from Jezebel's threat, fearing for his life. Then he sits down and essentially says, "I've had enough, God. Just let me die!"

Elijah had just defeated the prophets of Baal by calling down fire from heaven through his prayers, and this is after his prayer to stop the rain had been answered. You would think his faith would've been bolstered by these events, yet he's still frightened, discouraged, and ready to give up.

This is just a man like us.

We may, at times, become so discouraged, tired, and afraid that we ask God to just kill us, or perhaps, like Job, we simply wish we'd never been born (Job 10:19).

We may see God work in miraculous ways, and yet be fearful at each new trouble, but our prayers are still heard when we're obedient to what the Lord has called us to do.

God wasn't harsh with Elijah because of his response but sent an angel to minister to him, saying, "Arise, eat; because the journey is too long for you" (1 Kings 19:7).

The Lord gave Elijah a task knowing it was too long and that Elijah was incapable, then provided what was needed in order to accomplish it, even in the midst of Elijah's pity party.

God will come alongside where he calls us; we're to remember the victories he's given us in the past and pray, because prayer changes things (James 5:16).

"Let's hold firmly to the confession of our hope
without wavering, for he who promised is faithful."
—Hebrews 10:23

A promise is only as good as the character of the person who makes it. If someone is unreliable or has ill-will toward us, we're not going to have much hope in their promises, no matter how wonderful they might sound.

But we believe a promise that comes from someone who not only has the power to keep it but who loves us and intends good for us.

Often, when we begin to doubt God's promises and our hope begins to falter, what we really need to address is how well we know the Lord. Have we begun to believe the seeds of mistrust, pride, and selfishness Satan has been sewing in our minds since the beginning (Genesis 3:1–5)? Have we begun to doubt whether God really means good for us as he says in Jeremiah 29:11 and Romans 8:28? Have we begun to doubt whether God is really good in and of himself as it says in Psalm 34:8 and Psalm 106:1? Have we begun to doubt God's omnipotence as spoken of in Mark 4:41 and Romans 1:20?

We could provide verse after verse discussing each of these attributes in our God. He is all-powerful, he is holy, he cannot lie, and he loves us with an everlasting love.

When our hope begins to wane, we need to spend some time basking in who God is, because confidence in the Promise-Giver brings confidence in the promise. He is faithful.

"Do you not know? Have you not heard? The
Everlasting God, the Lord, the Creator of the ends
of the earth does not become weary or tired.
His understanding is unsearchable."
—Isaiah 40:28

The Lord is forever; he knows everything from the beginning of time to the end. He made everything and knows all the inner workings of the world. More importantly, he knows each person he created. He never tires, and all the books in the world could not contain his wisdom.

Do we know this? We have heard it, but do we live like we believe it? Have we taken the knowledge into our lives as if we're confident in it?

What does it mean for our daily life?

It means we can trust his guidance. We don't have to worry if he's capable of taking care of us or not. We don't have to worry whether he's taken a break or has stopped paying attention. He sees us.

It means that whatever we think we know is like a newborn baby's knowledge compared to his. We don't have to stress about what the best decision is. We only have to trust his unsearchable understanding, seek his wisdom (James 1:5), and follow him. Our wisdom has limits, but his does not. We will grow tired, but he will not.

And as a good father leads and cares for his children, our heavenly Father will lead and care for us. We can trust that his heart is for us, not against us (Psalm 56:9; Romans 8:31).

In infinite trust, we can walk beside him without the fear of man or this world's troubles.

"But the goal of our instruction is love from a pure
heart, from a good conscience, and from a sincere faith.
Some people have strayed from these things and have
turned aside to fruitless discussion, wanting to be
teachers of the Law, even though they do not
understand either what they are saying or the matters
about which they make confident assertions."
—1 Timothy 1:5–7

Many Christian leaders seem more interested in proving themselves right than in discipling souls, but we should all be more interested in transforming hearts than we are in satisfying pride.

So before we speak instruction, let's ask ourselves a few questions.

Are we speaking from love? Is it from a sincere desire to help the other person, or do we feel disdain for them even as we speak?

Do we have a pure heart and a good conscience? Is there some secret sin we haven't confessed, some area we haven't submitted to God, or some work of the Lord we're resisting? If so, it's better to stay silent until we've given the Lord full rein in our lives.

Do we have a sincere faith not only speaking but also living out the Lord's instructions?

Could the conversation fall into the category of fruitless discussion? Will the outcome have an impact in the eternal kingdom of God, or are we just trying to prove a point without the wisdom of the Holy Spirit?

Asking these questions would prompt thoughtful, kind discussion rather than heated debates that spark division. It would nurture a chance at becoming the body of Christ working in unity and loving one another fervently as we're charged in the Bible.

Before giving instruction, we should always look for purity and sincerity in our hearts, our conscience, and our faith.

"Your speech must always be with grace,
as though seasoned with salt, so that you will
know how you should respond to each person."
—Colossians 4:6

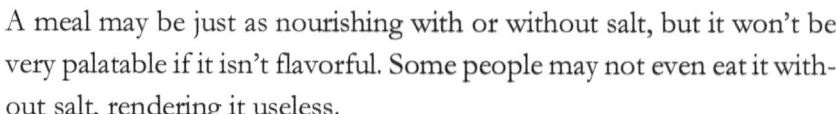

A meal may be just as nourishing with or without salt, but it won't be very palatable if it isn't flavorful. Some people may not even eat it without salt, rendering it useless.

The same is true of our words. If we speak truth in a hurtful way, others may not receive it. But when we work to season our words with grace, people are far more likely to take that truth into their hearts and be nourished by it.

When something difficult needs to be said, we ought to be "slow to speak" (James 1:19) and consider whether we can respond with grace.

We take a pause, check in with the Holy Spirit, say a prayer (or several!) and evaluate our hearts and what we want to say to make sure it is both true and Christlike.

We take that pause even if it creates an awkward silence, even if it means we lose a fight, and even if it means we never get to make that really great point.

After this, if we find our words cannot be spoken with grace, we should step back from the interaction. We may be able to come back later and reply with grace, but sometimes, it's not for us to respond at all, and we will benefit from the lesson in "taming the tongue" (James 3:1–12).

Difficult words are much more likely to be heard when they are spoken kindly in love.

"Behold, I go forward but he is not there, and
backward, but I cannot perceive him; when he
acts on the left, I cannot see him; he turns to the
right, but I cannot see him. But he knows the
way I take; when he has put me to the test,
I will come out as gold."
—Job 23:8–10

Job was at his lowest point. He couldn't feel God moving; he couldn't see God moving. But even though it didn't feel like it, he was absolutely certain that God was still working on all sides.

He never doubted that God still saw him. "He knows the way I take."

When we're walking a hard road, when we don't understand why, and when it feels like God isn't working, we can be certain that he is. He's on the right hand and the left . . . he goes before and behind (Psalm 139:5).

He's on every side. He sees us. He knows what we're going through.

And what's the outcome at the end of this unknown? The perfection of our faith. We are in the fire; it is burning off the doubts, fears, selfishness, misplaced confidence in worldly endeavors and comforts. On the other side, we will come out like gold—purified, proven in faith, beautiful, and shining for all to see.

And the purest gold is the softest gold, able to be molded by the Craftsman into the shape he has planned for it.

We can trust that this fire, though painful and confusing, is creating in us the ability to become what the Lord intends . . . to be used to bring about the highest fulfillment both in our lives and for his kingdom.

"But you will be betrayed even by parents, brothers and
sisters, other relatives, and friends, and they will put some
of you to death, and you will be hated by all people
because of my name. And yet not a hair of your head will
perish. By your endurance you will gain your lives."
—Luke 21:16–19

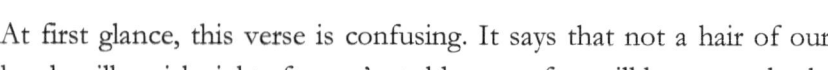

At first glance, this verse is confusing. It says that not a hair of our heads will perish right after we're told some of us will be put to death.

In our minds, death is perishing! But in the kingdom of God, death has been swallowed up in victory (1 Corinthians 15:54). It's merely the doorway we must pass through for our souls to begin our true, forever lives.

We can rejoice in any persecution because it will bring the opportunity for testifying about our God, the salvation of our souls, and identification with Christ in his death and sacrifice (Matthew 5:11–12; Matthew 10:16–28; Luke 21:13; 1 Peter 1:6–9).

We should not be surprised when betrayal or persecution comes (1 Peter 4:12–19). The world hated, accused, and condemned our Lord without cause. The same may happen to us (John 15:18–25), but many may come to him through our suffering.

As believers, let us not fear those who can harm the body, but only the one who holds the eternal destiny of our souls (Matthew 10:28). Even if our body is killed, we will gain our true lives through endurance (Matthew 10:32–33).

This earthly life is like a shadow, and it should not control us (1 Chronicles 29:15; Psalm 144:4); what perishes with the body is not our real life.

Everything that matters will come with us into eternity.

"The refining pot is for silver and the furnace for gold,
but the Lord tests hearts."
—Proverbs 17:3

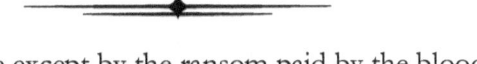

None of us are pure except by the ransom paid by the blood of Jesus, but the Bible tells us many times that going through the refiner's fire burns off the dross.

When the Lord allows hard things and discipline into our lives, if we let them, they will melt away all the unnecessary parts—the things that have us focused on this life.

The crucible and the furnace are painful, but they are also beneficial. They will test our hearts and reveal to us the places we have not yet allowed God in but are still holding to our earthly desires, selfishness, and the cares of this world.

When we look back at fires we've gone through and the dross it left behind, we can usually tell what the Lord was doing; there was a place we'd been allowing the devil a foothold, a fear that was controlling us, or sins we hadn't given up.

And each time we go through the fire, the impurities it brings to the surface are diminished.

As we mature in the Lord, he often reveals sins that five years earlier, we wouldn't have had the slightest pang of conscience over. But he tests hearts, and he knows where that sin still resides, even if it comes out in more and more subtle ways as we are sanctified through him.

If our goal is to be like Jesus, we can expect the refiner's fire to come, and we can welcome it when it does. It does not burn indiscriminately but burns away that which is impure and unnecessary for the kingdom of God.

"Yet those who wait for the Lord will gain new strength;
they will mount up with wings like eagles, they will run
and not get tired, they will walk and not become weary."
—Isaiah 40:31

When we become weary, it's often because we haven't waited on the Lord in some instance. We have not sat long at his feet or allowed him access to some area of our lives, or we've chosen distance from him in some area of selfishness, pride, anger, or other sin.

Perhaps we've plowed ahead in our own plans and our own strength because we want something and haven't checked in with him.

But the eagle flies best by the power of the wind. It soars not with its own strength, but by waiting for the moments when the wind is right to carry it. An eagle can fly in its own power, but it can only carry the smallest of weights without the wind's strength.

That's true of us as well. If we try to lift our own weights without waiting for the Lord, we will quickly grow tired. We won't be equipped to bear the burdens and temptations of this world. We might be able to carry some things for a time, but even small weights will quickly become too heavy. We will grow weak and fall in our weariness.

The Lord is our strength, and when we run ahead of him, we will always wear out. We will not be able to take up our cross and follow him (Matthew 16:24).

But when we wait for him, the Holy Spirit becomes like the wind to the eagle, bearing us up and giving us strength for our flights and our burdens.

"Be devoted to one another in brotherly love; give preference to one another in honor, not lagging behind in diligence, fervent in spirit, serving the Lord; rejoicing in hope, persevering in tribulation, devoted to prayer, contributing to the needs of the saints, practicing hospitality."
—Romans 12:10–13

How beautiful would the body of Christ be if we employed these instructions!

Are we devoted to one another in brotherly love, or do we see our brother as a burden?

Do we give honor and preference to others instead of seeking our own ends first?

Do we employ diligence in studying the Word and following God?

Are our spirits fervent in loving God and others, or are we weak and careless in our faith and relationship with him?

Are we serving the Lord faithfully, living lives of obedience and following where he leads, or are there areas of sin we are holding on to and calls to service we have not yet answered?

Are we rejoicing in God and his eternal hope, or are we staggering in despair and hoping in the things of this world?

Are we persevering even in tribulation, or do we doubt and turn away from the Lord when difficulties come?

Are we devoted to prayer in a way that proves we actually believe it changes things, or do we treat it as a weak platitude when there's nothing we can do with our human hands?

Are we contributing to the needs of other believers, or do we hold our possessions tightly because we fear we will not have enough?

Do we practice hospitality or keep others at arm's length because it's inconvenient or difficult?

We can use these questions to discover if we're living out the kind of faith and love these verses describe.

"Far be it from me to boast,
except in the cross of our Lord Jesus."
—Galatians 6:14

Paul is referencing those things we tend to wear proudly as badges of honor for our Christian faith. In his day, it was being circumcised versus being uncircumcised. Today, it may be something like, "I go to church every week," or "I never cuss," or "I've never_____" (fill in the blank) that makes us feel spiritually superior.

But to do this is to live like the Pharisees, taking joy in others' weakness. It makes us feel good to think we are better than them—"thank you that I am not like other people" (Luke 18:11–12).

This attitude cripples love. As long as we continue this way, we cannot truly wish for others' good, because to raise them up means we have less to feel good about within ourselves.

When we take our eyes off ourselves and put them on Christ, remembering his sacrificial love—that "while we were still sinners, Christ died for us" (Romans 5:8)—then we can truly love others the same way, wishing for their greatest good.

It's freeing to boast only in the cross; our self-image is no longer defined by comparing ourselves to other people, whether good or bad. Whatever earthly advantages or disadvantages we may have, we are all equal before the cross.

We recognize that he is the reason for anything in us worth boasting of, so we point to the source, and we are then free to love as he loves.

"Therefore, my beloved brothers and sisters, be firm,
immovable, always excelling in the work of the Lord,
knowing that your labor is not in vain in the Lord."
—1 Corinthians 15:58

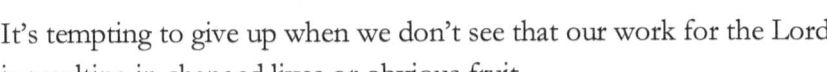

It's tempting to give up when we don't see that our work for the Lord is resulting in changed lives or obvious fruit.

But this verse assures us that if we are seeking the Lord and following him, that work will always matter. We don't have to wonder.

Galatians 6:9 says, "Let's not become discouraged in doing good, for in due time we will reap, if we do not become weary." That's the important thing; even when we don't see the results, we are to be steadfast, keep going, not waver, and keep doing what he's called us to do.

The farmer does not reap if he gives up mid-season. He must continue tending, waiting, watering, weeding, pruning, protecting from pests, and trusting the Lord to bring the harvest.

For all of our seventy or eighty years on this earth, we're to continue tending what the Lord has put in our lives so we are fruitful for his kingdom. The life we live in Christ is always worth it even when difficult; we have his presence (Psalm 23:4), peace (Philippians 4:7), and the assurance of eternity with him ahead to carry us through (Hebrews 12:2). We may see small harvests here and there along the way, or we may not see a real crop until eternity.

But the Lord has promised that a harvest will come, and our labor will not be in vain.

"Behold, to obey is better than a sacrifice, and to pay
attention is better than the fat of rams."
—1 Samuel 15:22

We often choose sacrifice—the ritual of religious duty—over obedience and paying attention to the Lord.

But our lives with Christ are not lives of fill-in-the-blank dos and don'ts. They are lives lived in an ongoing essay of obedience and paying attention.

The fill-in-the-blank life will have us checking off tasks on a moral to-do list without ever learning who the Lord is. It's straightforward—a facts and figures knowledge that means little to us as long as we pass the test. It has us seeing God as a distant deity we must pacify, doing just enough to keep him on our side.

But the essay life will have us walking in humble obedience and paying attention to the Holy Spirit minute-by-minute, day-by-day. The essay life is open-ended. We see and understand the beauty and depth in the story of God's Word, and that translates into a life that continues to tell his story. It's not only duty that constrains us but love and a desire to know the Lord more each day. He's our heavenly Father who knows us intimately and wants us to know him as well (Galatians 4).

The Word tells us repeatedly that God doesn't want our religious performance; he wants our hearts turned toward him in love and trust.

As we follow Christ's example of love and obedience, our lives themselves become the sacrifice that pleases the Lord (Romans 12:1–2).

Let's not settle for fill-in-the-blank lives of rote religion. Let's learn to know, love, and follow our heavenly Father.

"The mind of a person plans his way,
but the Lord directs his steps."
—Proverbs 16:9

Most of us make plans and have goals; that's good. But those goals should always be held loosely. Our only unwavering goal—the one we will not stray from no matter what—should be to follow where the Lord leads.

If there is some plan or goal we feel we cannot live without, we're unwilling to give up if the Lord asks, or something outside of that we're unwilling to do if the Lord leads, then our steps are headed in the wrong direction.

Holding on to our plans and wants against the Lord's guidance or biblical wisdom will always lead to fruitless dissatisfaction or destructive consequences.

When the Lord directs our steps away from what we've planned, we follow without question. He will not lead us astray; all his ways are perfect (Psalm 18:30). Following him keeps us in the refuge of his wings and will lead to the truest satisfaction we can ever have in this life.

He does not direct us away from what we desire in order to punish, but to free us from the earthly snares that our enemy sets to trap us. Whatever we give up by following the Lord closer and closer each day will be replaced by the ability to love God with our whole heart, soul, and mind and by the power of the Holy Spirit working through and in us.

Through submitting our plans to him, every other thing in our lives will become more full, true, good, and complete.

"For you showed sympathy to the prisoners and accepted
joyfully the seizure of your property, knowing that you
have for yourselves a better and lasting possession."
—Hebrews 10:34

We are so vocal about our rights. I can't imagine many Christians joyfully accepting the seizure of our property . . . or accepting the seizure of our property at all. We would be railing against it, trying to find justice, and many would gladly do violence to prevent or oppose it.

But if our hope is not in this world—in what we own and see and touch—if we truly know we have a better and a lasting possession coming, the loss of these things will not derail us.

The loss might be hurtful, frustrating, disappointing, and sad, but can we joyfully accept it nonetheless?

Can we show others that our satisfaction is not in our possessions?

Can we, in the midst of the plundering of our property, be so unconcerned with it that we continue to support other struggling believers and still do the good works to which Christ has called us?

Can we love our enemies while they're still doing us evil (Matthew 5:43–48)?

Can we give those doing us harm not only what we're compelled to give by force but more (Luke 6:29)?

Can we respond with the same spirit Jesus exhibited when he healed Malchus after Peter cut off his ear (John 18:10–11) in the Garden of Gethsemane (Luke 22:51)?

Can we show the world that we don't care about our rights as much as we care about their souls?

Will we be ready and able to represent Christ in the middle of the seizure of our property if it ever comes to that?

"Rest in the Lord and wait patiently for him."
—Psalm 37:7

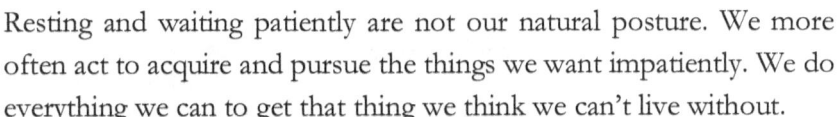

Resting and waiting patiently are not our natural posture. We more often act to acquire and pursue the things we want impatiently. We do everything we can to get that thing we think we can't live without.

Three things can happen when pursue things without waiting on the Lord and his direction:

1) We don't get the thing anyway, but now we've wasted time, energy, and other resources pursuing it, leading us to despair, frustration, overwhelm, and feelings of inadequacy. It's the unrealized dream.

2) We get the thing, but it's not the good we expected. It's difficult, it creates new burdens we didn't imagine, or it's spoiled by something nearly the moment we get it. It's the longed-for spouse that reveals a dark side only after the wedding. It's the Ishmael that Abraham and Sarah got.

3) We get the thing, and it leads us away from the Lord. We placed it above him, and now it's crushed out even the desire for him we had. It's the deceitfulness of riches that choke out the Word in our lives (Matthew 13:22).

By resting in the Lord and waiting patiently for him, we free ourselves from the control these things have over us and the consequences of pursuing them against the Lord's will. The waiting generates that godliness accompanied by contentment that is great gain (1 Timothy 6:6).

But we do have to work at it. We must intentionally set our desires in the Lord's hands and affirm that we trust him whether he provides or does not.

Waiting anxiously will lead us into unrest, strife, and anxiety.

But resting and waiting patiently in our good Father will bring us peace, hope, and joy.

"At the dinner hour he sent his slave to tell those who had
been invited, 'Come, because everything is ready now.'
And yet they all alike began to make excuses."
—Luke 14:17–18

———————◆———————

God invites everyone to the eternal banquet—he is "not willing for any
to perish, but for all to come to repentance" (2 Peter 3:9)—but those
who find their satisfaction in this world will often have some reason to
refuse—something they believe is more important.

"I have business," "I'm getting married," "I have things to take care
of (Luke 14:18–20)."

So the master invites those considered to be undesirable—the have-
nots of the world.

Those people could see that their need was not filled by the fleeting
value of the things of this world. They knew that money, health, and
power are all too transient, and they wanted a lasting, eternal abundance.

We should never decline God because we've become happy, content, fulfilled, absorbed with, or distracted by the things of this world.
He might invite us to some task that takes us away from a life we've
meticulously built and now place our hope in, just like the rich young
ruler. Jesus told him to sell all he had and follow, but the man would
not because his faith was in his possessions. He "went away grieving;
for he was one who owned much property" (Mark 10:22), but that grief
brought him no closer to God.

Our excuses might mean we're trusting in and filling our hearts with
things other than God. Let's not forfeit our place at the table by allowing earthly blessings—the deceitfulness of riches (Mark 4:19)—to blind
us to our one true need. Let's choose eternal joy and lasting worth.

"Blessed be the name of the Lord from this time on and
forever. From the rising of the sun to its setting, the
name of the Lord is to be praised. The Lord is high
above all nations; his glory is above the heavens. Who is
like the Lord our God, who is enthroned on high, who
looks far down to the heavens and the earth?"
—Psalm 113:2–6

"The name of the Lord is to be praised," but most of us don't know how to do that in our daily lives. It's not as hard as we make it.

When we love a movie or a book, we talk about it and try to get others to watch or read it so we can share it with them. When we love someone, we tell others how great they are. If we get engaged or married, we want everyone to know about it and to celebrate with us. When we see a magnificent sunset or go on vacation, we share pictures and love telling others about our favorite places so perhaps they can enjoy them too.

Praising is not a show we put on; it's what we're doing every time we tell someone how the Lord spoke during our prayer time, every time we share how a Bible verse showed up just at the right moment, and every time we talk about how he's bringing life to our souls.

The natural outpouring of our love for God will be to praise him from this time through forever and from the rising of the sun to its setting. "Great is the Lord, and highly to be praised!" (Psalm 145:3).

"Every place on which the sole of your foot steps, I
have given it to you, just as I spoke to Moses. From
the wilderness and this Lebanon, even as far as the
great river, the river Euphrates, all the land of the
Hittites, and as far as the Great Sea toward the
setting of the sun will be your territory."
—Joshua 1:3–4

The Lord promised that all this land would be the Israelites' if they
simply walked the ground and claimed it—but they never claimed it in
its entirety. They left a large portion of it empty and never trod it with
the soles of their feet.

We do the same thing. The Lord gives each of us something here
in this life that is set apart for us—specific good works (Ephesians
2:10) and a specific path for each of us to walk (1 Corinthians 7:17)—
but for it to become part of our lives and legacies, we must walk in his
path and heed his direction. There are some promises in the Bible that
belong to every believer, but there are many more that require action
and obedience before they come to fruition in our lives. We must tread
the ground to claim the promise.

The obstacle might be fear, time, distraction, or laziness, but we
need to persevere in spite of that in order to start walking in the fullness
of all God has planned for and promised us.

How many good works do we leave undone and promises do we
leave unclaimed because we haven't stepped out?

"Only, as the Lord has assigned to each one,
as God has called each, in this way let him walk.
And so I direct in all the churches."
—1 Corinthians 7:17

◆

Each of us is called to a unique journey. Our inclination is to look at other peoples' lives to figure out what "worked." We want to follow the pattern for happiness and success.

But that's not how it works in the kingdom of God. As we live in this world for him, we can't predict where he might have us go or what he might have us do based on worldly wisdom.

Success and failure are measured differently in the Christian life. Christ will not look at us at the end of time and say, "Your house wasn't very nice after all," or "You really should've had a more prestigious job," or "If only you'd been more well-known and respected."

His only metric for success or failure is following him. He will say, "Well done thy good and faithful servant" according to that and that alone.

The path for following Christ might not make sense to the world and its approved formula for doing things "right," but it's the only road that will lead to true fulfillment, joy, and peace in the end.

Chasing the world's advice will have us running in circles, always certain we're not measuring up to its standards for finances, talent, or appearances, etc. Its aim is an ever-moving target.

And even a good, God-ordained path for one believer might be a bad path for another.

Our aim is to walk alongside God on the path he's assigned and called us to as individuals, not to make our lives a cheap copy of someone else's.

"I believed when I said, 'I am greatly afflicted.'"
—Psalm 116:10

Sometimes in this life, we will be greatly afflicted. We're not alone. This psalmist and many others in the Bible experienced great affliction—David, Daniel, Joseph, Ruth, Esther, Paul, and even Jesus.

We don't have to pretend we're fine when things are hard.

The psalmist acknowledges the difficulty of his circumstance, yet still believes. In this chapter, he goes on to give the Lord thanks and praise for salvation, provision, compassion, rescue, and freedom.

We can walk through the affliction in this way—praising and remaining faithful even in the middle of the difficulty.

We can say, "I believe even when I don't see the way out, when I don't like what's happening, when I feel too tired to move forward, when I don't know what I'm doing, when I've made a terrible mistake, when my finances aren't enough, when my car breaks down, when my future seems dark, when my friends and family have abandoned me, when the world seems full of disappointment, frustration, and sorrow, when I've been betrayed, when serving the Lord has me walking right into danger, and when everyone seems against me."

We can cry out to the Lord in desperation but also turn to thanks and praise. When we look at the times thankfulness is mentioned in the Bible, it's often brought up in context with remembering all the Lord has done for us so we will be encouraged. It's like building a monument as a reminder of the Lord's faithfulness in the past so we won't forget it when hard times come.

Let's build our monuments of praise and thanksgiving so when we are greatly afflicted, we can say, "I believe, even when . . . because . . ."

"This is the day which the Lord has made;
let's rejoice and be glad in it."
—Psalm 118:24

Some days are hard to rejoice in. We wake up dreading whatever the day holds and feeling like we don't have anything to look forward to. Maybe our day is full of illness, a broken-down car, a rebellious child, or a stack of bills we don't know how we're going to pay.

But the truth is, we only ever have "this day." If we trust that the good things are the Lord's blessing, know that some of the hard things are his teaching and discipline which prepare us for his purpose, and if we believe the rest of the difficult things we face will be turned to good even if they're the result of sin and evil, then we can rejoice every day.

As we follow the Lord, we rejoice because he can transform it all, no matter how unlikely or how terrible the situation—Joseph, in the pit, in slavery, in the dungeon; Ruth, widowed, a stranger in a strange land with no one to provide for her; Elijah, alone on the run from a bloodthirsty queen; Jesus, betrayed, sentenced unjustly, tortured, and murdered.

God turned all of this around—brought beauty from ashes, gladness from mourning, and praise from despair.

Rejoicing is an act of trust in the future we know God has promised us. It reminds us of the source of good things, staves off the dread in difficulty, and renews our hope. It changes our attitude and puts our mind back on Christ instead of on our circumstances.

So whether we feel like we're sinking in the waves or our barns are overflowing, let's rejoice in this day and put our eyes on Christ.

"Not having a righteousness of my own derived
from the law, but that which is through faith
in Christ, the righteousness which comes
from God on the basis of faith."
—Philippians 3:9

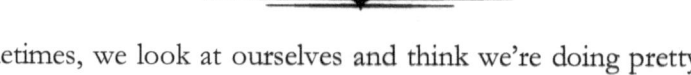

Sometimes, we look at ourselves and think we're doing pretty good. We haven't done anything overtly sinful or obvious to the outside world recently.

But Jesus makes it clear that this type of righteousness is just like whitewashing a tomb. The outside might look good, but inside, it's still dead. He tells us that it's not only our actions that incriminate us, but our motives and our thoughts.

And if we're looking at those honestly, we can usually see the fear, hypocrisy, lust, selfishness, pride (and more) that rears its head over and over each day.

It's easy to let this discourage us when we truly want to be like Christ. But wallowing in our failures and letting them drag us down into despair is just another trick of the devil (2 Corinthians 7:10). He tempts us to sin then uses our shame over that sin to keep us from running to Christ.

It's another way to keep our eyes on ourselves instead of on Jesus.

Jesus is not shocked by our failures, and we shouldn't be either.

When he rescued the woman caught in adultery, he implored her to "Go and sin no more," but he did not shame her (John 8:1–11).

When Peter had denied and abandoned him, Jesus did not scold and belittle. He sought Peter out and renewed his calling.

When we fall short (Romans 3:23), the answer is to repent, turn our eyes back to the Lord, run to him, and accept his grace.

Our faith is not in ourselves, but in him.

"The one who has found his life will lose it, and the one
who has lost his life on my account will find it."
—Matthew 10:39

We spend a lot of time trying to "find our lives." We want to make our mark, have a successful career, be comfortable financially, and have trouble-free relationships and lives.

But this says the way to "finding our lives" is through seeking the Lord and submitting all our wants and desires to him rather than spending our time scraping and clawing for what we think we need.

Giving up our right to ourselves is the way to true life. It's counterintuitive. We're taught to chase our dreams and do what makes us happy, and that makes sense to us.

But the Word tells us that will only end with us losing the thing we sought. It says that seeking God and righteousness is the way to finding all the things our soul actually needs (Matthew 6:33).

What we need may not be in the direction of our dreams nor what we believe will make us happy, but it will always be worth it in the end, because we don't actually know what will make us happy. God does.

When we're unwilling to let go of a desire, insisting that we must have or experience something in this life, our hearts are saying, "I can't trust God in this area; he's not enough. I must get it regardless of whether he intends it or not."

But trusting the One who knows everything and giving him the right to direct our steps is the path to life even when it means releasing our worldly expectations and desires.

When we're willing to lose our life, we will find it.

"By faith Abraham, when he was called, obeyed by going
out to a place which he was to receive as an inheritance;
and he left, not knowing where he was going."
—Hebrews 11:8

When God tells us to go but doesn't say where, it's scary. We rarely—
if ever—even leave our homes without planning the destination.

But he always has a reason, and it's always for good.

It might look crazy to the rest of the world—other Christians might
even question. "But do you have a plan? God wouldn't want you to go
without a plan!"

But when the contest is between our plan or the Lord's direction,
he doesn't want us to follow the plan; he wants us to follow him. He
knows the plans and purposes for our lives. He knows the way when
we can see no way. And his way is often something we never could
have imagined.

The truth is that every time we leave our homes, though we think
we know where we're going, our destination may change. We might
not end up where we intended. There is no guarantee in following our
own plans even though they often feel more certain than the Lord's.
We will never be on more solid ground than when we are following
him, though we may not know the next step in front of us.

When he calls, we should always follow his lead. We should neither
hesitate—even if it doesn't make sense to us—nor forge ahead trying
to make things happen our own way and attempt to guess where he
has us headed.

We wait on the Lord and take each step at his direction. We might
not know where we're going, but he does.

"Incline your ear and come to me. Listen, that you may
live; and I will make an everlasting covenant with you,
according to the faithful mercies shown to David."
—Isaiah 55:3

Listen, and come. These are the things we're told to do. It's just another
way of saying, "believe," because who do we listen and come to? The
people we trust, the people we believe want good for us, and the people
we love.

If we listen and come to the Lord, we're believing in him. True listening will result in acting on what we hear (James 1:22), not just letting
the words pass our ears.

When we come to the Lord, we know that he will come near to us
(James 4:8). The result? We live! Many versions say our "soul" lives,
and "lives" is also translated as "recovers" or "is restored."

When our souls feel dead or dying, our action should be to listen to
and come to him. This isn't a brief encounter on Sundays, but an everyday act of learning about him and his heart for us and reading and
meditating on his Word. What do his Words mean for our day-to-day
lives, our hearts, our actions, and our thoughts? How can we bring
them into his truth?

We tend to settle for a weak, withered soul now because we're feeding it what the world offers. But when we nourish it by listening to the
Lord and coming to him, we come alive now and come into that everlasting covenant and faithful mercy. It's like CPR for a dying soul, giving us the only thing that will truly sustain—God's presence in our
lives.

"Be merciful, just as your Father is merciful. Do not
judge, and you will not be judged; and do not condemn,
and you will not be condemned; pardon, and you will be
pardoned. Give, and it will be given to you. They will pour
into your lap a good measure—pressed down, shaken
together, and running over. For by your standard of
measure it will be measured to you in return."
—Luke 6:36–38

By the measure we give, the Lord will give to us. That's a sobering
thought.

What would God's condemnation toward us look like if he were
standing in front of us and modeling our own behavior toward others?

Are we hardhearted? Harsh in judgment? Unforgiving? Selfish?

In Matthew 18:21–35, the master does not forgive the servant the
great debt after the servant is unforgiving to the one indebted to him.
It's even in the Lord's Prayer: "Forgive us our debts, as we also have
forgiven our debtors" (Matthew 6:12).

If we're unwilling to forgive, we will not be forgiven.

On the other hand, are we generous? Patient? Merciful? Forgiving?
Kind? Encouraging?

If we can say yes to those, what a prize we can expect!

These things will be poured into our lap in return with unmitigated
bounty.

It's human nature to judge others harshly, and it's difficult to forgive, but as we become more and more merciful as our Father is merciful, we will draw others to him by passing on his grace and kindness.

The world expects reciprocity and payback. They don't expect kindness and mercy.

It's our job to show them that God is ready to give it.

"If I say, 'Surely the darkness will overwhelm me, and
the light around me will be night,' even darkness is not
dark to you, and the night is as bright as the day.
Darkness and light are alike to you."
—Psalm 139:11–12

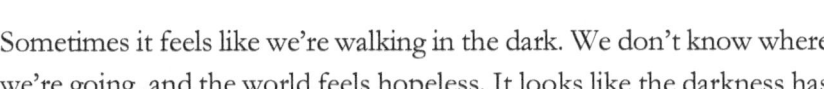

Sometimes it feels like we're walking in the dark. We don't know where we're going, and the world feels hopeless. It looks like the darkness has won.

If we're looking at our circumstances, that might seem true. There may be no earthly way out, as there was no way for the Israelites to cross through the sea, no way for Shadrach, Meshach, and Abednego to survive the fiery furnace, no way for Abraham and Sarah to have a child, and no hope when Jesus died.

But when we look at the Lord's work in those and other circumstances, we can see that there was still a way, even when death was sure and all earthly hope was lost.

He is the God "who makes a way through the sea and a path through the mighty waters" (Isaiah 43:16).

We look to the hand of the Lord. If it seems he is slow to respond, we keep praying, seeking, asking, and knocking (Luke 11:9–13). He will not fail to send the good gift of the Holy Spirit to guide us.

When we find ourselves in the dark unable to see the way, we operate by faith, not by sight (2 Corinthians 5:7). We can be unconcerned when our sight does not show us the way, knowing that the Lord can see where we cannot. The dark is not dark to him. It's as bright as the noonday sun.

"To me they listened and waited, and they kept silent
for my advice . . . And now I have become their
taunt, and I have become a byword to them.
They loathe me and stand aloof from me."
—Job 29:21 & Job 30:9–10

The world loves a success story. They want advice about how to get there too, and they want to be associated with that success. They hang on every word to find out how to accomplish their own goals.

But what happens when that success story collapses?

The world's first reaction is suspicion. Like Job's friends, most people will think, "They must've done something wrong. Maybe they deserve this loss."

They start thinking that person must not be as smart or as great as they thought; they stop flattering and begin to shun.

We like to believe that success is always earned and failure is always deserved, but the Bible shows us over and over that this isn't true.

"He causes his sun to rise on the evil and the good and sends rain on the righteous and the unrighteous" (Matthew 5:45).

This world is broken. Bad things will happen in life no matter how diligently we work, how devoted we are to serving God, or how intelligent and talented we are. Sometimes bad things actually happen because of those things, as we can see with Job.

May we look upon those whose worlds are collapsing and have compassion for them rather than suspicion. May we not distance ourselves from them in their time of need. May we remember that Job was blameless before God; he was not being punished.

And may we remember the same for ourselves when our hard-won successes fall away through no fault of our own.

"We have nothing here except five loaves and two fish."
—Matthew 14:17

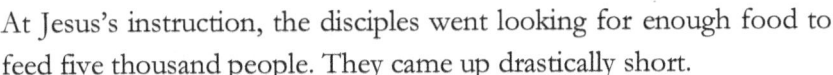

At Jesus's instruction, the disciples went looking for enough food to feed five thousand people. They came up drastically short.

When they told Jesus what they had, he didn't tell them to try harder or go find more. He didn't mock them for mentioning the meager amount they had. He simply said, "Bring them here to me."

When Jesus asks something of us, our job is simply to do what he asks in service to him—to gather what we have and bring it to him.

What we give him will not be enough to make a difference in any earthly sense, but giving it means we get to be a part of what he is doing. He takes our not-enoughness and multiplies it to the Father's glory.

He transforms it into enough. We should never be ashamed when we have less to offer than someone else. Whether it's less talent, money, time, or intelligence, if we give it to the Lord, he multiplies and transforms it to his glory.

Jesus said that the widow who gave her two last coins gave more than all the rich people who had put in large amounts (Mark 12:41–44). It's not about how much we have to give; it's about giving what we have.

Let's stop thinking we couldn't possibly make a difference and remember that it's not about what we can do; it's about what God can do when we give where he asks.

"'Teacher, which is the great commandment in the Law?'
And he said to him, "'You shall love the Lord your God
with all your heart, and with all your soul, and with all your
mind." This is the great and foremost commandment.'"
—Matthew 22:36–38

What does it mean to love God with all our heart, soul, and mind?

God must be first in our emotions, our will, our motives, our desires, our thoughts, and our intellect.

Some try to love him with their emotions but not with their will. Some try to love him with their thoughts and intellect but leave those pesky emotions out of it altogether.

This commandment reminds us that all three aspects must be involved in order to love God with our whole selves.

If we try to love him with our thoughts and emotions but aren't willing to love him in our souls—the seat of our will, desires, and effort—our love will be incomplete. If we try to love him with our wills through obedience and our minds through learning but don't train our emotions to line up with his Word, we cripple our ability to love.

Leaving any of these things out is like tying one hand behind our back while building a house. We might make progress, but it will be slow, cumbersome, and much harder than it has to be.

Even worse, we might be working against ourselves. Every time we get a truth nailed up in our thoughts, our emotions may take it right back down.

When we engage all of ourselves, we train ourselves to think, feel, and act according to the Word of God. This takes time and intentional effort, but the outcome is not only loving God, but internal peace and healing.

"Two are better than one because they have a good
return for their labor; for if either of them falls, the
one will lift up his companion. But woe to the one
who falls when there is not another to lift him up!
Furthermore, if two lie down together they keep warm,
but how can one be warm alone? And if one can
overpower him who is alone, two can resist him. A
cord of three strands is not quickly torn apart."
—Ecclesiastes 4:9–12

———————◆———————

This is often taken to be a passage only about marriage, but shepherds, travelers, soldiers, and the like would all "lie together" at night to stay warm. This is about our need for community within the whole body of Christ.

We're not made for isolation. We need others to help and work alongside us. We need support when we stumble, whether in body or spirit. We need a listening ear when circumstances are harsh. We need protection when we're threatened.

True fellowship is difficult in our culture. We're not encouraged to be honest about our struggles, ask for help, or reach out when others need it, but that's what the church is meant to be. We're supposed to love one another fervently, welcome with generosity even when it's inconvenient, and serve one another in the ways God has equipped us (1 Peter 4:8–10). None of this happens by accident.

Finding this type of community requires stepping out of our comfort zones and facing rejection. We've learned not to prioritize this kind of life, and most of us are busy and stressed. That's all the more reason to live this way; as we reach out, we'll often discover we've built a deep fellowship that is also helping to bear our own burdens.

"Therefore, if anyone cleanses himself from these things, he will be an implement for honor, sanctified, useful to the Master, prepared for every good work. Now flee from youthful lusts and pursue righteousness, faith, love, and peace with those who call on the Lord from a pure heart. But refuse foolish and ignorant speculations, knowing that they produce quarrels. The Lord's bond-servant must not be quarrelsome, but be kind to all, skillful in teaching, patient when wronged, with gentleness correcting those who are in opposition."
—2 Timothy 2:21–25

Do we long to be vessels of honor rather than dishonor in the Lord's house? Do we want to be prepared for the good works he's laid out for us?

Then here is our to-do list:

- Flee youthful lusts.
- Pursue righteousness, faith, love, and peace from a pure heart.
- Refuse ignorant speculations and quarreling.
- Be kind.
- Be skillful in teaching the Word.
- Be patient when wronged.
- Correct others gently.

Flee. Pursue. Refuse. These require action and intent.

And the order is not accidental; we must flee youthful lusts in order to pursue righteousness, faith, love, and peace, and have a pure heart. We must refuse ignorant speculations and quarreling if we're to be kind. We must be skillful in teaching the Word and patient with those who are in opposition if we want to correct them rightly and gently.

Many of us never make it past the first two. We are, as Paul says, still living as ordinary people—fleshly rather than spiritual and fed on milk rather than solid food (1 Corinthians 3:1–3).

May we turn our hearts from earthly pursuits to the inestimable task of becoming vessels of honor.

"Put on the full armor of God, so that you will be able
to stand firm against the schemes of the devil."
—Ephesians 6:11

The armor of God tells us what is needful if we're to stand firm against the devil:

- Truth
- Righteousness
- The Gospel of peace
- The Word of God, which is the Holy Spirit's weapon (Ephesians 6:14–17).

- Faith
- Salvation

We must consistently check whether we're believing and living God's truth and promises or the false beliefs of the father of lies (John 8:44).

We must seek righteousness above all (Matthew 6:33) lest we give the devil a foothold through our sin (Ephesians 4:27).

We must stand so firmly on the Gospel of Jesus Christ that no earthly circumstance can shake our peace (Philippians 4:7), and we must—as far as it depends on us—live at peace with all men (Romans 12:18).

We must truly believe that God is faithful even in the dark times. Doubts about what God said and who he is will leave us open to the enemy's darts. Those are the first lies Satan used to deceive (Genesis 3:1–5).

Salvation through Jesus Christ, as the helmet, is essential. Without it, we are vulnerable even if all the other armor is in place.

And the Word of God, wielded by the Holy Spirit within us, is our sword; it's our only offensive weapon. With it, Jesus rebuked and triumphed over the devil. So can we. The Spirit will bring to mind what we have diligently learned and also teach us "all things" as we need them (John 14:26).

With this armor, we are truly able to stand against the schemes of the devil.

"For this is what the Lord God, the Holy One of Israel,
has said: 'In repentance and rest you will be saved, in
quietness and trust is your strength.' But you were not
willing, and you said, 'No, for we will flee on horses!'
Therefore you shall flee!"
—Isaiah 30:15–16

———◆———

The Lord says we find our salvation in repentance, rest, quietness, and trust. How peaceful that sounds and how rarely we employ it!

When worldly troubles loom, our impulse is to grasp for human means to escape and solve. We trust our modern "horses"—money, insurance, retirement plans, public servants, governments, knowledge, talents, or appearance—to save us.

When trouble comes, we rarely check that our hearts are right with the Lord, then turn quietly, restfully, and confidently to him.

If we don't have enough money in the bank, our protection is failing, we realize we're somehow not enough for the people in our lives, or we're not achieving what we hoped, we begin to feel the enemy's breath at our backs, and we jump on our metaphorical horses, scrambling to find an earthly way to make sure the danger doesn't catch us instead of repenting where there is something to repent of, following the Lord, resting quietly in him, and trusting his promises.

While having horses—or any of these other things—isn't sinful, trusting them for our salvation is, and if we choose to flee using earthly means, then fleeing becomes our fate.

But when we're walking with God in repentance, quietness, and rest, he is our salvation even when we see no way to overcome. We must trust in him instead of in the things we can see.

> "But when Jesus saw this, he was indignant and said to
> them, 'Allow the children to come to me; do not forbid
> them, for the kingdom of God belongs to such as these.'"
> —Mark 10:14

Have you ever felt like someone blocked you from coming to Christ?

These days we can't stand in front of Jesus physically, but it might feel like someone saying, "You're too far gone, not important enough for him to bother with, too weak, or too bad."

Friends, anyone who makes us feel like we can't approach the King doesn't understand the King at all. They have mistaken him for the ruler of an earthly empire, full of self-importance and ceremony—only to be approached by dignitaries and people dressed in finery.

Our King came for the weak, the wounded, the children, the poor, the sick, the downtrodden, the strangers, and the sinners. He came to heal and redeem the broken and help us out of our mess. He gives dignity to the lowly and strength to the weak.

We approach him as one of the weak or not at all. If we come dressed in our best, thinking we have a right to his audience—that we deserve to be in front of him more than others do because of what we can bring or make of ourselves—we don't understand who he is or who we are.

We are all the downtrodden, the children, the humble, and the sick. And we can be thankful we are, because to such belong the kingdom of God. "I have not come to call the righteous to repentance, but sinners" (Luke 5:32).

"For this is the love of God, that we keep his
commandments; and his commandments are not
burdensome. For whoever has been born of God
overcomes the world; and this is the victory that
has overcome the world: our faith. Who is the one
who overcomes the world, but the one who
believes that Jesus is the Son of God?"
—1 John 5:3–5

Believing that Jesus is the son of God is the very foundation for over-coming the world. If we believe he is who he says he is, then we must also believe all he said and did as truth, and we will strive to live our lives according to those teachings.

When we're young Christians, we often test his words like a toddler tests the "no" spoken as he reaches for a hot stove. He does not yet fully believe the words of his parents.

But as we grow in Christ, we should also grow in our faith in his commandments as truth—not as burdensome but for our good, be-cause of his love. He does not want us to be burned.

Anything we do that ignores his commands is contrary to the belief that Jesus is the Son of God, and it will lead to us succumbing to the world rather than overcoming it, because that is not walking in faith.

Only the one who believes Christ is the Son of God will overcome, and that is through the active faith that leads to following his instruction.

We need to look carefully at our lives and take note of the attitudes, beliefs, thoughts, and actions that are not in line with belief in Jesus. Those are the things keeping us from overcoming the world.

"Peace I leave you, my peace I give you; not as
the world gives, do I give to you. Do not let
your hearts be troubled, nor fearful."
—John 14:27

The world says peace is when there are no troubles, no fears, and no struggles in our lives, but that's not how our Lord gives peace.

He gives the peace that comes from the Holy Spirit living within us—the peace that exists even when it sees all the pain and turmoil in this life. When we trust God, we have the ability to face the difficulty, the hurt, and the suffering—we know those things are passing away. We know the end of the story and that as believers, that end is eternal joy in his presence.

He gives us the peace that comes from knowing he will use all things for good when we are following him, even if the thing itself is terrible (Romans 8:28).

He gives the peace that passes understanding (Philippians 4:7) when the sufferings of this world come, because we know that our suffering here does not even tip the scales against the eternal weight of glory (2 Corinthians 4:17).

And as one of the fruits of the Spirit, he gives the internal peace that no law or power in this world can take from us (Galatians 5:22).

The world's peace is a roller coaster dependent upon circumstance, our moods, and the shifting opinions of society. The Lord's peace is constant and steady, a solid thing, immovable, because it comes from him and depends on him. It is the unchanging constant throughout the course of time (Hebrews 13:8) and the only firm foundation (Matthew 7:24–25).

"But whoever wants to become prominent among
you shall be your servant, and whoever desires to be
first among you shall be your slave; just as the Son of
Man did not come to be served, but to serve,
and to give his life as a ransom for many."
—Matthew 20:26–28

Can we choose to be servants and slaves? Can we lay down our lives in the service of Christ for the sake of others?

We want greatness to mean we are commended and comfortable.

In the kingdom of God, it often means we're rejected and despised.

In 2 Timothy 2:10, Paul says, "I endure all things for the sake of those who are chosen, so that they also may obtain the salvation which is in Christ Jesus and with it eternal glory."

Paul endured beatings, nearly leading to death; thirty-nine lashes five times; beatings with rods three times; one stoning; three shipwrecks; being adrift at sea; danger from rivers, robbers, his own people, Gentiles, and from false brothers; much toil and hardship; sleepless nights; hunger and thirst; cold and exposure; and the daily pressure of anxiety for the churches (2 Corinthians 11:23–28).

No one could look at his life and say he was showered with praise or comfortable. Yet he is great in the kingdom of God.

We're unlikely to live the depth of hardship Paul did, but we're all called to be servants in the kingdom of God.

We don't have to grow bitter if others don't praise us. We, like Paul, can "endure everything for the sake of the elect." We, like Jesus, don't have to be concerned with whether we are served by others. We can serve with joy and not expect servants of our own.

"He has told you, mortal one, what is good; and what
does the Lord require of you but to do justice, to love
kindness, and to walk humbly with your God?"
—Micah 6:8

We tend to judge ourselves by what we accomplish and how successful
we look. This leads to frustration and overwhelm, because there are
innumerable worldly things we need to do to make this "success" happen.

Are our homes clean? Are our careers and relationships flourishing?
Are we exercising daily and eating healthy? Are our kids doing well in
school? Is the lawn tended and manicured? Do we have the latest fash-
ions? Have we read meaningful books and also kept up with the news?
Do we have it all together emotionally?

We really can't do it all, and there are seasons in which we can only
do the bare minimum. We feel behind and like we're failing at everything. There are so many things on our plate, and most of them are
falling off.

The Lord does not look at us in frustration when our to-do lists
keep piling up. He is not bothered if our toilets go unscrubbed or our
hedges untrimmed.

What does he care about? That we do justice, love mercy, and walk
humbly with him.

We can do that even when our daily life looks like a mess to us or
anyone who happens to be looking on.

Let's stop judging ourselves on how many tasks we accomplish, but
rather according to the Lord's requirements. At the end of the day, we
may be further behind than we began, but if we've done these three
things, we are successful regardless.

> "Be devoted to one another in brotherly love;
> give preference to one another in honor."
> —Romans 12:10

"Love one another" is something we see all over the Bible.

It's easy to forget this means anything extraordinary, so I love how the next sentence takes it to a new level. "Give preference to one another in honor." Some versions say, "Outdo one another in showing honor."

There are about a thousand ways we try to outdo one another: in performance, success, by possessing the latest gadget or the nicest car, by dressing or looking a certain way, and by comparing our kids to other people's kids. We can even try to outdo one another in our religious zeal and end up like the Pharisees: "God, I thank you that I am not like other people: swindlers, crooked, adulterers, or even like this tax collector. I fast twice a week; I pay tithes of all that I get" (Luke 18:11–12).

But what if we each tried to outdo one another only in showing honor? Imagining a world like this makes me take a deep breath and smile, because it would mean no one was trying to overshadow anyone else. No one would be oppressing others, but rather lifting them up. We would all be happy to rejoice in others' success even if it surpassed our own.

So let's take that deep breath, relax into the lives we have instead of the ones we don't, stop worrying what standards others are judging us by, and live free of all the other cumbersome "outdoing one another" that keeps us in the trap of comparison, insecurity, and fear of the opinions of others.

Let's attempt to outdo others only in showing honor and wow them with our love.

"But godliness actually is a means of great gain
when accompanied by contentment."
—1 Timothy 6:6

People living in contentment don't have everything, but they don't need to have everything. They may live paycheck-to-paycheck. They may not wear fancy clothes or drive a nice car. Their house might need work. They might not get recognition or appreciation for the things they do. They might not have the type of relationships they wish they did.

Yet, being near a content person is calming. They live in peace and hope regardless of their circumstances and even when things look bleak.

How do we grow this contentment?

As we walk in godliness and obey the Word of the Lord, the truth becomes more and more clear in our lives. The Word becomes living and active.

We recognize that what it asks of us really is the path to the easy yoke and the light burden. The last really shall be first (Matthew 20:16) and seeking the kingdom of God and righteousness first really is the path to having anything else of worth (Matthew 6:33). The approval of man really is empty (Matthew 6:1), and whatever we give up for Christ really will be repaid many times over both in this life and the next (Matthew 19:29).

These truths don't feel true until we're walking in them. Our human nature tells us that seeking what we want will bring us contentment, but what we find there is abundance without fulfillment and fleeting pleasure without lasting joy.

As we walk in godliness by the power of the Holy Spirit, we find the opposite is true. We're renewed rather than depleted as we serve. We have joy even in the midst of pain. We're content even when we lack things we desire.

"Today, if you will hear his voice,
do not harden your hearts."
—Psalm 95:7–8

When the Lord prompts us to do something or we feel the nudge of the Holy Spirit telling us not to do something, it's easy to silence that voice in the moment.

"This is just a small thing; it won't matter. I'll listen next time."

When we do this, we harden our hearts and make his voice a little bit quieter every time.

If we continue down this path, we slowly quench the Spirit (1 Thessalonians 5:19) and show that he is not truly our Lord. John 10:27–28 says, "My sheep listen to my voice, and I know them, and they follow me; and I give them eternal life."

If we are his sheep, we will follow him, and if we love him, we will keep his commandments (John 14:15; John 14:21; John 14:23). We won't do it perfectly and there is so much grace for our stumbles, but our true desire and sincere effort should be to grow in the grace and knowledge of the Lord (2 Peter 3:18), to move beyond the elementary teachings and become mature believers (Hebrews 6:1), and to learn, by practicing our faith, to discern between good and evil (Romans 12:1–2).

Every tiny whisper the Lord speaks to us, whether it's through his Word or the Holy Spirit, is taking us down a path closer toward that maturing, but hardening our hearts to those whispers will take us away from him. The small steps along that path are just as important as the big ones.

> "Stop striving and know that I am God; I will be exalted
> among the nations, I will be exalted on the earth."
> —Psalm 46:10

As believers, we can stop bustling anxiously from one thing to the next, stop trying to control our circumstances, and stop worrying about everything . . . and we can do it all in confidence of our God.

The worldly phrase we all know for this is to "stop and smell the roses," but the impact of that statement pales compared to how God puts it: "Stop striving and know that I am God."

Sometimes there aren't any roses. Sometimes everything around us stinks. Sometimes stopping to smell the roses just reminds us that—right now—we can only see thorns.

But God is always there in his fully present, all-powerful god-ness. No matter what we see around us, he is Immanuel—God with us.

And no rose has power over the circumstances of our lives.

We could be in the middle of a rose garden, but it might bring, at best, only a few moments of peace before the difficult realities all around us take over our thoughts once again.

But God is still God no matter what. He is the same yesterday, today, and forever (Hebrews 13:8). He is still in control. We can look around at the roses or the stink and the thorns and know that he is working in and through it all.

Instead of striving, we can rest in who he is—our fully good and loving, omnipotent God—and the rest, peace, and confidence we have in him will be a testimony of his goodness and sovereignty to those around us.

> "For as the rain and the snow come down from heaven,
> and do not return there without watering the earth and
> making it produce and sprout, and providing seed to the
> sower and bread to the eater; so will my word be which
> goes out of my mouth; it will not return to me empty,
> without accomplishing what I desire, and without
> succeeding in the purpose for which I sent it."
> —Isaiah 55:10–11

Sometimes we say things at the Lord's prompting, and it feels like we just watch it fall to fallow ground, yielding nothing.

Maybe we don't receive the reactions we hoped—or any reaction at all. Maybe no one suddenly accepts Jesus Christ, turns their life around, or responds to the truth in what was said. Maybe they even respond badly.

That doesn't mean the words were useless. If we're speaking God's Word, it's planting seeds all along the way. Some may sprout and some may not; that depends upon the soil where they land (Matthew 13:1–23), but those words are never spoken in vain.

Most seeds take time to sink deep into the soil and begin to sprout . . . sometimes a very long time.

And we may never know even if the fruit does thrive; maybe we're there for the planting, but someone else is there for the harvest (John 4:37–38).

We can continue planting those seeds in hopeful confidence, because if we're faithful to plant, the harvest will eventually come (Galatians 6:9).

The Lord's Word will not return void.

"Do not be haughty in mind but associate with the lowly.
Do not be wise in your own estimation."
—Romans 12:16

If we're humble, we won't be afraid to be seen with the lowly. This verse makes us think of the poor and the homeless, but let's make it relatable—it's the lady nobody likes, the awkward person who always says the wrong thing, and the guy at work with no hygiene.

If we're humble, we won't need to seem more important than others. We won't need to hobnob only with the most popular or successful people in the room. We'll always treat the lowly as equals, though some may think it's degrading to do so. We also won't hesitate to get our hands dirty and do what many consider the lowly jobs. If we're humble, we can do these things even if we're put in a prominent position, because we aren't "believing our own press," as they say.

Others may see us as a giant in some area—industry, intellect, wisdom, talent, or charisma—but if we're humble, we won't let the root of pride burrow into our hearts. We will know we are human like all others and that only the power of the Holy Spirit makes us truly good. All believers are on equal ground before Christ.

And humility is part of our protection against falling into that sin. If we start believing we're better than others or wise in our own estimation, we begin trusting in ourselves and our own worldly abilities and talents instead of leaning on Jesus Christ, and that will lead directly to a fall (Proverbs 16:18).

"Do not store up for yourselves treasures on earth,
where moth and rust destroy, and where thieves break
in and steal. But store up for yourselves treasures in
heaven, where neither moth nor rust destroys, and
where thieves do not break in or steal; for where
your treasure is, there your heart will be also."
—Matthew 6:19–21

If we ask ourselves regularly where our hearts are—and answer honestly—we will often find they are holding on to the temporary things of this earth.

The following questions bring some clarity:

- What are we focused on to the exclusion of other things?
- What brings anxiety to our hearts?
- What do we think about when we first wake up in the morning?
- What causes the most tension in our relationships?

If we put our treasure and heart's desire in Christ and become completely taken up with him, we won't be fazed by the gain or loss of earthly things. We'll recognize the truth that the earthly is all temporary and will fade away with age, destruction, or theft. Above all, we will want to live for the things that count for eternity.

May we always be checking where we've put our hearts and our treasure and redirecting when necessary.

This is not a one-time action. We must be alert to each new worldly temptation. Some of them can look very like heavenly gifts until our motives are brought to light. For instance, if our motive for godly work is so that others will believe we are good, then our treasure is in the opinion of man.

Our heart for the Lord's good works is building eternal treasure when it isn't set on any earthly outcome or reward (Matthew 6:1).

> "He lets me lie down in green pastures; he leads me beside quiet waters. He restores my soul; he guides me in the paths of righteousness for the sake of his name. Even though I walk through the valley of the shadow of death, I fear no evil, for you are with me; your rod and your staff, they comfort me."
>
> —Psalm 23:2–4

Sometimes it's good to remember that along with the green pastures and the still waters, our good Shepherd might also take us through the valley of the shadow of death. He has not stopped leading us, even there. The difficult path might be the only one that leads us home.

We do not have to fear it, because we trust our Shepherd.

With his rod and staff, the Lord directs, corrects, and protects us.

We often choose to be more frustrated than comforted by his direction and correction, but this passage teaches us that the proper attitude toward correction is to be comforted.

A toddler might be dazzled by a fire, but a good father will guide the child away from the danger over and over. The child doesn't understand, but we know the father is not being cruel or keeping a good thing from the child. This is protection.

The Lord does this for us when we become dazzled by the world and wander too close to its flames.

We often forget what this beautiful psalm tells us . . . first, that our circumstances may not always be pleasant, but we don't have to fear, and second, that the Lord may discipline and direct us where we do not want to go, but it is always for our eternal good.

"Be angry, and yet do not sin."
—Ephesians 4:26

We've been made to feel that anger itself is sinful, but it doesn't have to be.

Our reaction is where the issue usually arises; our anger too often comes out in rudeness, fear, hatred, or insults.

To be angry without sinning requires pausing before speaking and using kind words instead of quarrelsome ones (2 Timothy 2:24).

It requires abiding in the vine of Jesus Christ, disciplining ourselves in self-control, and allowing the Holy Spirit to be in charge instead of letting fleshly desires and rights take over our mouths.

If we're giving in to selfishness, the need to win an argument, the desire to put the other party in their place, or holding on to an offense and allowing it to turn to bitterness, we're letting that anger become sinful.

We must learn to respond with gracious words even in the middle of an argument and to adjust our actions so we're not tearing others down. They were made in the image of God and any failure on their part to reflect him should result in our pity, love, and prayers. We should also choose to hope and believe that others mean us good at heart rather than assuming the worst of their actions (1 Corinthians 13:7).

Whether they mean us good or evil, we're told to "Love your enemies and pray for those who persecute you, so that you may prove yourselves to be sons of your Father who is in heaven" (Matthew 5:44—45).

We must live this verse if we're going to be angry without sinning and show those around us that we are sons of the loving, merciful God.

"Therefore we also have as our ambition,
whether at home or absent, to be pleasing to him."
—2 Corinthians 5:9

Our goal should always be to please the Lord. If we have any other earthly ambition ahead of (or even in addition to) that, it will always be competing with what the Lord wants of us.

The beauty of this is that pleasing the Lord means freedom from the expectations of this world.

Paul goes on to say in verse 12, "We are not commending ourselves to you again, but are giving you an opportunity to be proud of us, so that you will have an answer for those who take pride in appearance and not in heart."

He was telling the church to stop being impressed by outward appearances, power, or grand gestures. "Recognize no one by the flesh," he adds (2 Corinthians 5:16).

Our only measure for ourselves should be whether we aim to please the Lord—in other words, where our hearts are. This doesn't mean we will necessarily do great things in the eyes of the world. It does mean that the fruit of the Spirit will be evident in our lives.

It's easy to get caught up in how we look to the world and worried about whether people see us as successful, smart, attractive, or worthy. But we're not seeking their approval, and God isn't worried about our appearance or our resume. We simply live our lives with the goal of pleasing him, and he is pleased.

We will not do it perfectly, but as long as living in humble service to him is our true aim, we will not miss.

"Now which one of you fathers will his son ask for a fish,
and instead of a fish, he will give him a snake? Or he will
even ask for an egg, and his father will give him a scorpion?
So if you, despite being evil, know how to give good gifts to
your children, how much more will your heavenly Father
give the Holy Spirit to those who ask him?"
—Luke 11:11–13

When I was little, I begged my mom for all kinds of things at the store—cheap toys, junk food, and useless trinkets. She almost always said no.

But the denial was because she loves me and wanted to give me good gifts instead—healthy food, lasting toys, an education, etc. I didn't understand good gifts; I only thought about immediate pleasure.

We're often like toddlers in our prayers. We ask for things to satisfy our pleasures, and God says no (James 4:3) because he wants to give lasting joy rather than cheap toys and healthy food that will help us grow rather than cookies for every meal.

So when we pray for the Holy Spirit, God will never meet us with refusal or something fearful instead. He will always give us this good gift.

The Holy Spirit is the promise of our salvation (Ephesians 1:13–14), our power to resist sin (Romans 8:12–13), our teacher of all things (John 14:26), our connection to the Father (John 16:13–15), and the power ensuring our eternal life (Romans 8:11).

The Spirit is real, powerful, and active in our lives, guiding us into truth and directing us into his good work (John 16:13; Acts 8:29; Acts 16:6–7).

"Whatever you do, do your work heartily, as for the
Lord and not for people, knowing that it is from the
Lord that you will receive the reward of the
inheritance. It is the Lord Christ whom you serve."
—Colossians 3:23–24

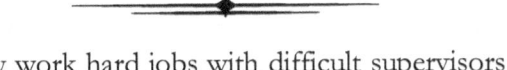

Many of us may work hard jobs with difficult supervisors and unreasonable expectations. The people Paul was writing to wouldn't have been strangers to a poor work environment. Many of his readers may have been slaves to cruel masters.

The message is the same for us as it was for them—that we do our duty faithfully and with integrity, not with that harsh supervisor in mind, but as if we are doing our work for the Lord . . . because we are.

We're ultimately serving him, and though bosses, supervisors, and slave masters may not deserve our best, the Lord does. He gave his best for us when we did not deserve it, and we certainly are not greater than he is.

This doesn't mean we must stay in the difficult situation if there is a way out. First Corinthians 7:21 says of slavery, "If you are also able to become free, take advantage of that." We can work to find a better job in an environment with healthy, godly leadership.

However, should our circumstances not change despite our best efforts, our integrity and work ethic should remain above reproach, because our service is always to the Lord.

Others don't determine the level of right actions expected from us; our actions must be right before the Lord.

"To those who have received a faith of the same kind
as ours, by the righteousness of our God and Savior,
Jesus Christ: grace and peace be multiplied to you in
the knowledge of God and of Jesus our Lord, for his
divine power has granted to us everything pertaining to
life and godliness, through the true knowledge of him
who called us by his own glory and excellence."
—2 Peter 1:1–3

"A faith of the same kind as ours."

Sometimes we feel like the authors of the Bible must've been superheroes of the faith, but they were flawed, struggling people just like you and me.

Our faith is the same kind as theirs—we've been given grace and peace through the knowledge of God and Jesus, and God's divine power has provided everything we need for life and godliness.

All the promises these pillars of the faith experienced apply to us as well, and we can live full lives for Christ through the same strength they did.

It requires commitment and obedience, though. As this passage goes on to say, "Now for this very reason also, applying all diligence, in your faith supply moral excellence, and in your moral excellence, knowledge, and in your knowledge, self-control, and in your self-control, perseverance, and in your perseverance, godliness, and in your godliness, brotherly kindness, and in your brotherly kindness, love" (2 Peter 1:5–7).

We must intentionally apply these things to our hearts, minds, and actions.

God works in us as we act on our belief that his way is the true way. We're transformed by our obedience. "As long as you practice these things, you will never stumble" (2 Peter 1:10).

"Let's consider how to encourage one another in love and
good deeds, not abandoning our own meeting together, as
is the habit of some people, but encouraging one another;
and all the more as you see the day drawing near."
—Hebrews 10:24–25

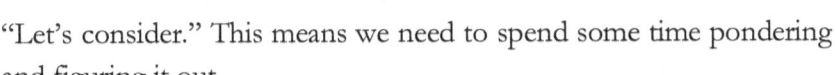

"Let's consider." This means we need to spend some time pondering
and figuring it out.

It probably won't come naturally, but part of our Christian lives is
to encourage others to "love and do good deeds."

So how can we do this?

First and foremost, we must be meeting together with other believers. If we aren't in community with them, how could we ever stir anyone to love and good works?

Second, one of the best ways to encourage someone in love and
good deeds is by being an example of actively loving them and looking
for ways to bear their burdens, bless them, and meet their needs as well
as the needs of others around us.

Love is winsome; it draws others to it and inspires them to pass it on.

Third, we can consider what has encouraged us in love and good
deeds in the past . . . and what has not. When have people encouraged
us in this way? How can we use that knowledge to do the same for
others, and how can we avoid reenacting attitudes that have kept us
locked in fear, insecurity, anger, harm, or inaction rather than inspired
us to love and good deeds?

It's our calling, especially as the world around us grows darker, to
spend time considering how we can encourage those around us to actively love others and impact the kingdom of God.

"To one he gave five talents, to another, two, and to
another, one, each according to his own ability."
—Matthew 25:15

In the Parable of the Talents, the master does not judge the servants based on their abilities. He knows what they're capable of and gives them responsibility accordingly. He isn't expecting anyone to do more than they're able; he only expects that they will not waste what they have been given.

We often either feel like we can't do as much as others around us or that we can't do things as well. We may not believe we're as smart, talented, or spiritually strong. We may struggle with learning disabilities or chronic health conditions that limit what we can do.

But God never judges us by comparing our talents and abilities to others'. He never looks at any of us and says, "Well, she's not as good as so-and-so because she can't _____." He created and arranged each of us in the body of Christ just as he desired (1 Corinthians 12:18) and has specific good works in mind for us—works tailored to our unique gifts and abilities (Ephesians 2:10). The work he has for us is work that we can do.

Our inabilities are never a point of shame, for even where we are weak, he is strong (2 Corinthians 12:9–10).

What he does ask is faithfulness with what we've been given. Our talents, abilities, skills, personality, and even our struggles are always to be invested in the kingdom of God, putting feet to the prayer "your will be done on earth as it is in heaven."

"The world is passing away and also its lusts; but the one
who does the will of God continues to live forever."
—1 John 2:17

The things the world promises and tempts us with will not last, but doing the will of God not only affects us and those around us in this life but carries over into eternity.

Doing his will requires us to:

- disciple others in the Word (Matthew 28:19–20).
- exhibit the fruit of the Spirit in our daily lives (Galatians 5:22–23).
- care for the poor, orphaned, sick, oppressed, imprisoned, and strangers (James 1:27; Matthew 25:31–46).
- do justice, love kindness, and walk humbly with God (Micah 6:8).
- forgive others as he has forgiven us (Matthew 6:14–15; Matthew 18:21–35; Ephesians 4:32; Mark 11:25).
- put to death the deeds of the flesh (Romans 8:12–13; Ephesians 5:3–9; 1 Peter 4:1–3).
- walk as Jesus walked (1 John 2:5–6).
- serve and love each other (John 13:35; Galatians 5:13; 1 Peter 4:8–11).

If we love him, there will be evidence of these things in our lives (John 14:23), and we will not only live forever in joy and peace with him, but the things we built by following God's will as we walk this earth will continue into eternity as well. Our life's example will have brought other people into forever with Christ.

Building up an earthly kingdom with temporary, earthly rewards—whether that is sin's short-term satisfaction, wealth, possessions, reputation, success, talents, or appearance—is like building a sandcastle. It will inevitably fall to nothing. Let's focus on the things that last.

"Jesus said to them, 'My food is to do the will of
him who sent me, and to accomplish his work.'"
—John 4:34

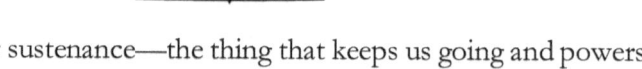

Our food is our sustenance—the thing that keeps us going and powers
us on. Physical food does this for the body. But what sustains the soul?

Some might say it's their children, their job, or a relationship. There
are an infinite number of things people might put in that place.

But as fellow heirs with Jesus Christ, we have a new nature like his
(2 Corinthians 5:17), and we have his mind (1 Corinthians 2:16). And
because we are now like him, our spiritual food—the thing that both
nourishes our spirit and spurs us on—is to do the work of the Father.

This is not a passive task. It's something we do—we are doers, not
just hearers (James 1:22).

Accomplishing the Lord's work will definitely include our children,
our jobs, our relationships, and many other good things in life, but
those things themselves are not the sustenance of our souls. If we treat
them as our soul's food, we will either consume them in the end, or
they will consume us. They're not meant to be the purpose, but they
are meant to receive the benefit of our soul's nourishment.

If we treat those things as an outflow of doing our Father's work,
they will reap the benefits in the outpouring of his Spirit, and we will
flourish as well.

If we look honestly at our day-to-day life, what is our food? What
are we using to fuel our souls?

"By faith Moses, when he had grown up, refused to be
called the son of Pharaoh's daughter, choosing rather to
endure ill-treatment with the people of God than to
enjoy the temporary pleasures of sin, considering the
reproach of Christ greater riches than the treasures of
Egypt; for he was looking to the reward. By faith he left
Egypt, not fearing the wrath of the king; for he
persevered, as though seeing him who is unseen."
—Hebrews 11:24–27

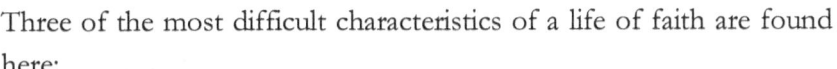

Three of the most difficult characteristics of a life of faith are found
here:

- to accept the difficulty following Christ affords us in this life
  rather than chasing the treasures of this world.
- to not fear or envy evil men.
- to live for the invisible rather than the visible.

Could we, like Moses, choose the humble life of a shepherd rather than
a life of royalty?

We know that the treasures of this life will always wither, fade
(Isaiah 40:8), rust, and be destroyed (Matthew 6:19). We know that evil
men will always get their due, even if it's not until eternity (Isaiah 3:11).
We know that the invisible is eternal while the visible is temporary (2
Corinthians 4:18).

In order to live lives of faith, we must intentionally, purposefully,
and consistently remind ourselves of these truths. When we're tempted
by the pleasures of this world (James 1:14–15), when we're afraid of
what man can do to us (Matthew 10:28), and when we're distracted by
the cares of the world, the deceitfulness of riches, and the desire for
temporary things (Mark 4:19) that choke out the Word in our lives, our
job is to turn our hearts back to the truth.

That is the life of faith.

"At that time the disciples came to Jesus and said,
'Who then is greatest in the kingdom of heaven?' And
he called a child to himself and set him among them,
and said, 'Truly I say to you, unless you change and
become like children, you will not enter the kingdom
of heaven. So whoever will humble himself like this
child, he is the greatest in the kingdom of heaven.'"
—Matthew 18:1–4

If we understand our place before God, there will be no vying for position. We will have no illusions of ruling with him in heaven, but rather fall down before his throne, even the greatest of us casting our crowns at his feet (Revelation 4:10–11). We will always see ourselves as children in his household, not masters.

We will know that there is only one Master—our heavenly Father. Only he is worthy of being greater than any other. We and all our brothers and sisters come on equal footing to his throne—helpless, dependent, and unable to earn our place in the kingdom.

This doesn't mean being a child requires nothing of us. What a father really wants from his children is love, relationship, trust, and obedience. And just as an earthly child is expected to grow, we're all to mature in the faith—to learn and grow in grace and knowledge (2 Peter 3:18), in maturity (Ephesians 4:11–16), and in obedience (James 2:26).

And how freeing to live as a child, trusting our Father's direction, knowing that he is capable of handling all that comes in this life, unconcerned with earthly position, and relaxing into the fact that he loves us wholly and is always with us!

"[Love] believes all things, hopes all things."
—1 Corinthians 13:7

What does it actually mean to believe and hope all things in love?

It means giving others the benefit of the doubt, trusting that their intentions toward us are good, taking their words at face value instead of trying to assume motives, and not living in suspicion because of our own insecurities.

When we think of those we love, we can imagine all the terrible things they might think of us or all the ways they might hurt us, but living in those thoughts will create a barrier of fear, lived by us and felt by them.

Or we can imagine that those people truly love us, want our good, and do their best to bring it about. We can realize that they probably also have areas where they struggle to restrain doubts and assumptions about our motives, feelings, and actions. By believing in those people, we will give them the courage to believe in us.

This doesn't mean we pretend hurts don't exist when they appear. When harm is done, we lovingly address it. We set boundaries and expectations.

But we don't create or imagine division out of nothing.

And this applies to all the relationships in our lives—family, friendship, professional, or romantic.

We will still be hurt sometimes, but that will happen whether we live in cynical expectation of it or not. And the cynical expectation not only hurts us; it creates an environment that fosters hurt in the other person as well.

When we choose to believe and hope, we renew both our relationships and our own hearts.

> "Rather, discipline yourself for the purpose of godliness;
> for bodily training is just slightly beneficial, but godliness
> is beneficial for all things, since it holds promise for the
> present life and also for the life to come."
> —1 Timothy 4:7–8

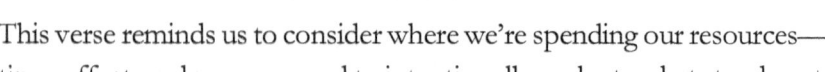

This verse reminds us to consider where we're spending our resources—time, effort, and money—and to intentionally evaluate what stands out.

Exercise is valuable; Paul isn't saying we can't or shouldn't do it. I also don't think he is minimizing the importance of being healthy. As the temple of the Holy Spirit (1 Corinthians 3:16–17), we're to be good stewards of our bodies as the instrument we use to carry out the good works he's assigned to us in this life (Ephesians 2:10).

But many of us spend far more of our resources on the external and temporary—looking younger, having the most fashionable clothes, the most toned body, or the fanciest car—than we do the internal and infinite.

Exercise for health can sometimes become exercise for vanity, and Paul is reminding us to keep our priorities straight. Neither exercise nor any other good thing in our lives should come before disciplining ourselves for the purpose of godliness.

That is pursuing a lesser good to the detriment of the eternal good.

And training for godliness actually trickles into every other area of our lives because it fosters the self-control and wisdom we need to be disciplined overall.

Are we spending the bulk of our resources on things that are only valuable for this life or on things that are valuable not only now, but also into eternity?

"But do not let this one fact escape your notice, beloved,
that with the Lord one day is like a thousand years,
and a thousand years like one day."
—2 Peter 3:8

Do you remember waiting for things when you were a kid? A month felt like an eternity when it was between you and your birthday, Christmas, or that vacation. The wait seemed unbearable.

Many of us can relate, finding it hard to be motivated by our eternity with Christ because it seems too far off. When things are hard or circumstances aren't what we want, another thirty, forty, or fifty years seems too hard, too long, and too much to bear.

Instead of looking at our future like children the month before Christmas—as an interminable wait they can't possibly endure—let's be like the parents who know it's just around the corner; a month will pass in no time at all.

We may look ahead at the difficult years and wish they would pass in a flash—wish we could feel confident the good thing was really on the other side of the wait.

God sees those years and wants us to trust that the wait will be worth it and that, afterwards, it will seem like no wait at all. Like parents with their children, he would love to see us living in eager excitement with contentment in the meantime.

God knows that being content in the waiting and through the difficult years seems impossible to us, but he also knows they will pass in a flash. Living in hopeful expectation is part of what he has for us on this side of eternity.

"Jesus began to point out to his disciples that it was necessary for him to go to Jerusalem and to suffer many things . . . and to be killed, and to be raised up . . . .. And yet Peter took him aside and began to rebuke him, saying, 'God forbid it, Lord! This shall never happen to you!' But he turned and said to Peter, 'Get behind me, Satan! You are a stumbling block to me; for you are not setting your mind on God's purposes, but men's.'"
—Matthew 16:21–23

Not everyone who speaks good things into our lives can be trusted to know God's will. Even well-meaning people who love us and love God may say things that tempt us away from the hard road necessary to accomplish the Lord's purposes.

They may say that no bad thing can come our way or that God would never allow us to suffer, but the Word says we will have trials (1 Peter 4:12–13), we will be hated (Matthew 10:22), and we will even be put to death (Matthew 24:9).

The belief that God will not allow difficulty or that a strong faith exempts us from worldly trouble will lead us to turn from him the moment difficulty arises. It creates a false sense of what God promises, so when the hardship comes, we start thinking he has not kept his word.

If our minds are set on men's purposes—comfort, prosperity, and health—any contradiction to those things will turn us away from God.

But if our minds are set on God's purposes, we will be focused on the eternal kingdom (John 18:36). Only from that foundation can we endure the trials of this world with our faith intact (Matthew 24:10–13).

"And they took him and threw him into the pit."
—Genesis 37:24

We seem to think that God's plan will keep us out of the pit, but that's not always true.

Sometimes we dig our own pits, and we usually know when that's the case. But sometimes we have no idea how we got there or why it's happening. Even then, we can trust that the Lord's hand is still working.

Daniel was thrown into the pit of lions because of his devotion to the Lord (Daniel 6).

Joseph was thrown into the pit by his brothers because he saw a vision from the Lord (Genesis 37).

Shadrach, Meshach, and Abednego were thrown into the pit of fire because they refused to worship anyone but God (Daniel 3).

Jeremiah was thrown into a pit to starve because he spoke the truth God told him (Jeremiah 38).

But what man means for evil, God means for good (Genesis 50:20).

There are many types of pits we could be in—isolation, abandonment, betrayal, illness, persecution, anxiety, financial trouble, or simple uncertainty.

And even if we've dug our own pit, we don't have to despair, because God is still our hope . . . the only one who can redeem, forgive, rescue, and give us a renewed purpose (Psalm 40; Psalm 103).

Being in a pit is objectively bad, but the Lord will work good through the bad for believers as he promises he will in Romans 8:28.

We hold fast to him and remember he's still working in our circumstances. The pit isn't fun, but God hasn't forgotten or abandoned us. He's promised he never will (Hebrews 13:5).

"Thomas said to him, 'Lord, we do not know where you are going; how do we know the way?' Jesus said to him, 'I am the way, and the truth, and the life; no one comes to the Father except through me.'"
—John 14:5–6

We are all too focused on knowing the end, the destination, or the goal when Jesus wants us to know and follow him.

He is the goal.

If we focus on him instead of being so concerned about where we're going, we can live with the peace of a child holding our father's hand, confident that he will not lead us astray.

The child is fully dependent on the father knowing where they are going. He doesn't know how to get anywhere, but he knows and trusts the father.

Let's trust our heavenly Father the same way, not worrying about the twists and turns we couldn't have predicted anyway, but holding fast to Jesus's hand as he guides us through this life. The road may sometimes seem dangerous or slow or like we've gone off track, but by following him, we never have to worry and will never lose our way.

It's when we get concerned about what's going on around us, take our eyes off him, and start trying to trust our own sense of direction or the way the world tells us we should go that we're in danger. We let go of his hand and begin to drift, like Peter sinking when he took his eyes off the Lord to look at the waves. But we only have to call out, and Jesus reaches out to take our hand once more and bring us back to the way.

Let us not be concerned with knowing what path we should take, but with knowing and following Christ—the only true way.

"For he will never be shaken; the righteous will be
remembered forever. He will not fear bad news;
his heart is steadfast, trusting in the Lord.
His heart is firm, he will not fear."
—Psalm 112:6–8

Does this mean the righteous person will never have trouble? No. The second sentence says he doesn't fear bad news, which means he may get some. First Peter 4:12 also tells us not to be surprised when we face trials.

Does it mean no one will ever oppress him? No. Daniel—a picture of faithfulness to God—was taken into captivity, made to serve the pagan king, and most likely made a eunuch. Jesus himself was tortured and killed.

Does it mean the righteous person will defeat every enemy? No. Hebrews 10:34 tells us the believers "accepted joyfully the seizure of their property" when it was the consequence of following the Lord's will.

So what does it mean?

It means when the bad news comes, the righteous man will not be full of fear. His heart will not waver, because he trusts the Lord no matter what.

When we're taken captive, made into servants, and our earthly goods are taken, our hearts remain in the Lord, unshaken, knowing these are fleeting troubles that will pass.

Indeed, when we're hated, excluded, insulted, and scorned as evil, we can jump for joy, for great is our reward in heaven (Luke 6:22–23)!

Our souls will be carried safely into eternity as we persevere in the Lord (2 Timothy 2:12; James 1:12). When we walk with the Holy Spirit, our faith isn't tossed about by the earthly waves of circumstance.

Our hearts are firm; we will not fear.

"And Jesus said to his disciples, 'Truly I say to you, it
will be hard for a rich person to enter the kingdom of
heaven. And again I say to you, it is easier for a camel
to go through the eye of a needle, than for a rich
person to enter the kingdom of God.' When the
disciples heard this, they were very astonished and
said, 'Then who can be saved?' And looking at them,
Jesus said to them, 'With people this is impossible,
but with God all things are possible.'"
—Matthew 19:23–26

When we are rich in anything—time, talent, money, health, intelligence,
beauty, etc.—our tendency is to rely on and put our hope in that thing
to the point that we can't imagine our lives without its benefit and
security.

To be servants of Christ, we must recognize that these riches are
not lasting or meaningful in the kingdom of God; they are temporary
circumstances in our earthly lives. Many of them fade over the natural
course of time, and if we have not become confident in God alone
before that happens, we will become bitter and disillusioned over their
loss.

We must be willing to give them up if he asks, knowing it's not our
richness that matters in the end; it's Christ's sacrifice and life in us.

Anything we aren't willing to give up when the Lord asks is an idol.

He knows we will be left empty if we're counting on our idols, so
he may make us destitute in this life so we won't be destitute forever.
If there's something in the way, he will make a way for us to come to
him. We still must choose to come, but the path will be possible.

"For consider your calling, brothers and sisters, that
there were not many wise according to the flesh, not
many mighty, not many noble; but God has chosen the
foolish things of the world to shame the wise, and God
has chosen the weak things of the world to shame the
things which are strong, and the insignificant things of
the world and the despised God has chosen, the things
that are not, so that he may nullify the things that are,
so that no human may boast before God."
—1 Corinthians 1:26–29

Do you ever feel foolish? Wish you were smarter? Worry that your lack of money, fame, power, or good health keeps you from doing anything worthwhile?

No need.

God chose us, knowing all our insecurities, flaws, and everything we lack. He esteems the poor (Psalm 113:7). He loves the downtrodden (Isaiah 61:1). His heart is for the powerless (Psalm 9:9). Through him, our weaknesses become strength: "He has said to me, 'My grace is sufficient for you, for power is perfected in weakness.'" (2 Corinthians 12:9).

When we know we're weak, we submit, obey, and our hearts are transformed; therefore, Christ can work through us. We're no longer tempted to do things our own way.

When our weaknesses leave us feeling defeated and insecure, let's remember that God's kingdom does not work like our earthly kingdoms. The last shall be first (Matthew 20:16). If we want to be great, we must be a servants (Mark 10:43).

Rather than letting our weaknesses drag us down, we can take them to Christ so he can use his mighty power to work in and through all our insufficiencies.

> "The kingdom of heaven is like a treasure hidden
> in the field, which a man found and hid again; and
> from joy over it he goes and sells everything that
> he has and buys that field. Again, the kingdom of
> heaven is like a merchant seeking fine pearls, and
> upon finding one pearl of great value, he went
> and sold everything that he had and bought it."
> —Matthew 13:44–46

We spend all our lives seeking to acquire things. Most of us scatter our wealth of time, money, and effort with little thought to what we're purchasing, but there is always an exchange.

Many of us have at least one thing we've been obsessively trying to purchase our whole lives, whether it's relationship, success, ease, escape, or wealth. Sometimes the thing we want is even a good thing, but what we know—because the Lord tells us—is that none of those things are worth anything compared to the kingdom of God.

Perhaps we've finally been able to acquire some of those things we've sought but found they still don't fill the deepest longings of our souls—the ache we thought they'd quench is still there.

We realize that we've worked long and diligently to buy the food that perishes (John 6:27–29).

Let us, instead, be willing to sell all our earthly trappings and trimmings—the worries and cares, the false hope of riches (Mark 4:19), our pride in ourselves, and the things our eyes desire and our hearts long for (1 John 2:15–17)—in our purchase of the one treasure worth more than all else.

Where are we placing our resources—both tangible and intangible? Have we yet committed all to the kingdom and heaven or are we still feverishly collecting trinkets and baubles?

"Now for this very reason also, applying all diligence, in your
faith supply moral excellence, and in your moral excellence,
knowledge, and in your knowledge, self-control, and in your
self-control, perseverance, and in your perseverance, godliness,
and in your godliness, brotherly kindness, and in your brotherly
kindness, love. For if these qualities are yours and are
increasing, they do not make you useless nor unproductive
in the true knowledge of our Lord Jesus Christ."
—2 Peter 1:5–8

Peter tells us to do these things after saying that God's "divine power has granted to us everything pertaining to life and godliness" (2 Peter 1:3).

On the one hand, if God's given us everything we need, we have no excuses. On the other, if this has been granted already, why must we do anything at all?

For the same reason a child who has access to a fabulous education must study diligently if they want to move forward.

The education is available, but if they don't apply themselves, it will be meaningless in their lives.

Once we've confessed, repented, and believed in Christ, all we need for life and godliness is available.

Now it's time to study and apply it with diligence "in faith." Outside of Christ's redemption, applying all these things will mean nothing; we won't have the Holy Spirit to live them out.

But if, through Christ, we're increasing in these qualities, we will not be "useless and unproductive in the kingdom of God."

So if we're feeling useless and unproductive, perhaps we can look at this list to discern where we lack application and diligence in these characteristics.

We want to hear the Lord's "well done" when we come before him, so let's commit ourselves, in faith, to diligence in all these things.

> "But if any of you lacks wisdom, let him ask of God,
> who gives to all generously and without reproach,
> and it will be given to him. But he must ask in faith
> without any doubting, for the one who doubts is like
> the surf of the sea, driven and tossed by the wind."
> —James 1:5–6

As Christians, we have access to the One who knows everything about everything from the beginning of time to the end. Why do we doubt and worry? God encourages us to ask for his guidance and wisdom and doesn't look down on us for not knowing already. We can ask him anything "without reproach."

The rest of this verse normally puts us in fear that we will not receive the wisdom because we have feelings of doubt.

But feelings of doubt are not the same as actions of doubt. We cannot help our feelings. In Mark 9, Jesus said the boy could be healed if the man believed, and the man replied, "I believe, help my unbelief!" Jesus did not scold him, and the boy was healed. The man was not punished for acting in faith where his feelings had trouble following.

We may feel tossed about internally, but as long as our external actions are still moving resolutely in faith, we are not "tossed by the wind."

So don't be afraid to ask the Lord for wisdom, and when you have doubts, simply continue walking in faith while praying, "I believe; help my unbelief."

Our Lord is not stingy with his wisdom and gives it in great measure to all who seek.

"From the end of the earth I call to you when my heart is
faint; lead me to the rock that is higher than I."
—Psalm 61:2

No matter where we are, how far we feel from the Lord, or how large
our trouble, when our hearts are faint, the answer is to call on and rest
in him, the only firm foundation.

No rock or foundation we could find for ourselves will carry us
above our trouble. We cannot understand the reasons for our trials nor
how to make it through them on our own strength.

But when we call on the Lord, though we be as far from him as we
can go, he will lead us to the rock that is higher than we are—higher
than our thoughts and higher than our troubles to the place where
there is no hint of shifting sand, only the firm foundation that will keep
us from being washed away with the wind and storms we endure.

At the end of the earth, it may seem he is not there or, perhaps,
even if we know he is there, that he is not paying attention. We may
ask, "Teacher, do you not care that we are perishing?" like the disciples
did in Mark 4:38. He may seem to be asleep while we are fainting in
fear. But he's sleeping because he knows the end; there is no danger.

The storm is still there, but in his presence, we will rise above it. He
will calm it when it's time, and in the meantime, we don't have to fear,
because he is the high rock, and he is always with us.

"Now we who are strong ought to bear the weaknesses of those without strength, and not just please ourselves."
—Romans 15:1

Where are we strong, and how have we used that strength?

Some who think themselves strong use their outward righteousness as a reason to look down on others who are weak; they're modern-day Pharisees.

We only need to look at how Jesus used his strength to see this is not the proper usage. Our strength is not for disdain, arrogance, selfishness, or forced subjugation, but for compassion, service, and sacrifice.

Do we use our strength to pursue our own desires, or do we use it to encourage and edify those around us?

Where our strengths are used to control, belittle, or please our flesh, they have become our downfalls. We have let strength lead us into pride.

Where our strengths are used to instruct, love, encourage, and serve, they're being used in accordance with God's plan. They have led us into Christlike humility. Any strength we have is not something we're simply to rest and take comfort in; it's to be used in service for others.

Bearing the weaknesses of others will often look like showing patience where none is deserved.

As we have patience with a toddler's first steps, giving reassurance, support, example, and instruction, we come alongside the weaker believer. We teach them truth. We encourage them in righteousness. We help them stand back up and try again when they fall.

Our strength is for pulling others up, not pushing them down.

"Be hospitable to one another without complaint."
—1 Peter 4:9

If you've ever been a guest somewhere the hosts were complaining or grumbling about all the work they had to do or griping about the number of guests, or even to a restaurant where you could hear the servers complaining about their jobs, you know it doesn't feel very hospitable.

Hebrews 13:17 says, "That they may do this with joy, not groaning; for this would be unhelpful for you." This is speaking of leaders shepherding their churches, but it's interesting that it addresses the same thing—if a service is done with groaning and complaint, it loses its benefit.

We can do the right things, but if we're doing them with a complaining heart, we're really not doing anyone any favors. It's like serving fruit that looks good on the outside but is rotten in the middle. And rotten fruit won't nourish anyone no matter how good it looks.

This is another reminder that heart-change—not just outward action—is what God is after. He doesn't want us only doing the right things; he wants us doing the right things with the right attitude.

He doesn't just want us to not murder; he wants us to not be angry (Matthew 5:21–26). He doesn't just want us to not commit adultery; he wants us to not be lustful (Matthew 5:27–30). He doesn't just want us to serve others; he wants us to serve others without complaining about it.

It's easy to feel that as long as we're doing the right things, we're good. This is just another reminder that God desires not only our right actions, but "truth in the innermost being" (Psalm 51:6).

> "'Teacher, we want you to do for us whatever we ask of
> you . . . Grant that we may sit, one on your right and one
> on your left, in your glory.' But Jesus said to them,
> 'You do not know what you are asking.'"
> —Mark 10:35–38

These disciples didn't yet understand that in the kingdom of God, the least is the greatest (Luke 9:48), and the greatest is a humble servant (Matthew 23:11–12). They sought glory and honor, not servanthood.

As Jesus went on to explain, "Whoever wants to become prominent among you shall be your servant; and whoever wants to be first among you shall be slave of all. For even the Son of Man did not come to be served, but to serve, and to give his life as a ransom for many" (Mark 10:43–45).

Any glory we have in heaven will not be because we had great power, position, or success in this life. It will be because we made ourselves servants as Christ himself did.

The most jeweled crowns in heaven will likely be worn by people no one ever heard of—the godly janitors, the ordinary women who love every child as their own, and the people who diligently and thanklessly provided for their families in unfulfilling jobs.

When we're willing to work for the kingdom of God despite the lack of notoriety or praise, we're serving like Christ. When we humbly set aside our own desires, comfort, and lives for the good of others, we're serving like Christ. When we live only for the hope of hearing the words, "well done," from our heavenly Father instead of any man's approval or earthly rewards, we're serving like Christ.

Let us seek to be servants, not masters.

"Therefore, everyone who hears these words of mine, and
acts on them, will be like a wise man who built his house
on the rock. And the rain fell and the floods came, and
the winds blew and slammed against that house; and yet it
did not fall, for it had been founded on the rock."
—Matthew 7:24–25

When the rain, floods, and wind come in our lives, what tumbles?

If Christ is our rock, then even when difficult circumstances arise,
though we might be shaken and unnerved, we won't be destroyed nor
our faith and hope unseated.

But we don't always recognize we've built on shaky ground until
things start to shift, so how do we prepare?

We can use the small winds of life as indicators—the rudeness of
the cashier, the driver who cuts us off, the wrong order at a restaurant,
or someone telling us no.

Our reactions to these things reveal if we have hidden beliefs built
on the unstable foundations of ease, convenience, pleasure, pride, ability, or what we feel we deserve. They can warn us that we won't
weather the real storms when they come.

We may also discover we have Christ firmly fixed as our foundation
in one area but not another; perhaps bumps in our career don't
threaten our faith, but difficulties in our relationships do.

We must continually take stock of our spiritual lives and make Jesus
alone our foundation in all areas. This is as simple as turning away from
sin (simple, but not easy) and as complex as digging into our own roots
of wrong belief to remove them.

Where we find unsteady foundations, we confess our lack of faith,
preach biblical truth to ourselves, and pray for the Lord's help in trusting him.

"He said, 'Naked I came from my mother's womb, and
naked I shall return there. The Lord gave and the Lord
has taken away. Blessed be the name of the Lord.'"
—Job 1:21

In the middle of his tragedy, Job was blessing, praising, and trusting the Lord.

He did not blame or rail against the Lord. He grieved, but within that grief, he still held on to his confidence in the goodness of God. He asked why, but he did not curse God, though his wife told him he should. He wished to die, yet he did not renounce his faith.

He kept his eternal mindset, recognizing that nothing he had in this world would be taken with him into eternity, and if God saw fit to take it before his death, in the end, there was no difference.

There will be times in our lives when we don't understand what God is doing and we feel abandoned by him. We may even—like Job—sometimes we wish we'd never been born (Job 3:1–16). It's okay to vocalize that and take it to the Lord in prayer and lamentation. It's okay to cry out in anguish.

Ultimately, what carries us through is knowing the end—that all we can see is passing away and our earthly sorrows will all be forgotten.

The things that will be carried into eternity cannot be taken away, and Job knew that.

May we all hold our lives on this earth so loosely that even when everything we have and everyone we love is gone, we can still bless the name of the Lord.

"Precious in the sight of the Lord
is the death of his godly ones."
—Psalm 116:15

Death is part of our broken world. We mourn, and that is right.

But for believers, death is also precious, because those who have died in Christ are now forever with God and free from the toil, turmoil, and suffering of this life. "He will wipe away every tear from their eyes; and there will no longer be any death; there will no longer be any mourning, or crying, or pain" (Revelation 21:4).

No more mourning, crying, or pain. No more struggles against this flesh. Perfect fellowship with Christ.

For a Christian, death is only sad from this side. The other side is glorious—the beautiful, complete fulfillment of God's promise, our inheritance.

Missionary Lilias Trotter said of the people who were martyred where she served, "One draws a breath of relief when they get safe home [to heaven]."

We can rejoice that our loved ones no longer endure the struggle brought about by living as strangers in a strange land.

Even without severe suffering or persecution, life, at its best, is still a fight that death releases us from—the fight to stay faithful to the Lord, to persevere until the end, to remain hopeful despite all the darkness, to be diligent to complete the good works God calls us to, and to resist the temptations of this world and our flesh.

We mourn our loss here when a believer passes on, but they have merely moved to that better country (Hebrews 11:16)—the one we all long for in our deepest depths.

The Lord welcomes his faithful servants home with rejoicing.

SEPTEMBER 14

"My flesh and my heart may fail, but God is
the strength of my heart and my portion forever."
—Psalm 73:26

It's not a surprise that, in this life, we will have times of weariness, struggle, pain, or illness. We are told it will happen (1 Peter 4:12).

Our bodies get tired and fail. Our hearts will grow heavy, seeing and enduring all the difficult things in this world. Our emotions will rise and fall like the tide.

But even in the middle of all that, God is our strength. Where we fail, he will not. Where we grow weary, he will not. Even if there are times we can see only sorrow in this world, we can hope in the next one, because he is our portion forever.

He is our strength in weakness, and when we bring that weakness to him and hand it over, we can trust that he will make something beautiful out of it.

And when this flesh fails completely, it's not the end for those who are in the Lord, but the beginning of our eternal inheritance. We will join him in perfect rest and joy.

There is no loss on this earth that will have the power to tarnish that joy in the slightest once we reach heaven (2 Corinthians 4:17).

Let's hold fast to the Lord's strength in the moments our own strength fails and continue to hope in that eternal portion he has ensured for those who trust in him.

"So that my imprisonment in the cause of Christ has
become well known throughout the praetorian guard and
to everyone else, and that most of the brothers and sisters,
trusting in the Lord because of my imprisonment, have far
more courage to speak the word of God without fear."
—Philippians 1:13–14

What does it look like to others when we suffer? Does it look like we've bound ourselves to Christ and believe that the suffering in our path will be used for his glory? Or does it look exactly like the world deals with suffering—in hopelessness, anger, confusion, overwhelm, and bitterness?

Would our attitude in imprisonment bring others to trust God or push them away from faith?

As Christians, our suffering should look different than the world's. We don't have to pretend we're enjoying it, but where others can see our strength and hope in the midst of difficulty, it will encourage and inspire them to overcome as well. It will show that our hope truly is in the Lord and not in what this world has to offer.

Paul's suffering didn't look hopeless nor inspire fear. Instead, it showed the power and truth of the Gospel he suffered for, and those around him were encouraged to greater trust in the Lord and more boldness to speak the Word—the very things which caused Paul's suffering in the first place.

Our confidence in the Lord even in our suffering will shine as a beacon of relentless hope to others, and our example will press them to a deeper trust in God that strengthens them and leads them to a heroic pursuit of his will even in their own sufferings.

> "For in hope we have been saved, but hope that is
> seen is not hope; for who hopes for what he already
> sees? But if we hope for what we do not see, through
> perseverance we wait eagerly for it."
> —Romans 8:24–25

———————◆———————

We tend to think of waiting as bad but hope as good. The truth is, we can't have one without the other. In fact, the words "hope" and "wait" are often translated interchangeably in the Bible.

If we are hoping, we are waiting, because we do not hope for what we already have.

Here's the difference: waiting can be done with a bad attitude and might lead to discontentment, anger, bitterness, or harmful behavior; hoping requires peace, trust, and confidence. In order to wait well, we must have hope. And hope requires trust and confidence.

If our hope is truly already placed where the Lord tells us it should be—in the lasting, eternal things of his Word, his promises, and our infinite inheritance with him—then we will endure and persevere even in our waiting. We will only become angry, in a hurry, and discontent where our trust and confidence in the Lord falters.

So when we're frustrated by a season of waiting, we can reflect on who God is—unchangeable, sovereign, true—and change the word "wait" to "hope" in our minds. "We're hoping, persevering, eagerly waiting, and trusting the Lord for what he has promised he will accomplish in his Word."

Some of what we wait and hope for will not be realized in this life (Hebrews 11:13), but we can still live with undying hope.

Our Lord has promised that the best is always yet to come.

> "My little children, I am writing these things to you so that you may not sin. And if anyone sins, we have an advocate with the Father, Jesus Christ the righteous."
>
> —1 John 2:1

When believers sin, Jesus stands at our defense. God is faithful and just to forgive us when we confess and repent (1 John 1:9). None of us are perfect for, "If we say that we have not sinned, we make Him a liar and His word is not in us" (1 John 1:10).

But there is also much expected of us as believers. Further down, 1 John 2:4 says, "The one who says, 'I have come to know him,' and does not keep his commandments, is a liar," and 1 John 2:9 says, "The one who says that he is in the light and yet hates his brother or sister is in the darkness until now."

Many who say they know God live in hatred of those around them, or they live without taking the Lord's commandments into consideration at all.

Though every believer will stumble, if we allow hatred to reign in our lives or make no effort to walk as Jesus walked, we are not in the light. The truth is revealed in our lives.

These passages are both a comfort and a warning—when we sin, we go straight to Jesus and repent. We aren't condemned because he paid our debt. At the same time, some who say and believe they're in the light are not.

This isn't contradictory; it's about lordship. Do we strive to follow God's commands and to love our fellow man? Do we live like God is our master, though we sometimes fail, or do we say God is our master without attempting to make him so?

> "If, however, you are fulfilling the royal law
> according to the Scripture, 'You shall love your
> neighbor as yourself,' you are doing well."
> —James 2:8

❖

When we think of loving our neighbors, we often think of the story of the Good Samaritan—helping those "neighbors" who need help even when they might not be in the category of people we consider desirable, even when it's inconvenient, and even when it costs us personally.

But we also need to think about what it means to love them "as we love ourselves."

This requires forgiving others the same way we want to be forgiven, without holding grudges or continually bringing up past failures. We don't punish them with our ongoing displeasure and irritation (1 Corinthians 13).

It requires considering how we hope others will treat us when we're having a bad day and aren't at our best. It's treating them with grace and gentleness.

We also love ourselves by taking care of our needs. To love others this way, we must pay attention to them. Our neighbors may not always tell us about their needs, but if we're attentive, we'll be able to see if they need our time, financial help, friendship, listening ear, or something else that is within our power to give.

Loving our neighbors as ourselves requires sacrifice.

This is the kind of grace-filled love we would do well to show others—the kind that says, "I'm willing to go out of my way to help you in your trouble." "I see your weakness and your failure, and I love you anyway." "You're not alone; I'm here to help."

It's the kind of love that Christ extends to us all the time.

> "Slaves, be obedient to those who are your masters according to the flesh, with fear and trembling, in the sincerity of your heart, as to Christ; not by way of eye-service, as people-pleasers, but as slaves of Christ, doing the will of God from the heart. With goodwill render service, as to the Lord, and not to people, knowing that whatever good thing each one does, he will receive this back from the Lord, whether slave or free."
> —Ephesians 6:5–8

We may not be slaves of earthly masters, but we can think of this as the responsibilities we have in our lives, whether to our employers, friends, or families. How do we serve the people in our lives?

If we're doing it begrudgingly or so that others will think well of us, we're missing the point.

Our duties toward others should be performed as if that person were Christ himself.

The Bible makes it clear here and in Matthew 25:31–46 that whatever service we do for others is done as to the Lord.

It also makes it clear that our reward will come from the Lord, not the people we're serving. Those people are fallen, and we may never get the desired response of gratitude or the same amount of effort and service in return. They may even fall into the category of "evil masters," as spoken of in 1 Peter 2:18.

The Bible doesn't change its requirements even for those evil masters. We must serve them with diligence and integrity, taking Daniel, Esther, and Joseph as our examples.

If we perform our service and work "as to the Lord," the reward from him will be greater than any we would've received from that earthly master.

"And do not be afraid of those who kill the body but are unable to kill the soul; but rather fear him who is able to destroy both soul and body in hell. Are two sparrows not sold for an assarion? And yet not one of them will fall to the ground apart from your Father. But even the hairs of your head are all counted. So do not fear; you are more valuable than a great number of sparrows."
—Matthew 10:28–31

It seems odd to our human minds that this says not to fear right before we're told that we may indeed be killed. It's hard to see how being murdered isn't something we should worry about, but God is telling us that being killed is not the worst thing that could happen.

We may face terrible things here—even to the point of being murdered.

But our soul's eternal destiny should be of far more concern to us than any earthly suffering or death. This life is not our highest priority; it will pass away.

But no matter what happens, we can trust that God loves us and he's paying attention. He knows every detail about our lives, down to each time we lose a hair. He even sees when a sparrow dies, and we're worth far more.

He cares when we are harmed even in body, but ultimately, the desire of his great love is to bring all of us to be with him in eternity.

Our earthly trials and sufferings do not mean he has abandoned us, even if we're being killed, because death is not the end.

"Jesus said to him, 'I am the way, and the truth, and the
life; no one comes to the Father except through me.'"
—John 14:6

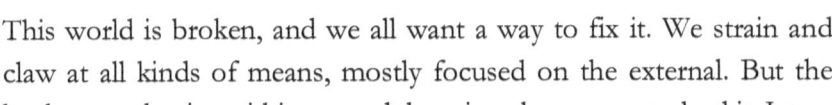

This world is broken, and we all want a way to fix it. We strain and claw at all kinds of means, mostly focused on the external. But the brokenness begins within us, and there is only one way to heal it: Jesus.

Without him, we try to concoct our own versions of becoming good enough for salvation. This will always be an impossibility . . . like a three-year-old trying to bake a cake. They might know a few of the ingredients, but they can't read the directions or operate the oven. They aren't capable, so the cake isn't going to be edible, and in the attempt, they'll probably get burned.

We will never find our own way to God. The recipe we end up with will not be "good," and in the process of trying to do it without him, we're probably going to injure ourselves and others.

History is full of people defining their own rules for getting to God. Even those who call themselves Christians have been establishing codes of morality that only serve to make those successful at it prideful and those who fail miserable.

But Jesus paid the ransom for us not being good enough, so we can stop trying to blaze a new trail to goodness. There is only one way, and it has been made ready for us. Following Jesus is the only thing that clears the path to our perfect King.

"All of you, clothe yourselves with humility toward
one another, because God is opposed to the proud,
but he gives grace to the humble."
—1 Peter 5:5

What does "humility toward one another" look like?

I think it looks like listening even when we disagree, living out kindness, gentleness, compassion, truth, and love.

The humble are teachable; they listen to the Lord's correction and direction. They do not choose their own way but allow themselves to be led by the Word of the Lord and the Holy Spirit.

What does "humility toward one another" not look like?

Gloating, selfishness, ignoring the wisdom of others, belittling, insulting, or controlling.

Philippians 2:3 tells us that humility looks like considering others more important than ourselves.

When we look objectively and honestly at our attitudes and the words we choose in our interactions with others, it's easy to see who we're considering more important.

And this verse tells us that God is not only displeased with the prideful; he actively opposes them.

When we walk in pride, we're making ourselves an enemy to our perfectly loving, wholly good, almighty God. Outside of his grace is a terrible place to be.

Our humility is based on the fact that we know we are nothing in and of ourselves. All that we are and all that we have is a gift from our God. There is nothing in ourselves worth being prideful over; we boast only in the Lord (Psalm 34:2; 1 Corinthians 1:31).

Let's be careful to approach God and others with the humility Christ himself showed to those around him.

"Were you called as a slave? Do not let it
concern you. But if you are also able to
become free, take advantage of that."
—1 Corinthians 7:21

Imagine this advice today with society's focus on success, prestige, and accomplishment.

- Are you a slave? Don't worry about it.
- Are you in a bad job? Don't worry about it.
- Are you held back by your finances, your health, your family? Don't worry about it.

It's not that God wants us to be in slavery or to be held back ("if you are able to become free, take advantage of that"). What he's telling us here is that our circumstances don't define the value of our lives.

We tend to focus on all the reasons we think we can't serve him well or do anything meaningful for the kingdom. God's making sure we know those reasons don't matter. In fact, the Bible essentially says, "Are you a slave? Be a really good slave, as if God himself were your master" (Ephesians 6:5; 1 Peter 2:18; Colossians 3:22).

The servant can be great in the kingdom of God. Those in poverty and those with terrible jobs, bad bosses, and difficult families can all be great in the kingdom of God. Our position, status, and power in this world are not factors in how well we can live for Christ.

Our circumstances might be less than ideal. He can use us anyway. He knows where we are. He hasn't abandoned us.

Don't focus on your circumstances. Focus on who you are in Christ. Focus on becoming who the Lord made you to be right where you are.

"Confess your sins to one another, and pray for one another."
—James 5:16

Many of us find ourselves increasingly isolated. Even if we're not alone in the physical sense, we're often alone in all the ways that matter.

Our world has glorified independence and shunned vulnerability, and social media has created an excess of artificial relationships based almost solely upon what can be seen from the outside.

For this to change, individuals—you and me—must step outside our comfort zones and start confessing our own sins. We must admit not only our need for help and support, but the responsibility we have toward each other. It will mean asking and being asked hard questions and giving and receiving tough answers.

This will often mean reaching out in uncomfortable ways. Not everyone will welcome it. Many church-goers prefer the superficial status quo. They don't want to need or be needed, and they don't want to be accountable to or for others.

But many are starving for connection.

Most of us have invisible burdens, invisible wounds, and invisible sins. We're lonely, isolated in our struggles, and don't feel like it's safe to be honest with anyone.

We can't love one another fervently (1 Peter 1:22), encourage one another toward love and good deeds (Hebrews 10:24), turn each other back to the truth if we stray (James 5:19–20), nor bear those invisible burdens (Galatians 6:1–2) if we won't open up about our sins and struggles.

Living in confession would prevent many secret temptations from growing into full-blown sin (James 1:14–15).

We must each humble ourselves in vulnerable confession and be willing to support and pray for others seeking to grow in grace and the knowledge of Jesus Christ (2 Peter 3:18).

"Do not be anxious about anything, but in everything
by prayer and pleading with thanksgiving let your
requests be made known to God. And the peace of
God, which surpasses all comprehension, will guard
your hearts and minds in Christ Jesus."
—Philippians 4:6–7

This verse is a recipe for going from anxiety to peace. God knows our worry is pointless. It does not change the circumstance nor help us cope with it.

But prayer changes things (James 5:16–18) and thanksgiving brings us hope in the midst of the trouble.

Why thanksgiving? In Scripture, talk of thanksgiving is often coupled with the phrase "to remember his steadfast love." Its purpose is to remind us of all the times God has shown his love in the past; this fuels the faith that he will continue to show that love both now and in the future.

Thanksgiving is not a vague action, but an intentional recalling of specific acts of God's faithfulness so that our trust is renewed. It's why the Lord had the Israelites build monuments; they served as a visual reminder to them and future generations of his rescue and help (Joshua 4).

Prayer and thanksgiving guard our hearts and minds in Jesus, preventing the darts of doubt and fear from destroying our confidence in God.

When anxiety rears its ugly head—which is sometimes many times each day—remember this formula. Take it to the Lord over and over. Recall his past protection and provision as well as the ultimate salvation he guarantees in Jesus through the Holy Spirit.

We can be at peace not because all is calm, but because we know the God who calms the storm.

"Therefore, since we also have such a great
cloud of witnesses surrounding us, let's rid
ourselves of every obstacle and the sin which
so easily entangles us, and let's run with
endurance the race that is set before us."
—Hebrews 12:1

Ridding ourselves of obstacles and sin is necessary; it's not given as an optional part of following Christ. If we're still choosing the world, its comforts, and our sins, we won't be able to run with endurance. A dedicated athlete does not eat doughnuts and pizza every meal, then expect to win the race; he must lay those things aside, just as we must lay sin aside (1 Corinthians 9:25).

It's not that we must be perfect. The Bible makes it clear that's impossible in this earthly body, but we must be constantly laying aside the weights and sins that keep us from being all-in with Christ. We cannot have two masters, and if we try, we will become entangled. Every choice to hold onto sin leads us further away from our heavenly Father.

As believers, our question will not be "How much sin is God okay with me keeping?" but rather, "How can I rid myself of this sin since it's an obstacle between me and my loving Father?"

If Christ is our true master, our aim will always be obedience because we trust God's Word.

The more we rid ourselves of obstacles, the more fully we will experience who Christ is (John 14:21) and the easier it will be to run that race as our endurance builds from training and practice.

> "Speak, for your servant is listening."
> —1 Samuel 3:10

Have you ever tried to listen to two conversations at the same time?

Once, my niece was talking directly to me while the other adults had a different conversation going.

Part of me wanted to be in both conversations, and eventually this ended in frustration from my niece. "No one is listening to me!" she said.

My first thought was, "I'm listening!" Then I realized that wasn't true—not really.

I was half-listening, and she could tell.

I wonder how often we do that to God. We're sort of listening to him, but we also have half an ear on the world's chatter to make sure we don't miss anything.

Maybe we really love God and want to hear from him in the same way I truly love my niece and wanted to know what she had to say, but to really hear him, we must shut out the voices of the world. We must focus on his voice to the exclusion of all others.

It's not easy. The voices of the world are loud. They make us fearful and self-conscious. We're afraid we'll miss something vital and get left behind. But the world's words are never worth missing something the Lord says to us.

And he often speaks in that still, small voice he used with Elijah in 1 Kings 19. He is speaking, but if we only listen to the loudest voice, we'll often miss what he has to say.

In John 10:27, Jesus says, "My sheep listen to my voice, and I know them, and they follow me."

Let's stop half-listening and turn both our ears to hear our good Shepherd as he guides and directs us each day.

"So then neither the one who plants nor the one who
waters is anything, but God who causes the growth."
—1 Corinthians 3:7

We like to live in the harvest, where the fruit of our labors is always visible. I'm so glad God gave us this illustration because watching any farmer will show us that's not how it works.

The fruit will come in its time, but it may look like nothing at all is growing for quite a while.

We plant; we water; we wait. We water some more and wait some more.

If the farmer didn't have the evidence of harvests witnessed year after year, putting all that seed in the ground would seem like a ridiculous waste of time. It would just look like digging a hole and burying a dead thing.

Many times, God asks us to plant. Maybe the "seed" looks completely dead to us, and we can't imagine how it could ever possibly grow. If we've never watched him work before, planting will likely feel like a waste of time. Yet before we even begin to see results, God asks us to spend more time and energy to water. It feels pointless and risky.

But if he asks us to plant and water, the rest is up to him. We may never even see the harvest. John 4:37 says, "One sows, and another reaps."

The planting and watering are never futile when we're doing them at God's direction. We can trust that he will bring the growth in his way and in his time, whether we are there to see it or not.

"Love is patient, love is kind, it is not jealous; love does
not brag, it is not arrogant. It does not act disgracefully,
it does not seek its own benefit; it is not provoked,
does not keep an account of a wrong suffered."
—1 Corinthians 13:4–5

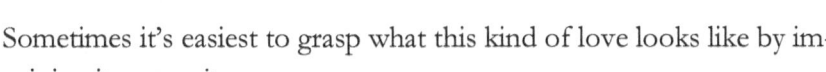

Sometimes it's easiest to grasp what this kind of love looks like by imagining its opposite.

So let's ask ourselves a few questions:

- Are we discontented and irritated when our expectations aren't met?
- Do we avoid helping others if we can?
- Are we frustrated because we envy someone else's life or progress?
- Are we excited about something in our lives because it makes us feel like we're better than other people?
- Does it make us happy when we've surpassed others in some area?
- Are we seeking our own desires at others' expense?
- Are we allowing ourselves to be easily offended and provoked into arguments or defensiveness?
- Are we holding grudges and allowing bitterness and unforgiveness to fester in our hearts?

If we fail these questions, it's often because we've stopped looking outward at how we can love others and gone back to looking inward. Our actions may be rooted in insecurity, fear, or selfishness; we worry that we won't get what we need or want if we don't exert control.

To discover how we can change, it may do more good to ask what it would look like to be on the receiving end of a 1 Corinthians 13 kind of love. We would know that person truly wants our good and cares for us. It would remove fear and comparison from the relationship, allowing us to live in honesty, confidence, and peace with that person.

Let's work on creating that for the people around us.

"Therefore, brothers and sisters, since we have confidence
to enter the holy place by the blood of Jesus."
—Hebrews 10:19

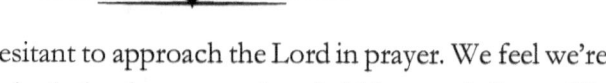

Sometimes we're hesitant to approach the Lord in prayer. We feel we're unworthy to enter the holy place, so we're afraid he won't listen. We worry that maybe there's no point.

But as Jesus died, the veil separating the holy place from the worshippers was torn in two from top to bottom (Mark 15:38). Prior to this, only the High Priest could enter the inner sanctuary of the temple. Jesus's sacrifice tore that barrier down.

He is now our High Priest (Hebrews 7:25–28), and as believers, we are one with him (John 17:23), so through his sacrifice, we can always approach the throne.

Hebrews 4:16 tells us to approach the throne with confidence "so that we may receive mercy and find grace to help us in our time of need."

"So that . . .." This is one of the reasons we go to him. By not doing so, we deny ourselves the help he wants to provide through the grace and mercy we receive in his presence.

If the leader of a nation gave us written permission to appear before him and make petitions as often as we needed, we would know what an honor that leader was granting. Yet we have a greater access to the King of Kings. Let's take him at his Word and not ignore this great gift.

We approach the throne in humility, knowing that in and of ourselves, we're not worthy, but we can still do so boldly because we have full access through Jesus Christ.

Our Lord wants to give us mercy and grace to help in our time of need.

"Or do you not know that your body is a temple of the
Holy Spirit within you, whom you have from God, and
that you are not your own? For you have been bought
for a price: therefore glorify God in your body."
—1 Corinthians 6:19–20

Do we still consider our lives and bodies our own? Do we think we should be able to do with them what we please rather than obeying the Word, conferring with the Holy Spirit, and allowing the Lord free reign in our actions? Or do we follow him even when it goes against our own desires, thoughts, hopes, dreams?

If we still consider our lives our own, we haven't yet fully surrendered.

Once we have, there may still be moments where our flesh tries to turn the other way, but the Spirit will check us faster and in more subtle ways on things that a year or two ago, we never would have recognized as rebellion.

There are times when the idea that this life is not my own rankles. I respond with resistance.

There is always the possibility of willful disobedience while we're in these bodies, but if we're maturing in our spiritual walk, that rebellion will lessen in frequency and intensity.

Our lives are not our own. They belong to the One who bought us with a price greater than we can ever comprehend. He ransomed us out of slavery and into freedom—a freedom in which we have given ourselves to him gladly to follow the good path he has forged for us. And it's the only path that leads to hope, joy, and eternity. Without him leading, we have no hope of finding the way.

"But the news about him was spreading even farther,
and large crowds were gathering to hear him and to be
healed of their sicknesses. But Jesus himself would
often slip away to the wilderness and pray."
—Luke 5:15–16

Our focus is so often on doing the work and meeting the needs in front of us that we forget to withdraw for prayer, but it's a vital part of our walk with the Lord. If we neglect it, the work and the meeting of others' needs will wither and turn to something more like that noisy gong or clanging cymbal talked about in 1 Corinthians 13.

Our withdrawal for time to pray and meditate on the Word is what keeps us abiding in the vine, overflowing with God's rivers of living water, and pouring out his love. When we don't abide in him and operate through the prompting of the Holy Spirit, we often end up doing works that sound good but that God never prompted.

Spending time in the Word and praying are essential building blocks of a thriving Christian walk with the Lord that will fuel love and help us impact the world for his kingdom.

Our spirits need this nourishment just as our bodies need food. We will not be healthy or functioning properly in the body of Christ without it.

Whether it's kids, jobs, or crowds clamoring for our attention, doing this might look, to them, like we're selfishly withdrawing from their needs and our duties, but Jesus's life shows that incorporating this into our lives is the only way to serve them well. Through following his example, we will also become an example to them, demonstrating our belief that time with our Lord is the most important thing in life.

OCTOBER 3

"I have heard of you by the hearing of the ear;
but now my eye sees you; therefore I retract,
and I repent, sitting on dust and ashes."
—Job 42:5–6

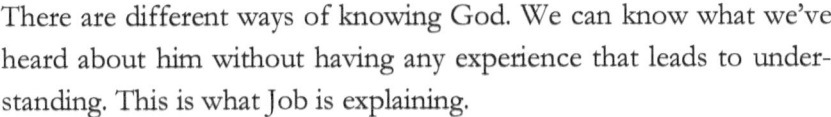

There are different ways of knowing God. We can know what we've heard about him without having any experience that leads to understanding. This is what Job is explaining.

When he finally did see God, he realized that trying to understand the Lord with his own human limitations had been nothing but foolishness. He retracts his former opinions and recognizes the limitations of his human insight. Now he's ready to trust God even when he doesn't have answers.

When we come to see the Lord as he truly is, our response is utter humility—the recognition of our own smallness before him, our complete dependence upon him, and the total submission we rightly owe him as the God who knows all from the beginning to the end of time.

The more we see of him, the more of ourselves—our pride, self-sufficiency, abilities, and understanding—we will turn away from in order to trust the only true power and wisdom of God himself.

And this utter humility will lead to us trusting him without question, to confidence in his guidance even when it doesn't make sense to our human sensibilities, and to following him with thanksgiving and praise even when we can't see the ultimate plan.

The world is broken because of our sin, but in his sovereign grace, he can and will use even the brokenness to bring about good as we follow and obey.

"Your kingdom come. Your will be done."
—Matthew 6:10

We've heard the Lord's prayer time after time, but it's easy to gloss over this phrase.

If I stop and ponder whether I really mean it when I say, "Your will be done," I'm forced to face the fact that there are times or areas of my life in which I don't—places where I'm not dying to my flesh.

There are some things I have walled off and held back from God. "No, this is mine, God. I don't want you to take it from me, ruin it for me."

But in this, we are like greedy little dragons, hoarding a treasure that does us no good in the dark recesses of our minds.

When we let God into them, he sweeps the dusty, grimy corners clean, opens the curtains, and lets the light shine in. He rearranges the furniture, lets in the fresh air, and sits there with us, redeeming the dark.

Often, if we examine our hearts, we will find that the thing we're afraid God will take from us is not actually bringing us the joy and peace we claim it is. Rather, it's enslaving us and making us anxious; it has a grip on our hearts that produces fear, insecurity, overwhelm, or sadness.

When we give God something we've been clutching tightly, there is a sense of relaxation in our souls. It brings rest and peace. We die a little more to self, sin, and the flesh. It eases the wantings that give us so much angst and sorrow (James 4:1-2).

It is always freeing to let the wantings go and let God in.

"Jesus wept."
—John 11:35

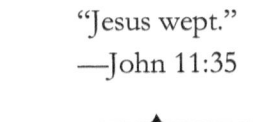

It's significant that Jesus—who is God in the flesh and who knew he was about to raise Lazarus from the dead—wept in this moment.

He had just seen Mary and others crying and mourning over Lazarus's death, and he was "deeply moved in spirit and troubled" (John 11:33). We often think of Jesus as being immune to or above our earthly emotions—perhaps even stoic and cold—but he wept for their pain and grieved for their grief.

He has compassion and empathy for our earthly troubles and needs (Matthew 9:35–36; Matthew 14:14–20; Mark 6:34) even though he knows they are not permanent and that we will be healed—sometimes in this life, sometimes not until eternity.

When we're living in pain and grief, we don't have to doubt whether our Lord sees us or cares about our sorrows and heartaches.

He sees us weeping and, even now, it moves and troubles him.

We don't always feel like that's true, just as they didn't. "If you had been here, my brother would not have died," Martha said (John 11:21).

Our normal human reaction is to think, "If you had been with us, Lord, this wouldn't have happened. We wouldn't be suffering right now. We prayed, but you're too late."

We have this story to remind us that God doesn't abandon us in those troubled times. He knows and sees, and he is always there with his presence and comfort. Complete healing and restoration is always the plan for those he loves and who love him, but he does not ignore our pain in the meantime; he sees it all and mourns with us in our mourning.

"I wrote to you in my letter not to associate with sexually immoral people; I did not at all mean with the sexually immoral people of this world, or with the greedy and swindlers, or with idolaters, for then you would have to leave the world. But actually, I wrote to you not to associate with any so-called brother if he is a sexually immoral person, or a greedy person, or an idolater, or is verbally abusive, or habitually drunk, or a swindler—not even to eat with such a person. For what business of mine is it to judge outsiders? Do you not judge those who are within the church? But those who are outside, God judges. Remove the evil person from among yourselves."
—1 Corinthians 5:9–13

These verses seem shocking. We normally see the opposite in our church culture—judgment for unbelievers and license to sin amongst believers.

Thankfully, there is grace and forgiveness for all who repent, but there is little attention given to the issue of those who say they've repented yet continue living in willful, repeated sin.

This has resulted in a church that looks almost no different than the world.

It's our job to speak truth to those who have strayed and potentially "save a soul from death and cover a multitude of sins" (James 5:19–20). We're not to consider them enemies, but to admonish them because we love them (2 Thessalonians 3:14–15), to restore them in gentleness (Galatians 6:1), and to address faults in a loving, orderly way so they have the chance to repent (Matthew 18:15–17).

Let's follow Christ's example of giving a gentle invitation to unbelievers while ensuring that our churches are free of those who only hear, but will not live, the faith.

"Jesus said to him, 'Because you have seen me,
have you now believed? Blessed are they who
did not see, and yet believed.'"
—John 20:29

We're all familiar with the phrase, "seeing is believing," but that phrase actually contradicts itself. If we see something, there's no need to believe it. No faith is required at all.

Even the people who love saying it don't believe it. We live by radio waves, wireless internet, and all sorts of other things we don't see.

And the most important things—love, joy, peace, hope, and so forth—aren't seen at all.

We don't see Christ in front of us the way they did when he was on earth, but those of us who walk with him know he's with us by how he guides, nudges, and gives us his strength. We see his presence in the world (Romans 1:20) and in other believers.

And the more closely we follow Christ, the more real his presence becomes . . . "the one who has my commandments and keeps them is the one who loves me; and the one who loves me will be loved by my Father, and I will love him and will reveal myself to him" (John 14:21).

1 Peter 1:8–9 says, "Though you have not seen him, you love him, and though you do not see him now, but believe in him, you greatly rejoice with joy inexpressible and full of glory, obtaining as the outcome of your faith, the salvation of your souls."

Because we believe though we do not see, we are blessed with inexpressible joy and filled with glory, obtaining the greatest gift of all—the eternal salvation of our souls.

"Take care not to practice your righteousness in the
sight of people, to be noticed by them; otherwise you
have no reward with your Father who is in heaven. So
when you give to the poor, do not sound a trumpet
before you, as the hypocrites do in the synagogues and
on the streets, so that they will be praised by people.
Truly I say to you, they have their reward in full."
—Matthew 6:1–2

It's easy to say we aren't doing things so people will see it, but how many times have we done good and taken offense when we didn't receive a "thank you"? Or become discouraged and been tempted to stop serving because no one seemed to notice? Or become angry and complained to others when our efforts weren't rewarded?

Though we genuinely want to do good, we often feel like it's only worth it if we receive some reward from others, and sometimes we don't realize that until we feel the frustration of not getting it.

When resentment arises within us because our good deeds haven't been noticed, let's remember that we shouldn't require worldly validation to continue on God's path, and our need for that recognition will lead us astray. Our motives determine our reward.

Do we want the attention of men? Then that will be our reward. Do we want to do what the Lord has called us to do regardless of whether or not men are impressed? Then our reward comes from him.

As believers, we can be free from the need for other men's approval, validation, or recognition.

Our true, lasting validation comes only from the Lord. Our reward is from him, and it is enough.

> "It is for discipline that you endure; God deals with
> you as with sons; for what son is there whom his
> father does not discipline? But if you are without
> discipline, of which all have become partakers,
> then you are illegitimate children and not sons."
> —Hebrews 12:7–8

The discipline we endure in the Western world rarely comes to the point of shedding blood (Hebrews 12:4), but we still must be trained to resist sin in the deepest part of our hearts. That discipline often comes through the death of some simple desire or expectation in this life. Our reactions when we don't get the things we want often reveal why we need the discipline—there's an idol exposed, or a sin brought to light.

The call of the Christian includes enduring the Lord's discipline—which may seem only like difficulty and pain in the moment—and living through it with our faith unshaken. That doesn't mean we must enjoy it or smile and dance all the way through; it just means that even when it's tough, we trust that God is with us.

We need this discipline just like a child needs the discipline of parents in order to become a responsible adult.

God is training us up, and if there's an area in which we're weak in endurance, patience, love, contentment, or anything else the Lord calls us to, he will work to strengthen it. That normally isn't pleasant (Hebrews 12:11), but it results in the ability to live a righteous life and set our minds on things above.

God is working peace, spiritual maturity, and righteousness through the discipline, and we can trust him even in the midst of it.

> "As for you, you meant evil against me, but God
> meant it for good in order to bring about this
> present result, to keep many people alive."
> —Genesis 50:20

We don't always enjoy the things that happen to us.

Joseph certainly didn't love being sold by his brothers, enslaved, and falsely imprisoned, but he lived there with honor and integrity. He acted in faith, though the sin of man and the nature of this broken world caused his hardship.

Sometimes things in our lives are unfair, objectively terrible, and nothing we would've ever chosen, but being depressed, bitter, unforgiving, or angry about the injustice of the situation won't change things.

We don't always get to pick what happens to us, but we can decide what we do while we're there.

We can grieve and ask God why while yet choosing to commit all our ways to him even in the darkness and uncertainty when we feel like we're in prison and no one is on our side.

Joseph's eventual release came simply because he asked two other prisoners why they looked sad (Genesis 40:7). Even in his suffering, he was still looking for ways to help others.

But he also didn't just settle in and accept that suffering was his inevitable fate. When Joseph interpreted the cupbearer's dream, he asked to be remembered to Pharoah, hoping for his release (Genesis 40:14).

Joseph did the good he could where he had been placed while still working for a godly way out of a terrible situation and hoping for a better future.

The cupbearer forgot Joseph for two years (Genesis 40:23), but God never forgot and worked miracles through his circumstances, using even the evil acts for good, just as he promised (Romans 8:28).

> "Call to me and I will answer you, and I will tell you
> great and mighty things, which you do not know."
> —Jeremiah 33:3

Without God, we must make all our decisions from within the confines of our limited knowledge and understanding. It's often impossible for us to know what the best decision is, but it's not impossible for God.

The key is remembering to call on him for our answers, walk daily with the Holy Spirit, and listen for his still, small voice in the midst of the chaos of the world. There are so many distractions—good and bad—shouting for our attention; we often go through life wringing our hands not only about the "great and mighty" things but also about our everyday concerns.

But if the Lord will tell us about the great and mighty things, he will also walk us through the common everyday ones. If we ask him for wisdom, he will give it (James 1:5).

He will guide us if we're listening to and seeking him—rather than the world—for answers. To do that, we must quiet the shouting voices and pressures of society so we can hear him, and we must know his voice. Jesus said in John 10:27, "My sheep listen to my voice, and I know them, and they follow me."

Quieting the world requires intention—a choice to stop all the bustle and focus on him. And knowing him requires time and dedication to studying the Word and spending time in prayer. None of this will happen accidentally or casually. Very few things of worth do.

Hearing his voice and understanding his Word becomes easier and easier the more closely we walk with him.

> "And while being abusively insulted, he did not insult in
> return; while suffering, he did not threaten, but kept
> entrusting himself to him who judges righteously."
> —1 Peter 2:23

Our flesh wants to defend our rights, to fight back, to take up the sword as Peter did in the Garden of Gethsemane.

But Jesus never got angry over his own rights. He lived the words: "do not be afraid of those who kill the body but are unable to kill the soul" (Matthew 10:28).

Reacting to injustice and suffering with calm peace as Jesus did can only be done by walking in the Spirit, not the flesh. This means we will be far more focused on the eternal than the earthly, even when the earthly circumstances threaten pain and danger.

And Jesus's example shows that he lived much in prayer and communion with the Father, even through the moments of betrayal, agony, torture, separation from God, and death.

How much more should we do the same? Without this deep intimacy with the Lord, we risk a fleshly response to the enemy's attacks.

Even when the world is unfriendly, dangerous, unjust, unfair, and even cruel, we don't have to live in fear, and we don't have to respond in anger. Earthly judges may fail us, but we can entrust our true, eternal selves to the God who judges righteously.

Before we respond with insults and threats or draw our worldly weapons, let's check if we are in the Spirit or the flesh.

> "When I am afraid, I will put my trust in you. In God,
> whose word I praise, in God I have put my trust; I shall
> not be afraid. What can mere mortals do to me?"
> —Psalm 56:3–4

When we are afraid . . . not *if*. Fear will come. So what will we do?

Put our trust in the Lord. Praise his Word.

And then what?

We shall not be afraid.

It sounds a little confusing, as if he's saying, "When I am afraid, I shall not be afraid."

And in a way, he is, because I don't think it means that all concern over the present danger will dissipate. But if, when we begin to be afraid, we take time to insert trust and praise of the Lord into our fear, it changes.

That trust and praise reminds us who's really in control and what really matters. "What can mere mortals do to me?"

We can face the difficult and painful things now even while trusting the Lord in all we do because no mere mortal is in charge of our ultimate fate. Man can harm the body but has no power over our soul (Matthew 10:28).

We've taken our thoughts captive, put our trust in the Lord, and turned our hope to the eternal. Anything man can do to harm is temporary, and in the Lord's strength, we will endure to the end.

Because of this, our actions can radiate trust even in the midst of terrifying situations—we can sing in the prison (Acts 16:25–26), face the giant (1 Samuel 17), and enter the fiery furnace calmly (Daniel 3:17–18)—but only when we react by intentionally injecting our fear with trust and praise of our almighty God.

"For we know that the whole creation groans and
suffers the pains of childbirth together until now. And
not only that, but also we ourselves, having the first
fruits of the Spirit, even we ourselves groan within
ourselves, waiting eagerly for our adoption as sons
and daughters, the redemption of our body."
—Romans 8:22–23

For those who struggle through this life—which includes everyone from time to time—this verse is a huge comfort. We groan, and creation groans.

This world, broken by sin as it is, will never fully satisfy us. Some have it easier than others, some have seasons of rest between battles, and some seem to have only strife and pain, but nothing in the Bible makes it seem like this life will be perfect, easy, or totally satisfying.

If we're going through hard things, we're in good company. Jesus, Joseph, Esther, the disciples, Ruth, Paul, Job, and countless others all struggled too.

It doesn't necessarily mean we're in the wrong place; it means we live in this broken world.

Sometimes the brokenness seems too heavy for us to bear, but there is always hope.

This passage continues, speaking of our adoption and the redemption of our bodies: "For in hope we have been saved, but hope that is seen is not hope; for who hopes for what he already sees? But if we hope for what we do not see, through perseverance we wait eagerly for it" (Romans 8:24–25).

The hope we await will never be fully realized in this life. God is guiding us through the difficulty now, and every moment brings us closer to our glorious eternal hope.

"Jesus stood and cried out, saying, 'If anyone is
thirsty, let him come to me and drink. The one who
believes in me, as the Scripture said, "From his
innermost being will flow rivers of living water.""
—John 7:37–38

Sometimes we feel empty, wrung out, and drained. When that's the case, we need to consider what we've been running to quench our thirst. Is it TV? Relationships? Food? An addiction? Work? Video games? Exercise?

If we've been filling our free time only with things other than Jesus, we can't expect to overflow with the rivers of living water, because this overflowing requires that we first come to him and drink. The inflow determines the outflow.

Some of the things listed above are not necessarily bad, but they are if they displace our time with God or if we expect them to take the role of our Comforter, the Holy Spirit. They will leave us emptier than we started rather than refreshed and refilled.

We all overflow with something. If it isn't the life-giving fruits of the Spirit promised to believers, we need to evaluate why.

It could also be that we need to dig into past hurts and get help to heal from those.

Whatever the reason for it, let's make sure that our emptiness sends us running to God instead of to some worldly quick fix that will not last. Let's fill our souls with the things of the Lord so his living waters are pouring out of us into the lives of others.

He is the only well that will never run dry.

"So if I, the Lord and the Teacher, washed your feet,
you also ought to wash one another's feet."
—John 13:14

This is a picture of how Christ cleansed us with his servanthood and sacrificial love. He did not demean us or look at us disdainfully; he lowered himself in humility and did the cleansing for us. Jesus is the only man that ever walked the earth who had no cause for humility. He was God himself in the flesh and would have been perfectly within his rights to destroy us all or demand we bow down and worship him by force.

Instead, he came in humility.

He died for us while we were still sinners (Romans 5:8). He came for those who know they're not righteous—the sick, not the healthy (Mark 2:17). He prayed for forgiveness for his murderers while still suffering from their wounds on the cross (Luke 23:34).

How much more should we, as the sinners that we are, approach others in humility, servanthood, and sacrificial love? We have no cause to think ourselves better than any other; it's only through Christ washing us that we are cleansed. We shouldn't look at the uncleanness of those around us with disdain and disgust, but with compassion and a desire to show them the same loving servanthood Jesus displayed.

Even while living in the middle of painful circumstances others have caused, we can serve them humbly, speak the truth that may lead them out of darkness, and pray they will find forgiveness.

There's no room for prideful leadership in the body of Christ.

"For who has shown contempt for the day of small
things? But these seven will rejoice when they see the
plumb line in the hand of Zerubbabel."
—Zechariah 4:10

Sometimes we get discouraged with all the small things—one tiny step after another. We want to see results. We want our efforts to be rewarded *now*.

But God rejoices over our small beginnings. He knows the only way to have a result is to be faithful in all the tiny steps along the way.

Even the first step of planning is rejoiced over—holding the plumb line to get everything straight before beginning the work of rebuilding the temple. There are no visible signs of progress—just planning, measuring, preparing.

It's easy to dismiss the importance and value in these early steps and long for the days we can already see the walls going up and the structure taking shape, but each step is necessary and worth celebrating.

Perhaps we're just beginning and others are showing contempt for our efforts because they can't yet see the visible rewards. Or maybe we're doubting the value of what we're doing ourselves—doubting whether it will ever amount to anything and feeling a bit overwhelmed by the breadth of the work ahead of us.

We can trust that the Lord is rejoicing over every tiny step we take along the way to obeying him and building the kingdom.

Let's rejoice over every new beginning and each small step. Many of them will seem tedious, but they are all getting us closer and closer to building something meaningful.

> "The cross of our Lord Jesus Christ, through which the
> world has been crucified to me, and I to the world."
> —Galatians 6:14

What does it mean for the world to be crucified to us?

It means that we no longer chase satisfaction in the here and now. We seek our fulfillment in pursuing the will of God (John 4:34). Though we still live here, we're no longer taken in by the "worries of this world, and the deceitfulness of wealth, and the desires for other things" (Mark 4:19). The spiritual world becomes more real to us than the physical world (2 Corinthians 4:18). We know that worldly pleasures will not last and seek instead to build up eternal treasure (Matthew 6:19–21).

We know our kingdom is not of this world, so we are not alarmed nor crushed when our earthly kingdoms crumble (John 18:36).

What does it mean for us to be crucified to the world?

We, like Christ, are willing to give ourselves up for the sake of others (Philippians 2:3). It is no longer our life, but his (Galatians 2:20). We are dead to sin (Romans 6:11), and now live for his glory and the sake of his kingdom.

"To live is Christ" (Philippians 1:21) frees us from the pressures of succeeding in any earthly goal.

All earthly ends may be frustrated, but when we make living for Christ our goal, then the purpose of every ordinary life is secure in him—whether we are parenting or working or living with a chronic illness that keeps us from pursuing other things.

No matter what we achieve—or don't—there's no such thing as a wasted life spent seeking God.

"Then his servants approached and spoke to him
[Naaman], saying, 'My father, had the prophet told
you to do some great thing, would you not have done
it? How much more then, when he says to you,
"Wash, and be clean"?'"
—2 Kings 5:13

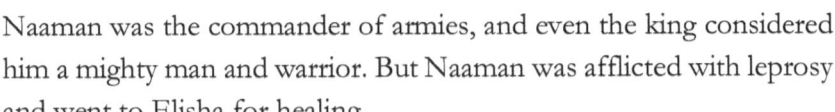

Naaman was the commander of armies, and even the king considered him a mighty man and warrior. But Naaman was afflicted with leprosy and went to Elisha for healing.

Elisha sent instructions for Naaman to wash in the Jordan River seven times.

Naaman was furious; he felt this was beneath the honor of his station. He should've been given some great deed or sacrifice to show himself worthy of his healing; there isn't anything special about dipping yourself in a river.

How often do people come to God and leave angry because he simply says, "Believe in me, and be cleansed" (John 6:28–29)? They want something that makes them feel good about themselves—some reason to say, "Look, the Lord forgave me because of this worthy deed!"

But all of us come to God unclean in sin as Naaman came to Elisha in leprosy. No great position in this world gives us a different route to his forgiveness.

And after our cleansing, he tells us not to go and receive honor, but to go and disciple (Matthew 28:19–20), to go and wash feet (John 13:14–15), to go and die (John 12:24–26). In all things, we are to be servants.

Many of us resist God's call because it has us serving in the low places rather than earning prestige in the show places, but if we come to him in humility, we will be cleansed like little children just as Naaman was (2 Kings 5:14; Matthew 18:3–4).

"The steadfast of mind you will keep in perfect peace,
because he trusts in you."
—Isaiah 26:3

———————◆———————

We would all say we want perfect peace. Here is the formula—to constantly, steadfastly fix our minds on the Lord and trust in him.

When fear, doubt, anxiety, insecurity, anger, selfishness, jealousy, bitterness, or any other unpeaceful thing arises in our hearts, we turn our eyes from it and back to the Lord. We stop looking at the circumstances, desires, and needs we have no control over. We choose to hand it all over to the Lord, and we find peace again.

Like Peter walking on the water, if we turn to the uncertain waves of this world, we will start to sink. If we look at the Lord, he will lift us back to confidence in him.

When our minds become anxious and troubled instead of full of his perfect peace, our first and intentional reaction should be to put our minds back on the Lord and fix them there.

We must unceasingly ask ourselves, "Is my mind fixed on the Lord? Do I truly trust him? Or am I looking around at the desires of this life, chasing other things, and becoming disillusioned by my circumstances?" We must do it every time those things come up, over and over and over.

Perfect peace follows when we trust him with those things instead of striving with them because as it says in the next verse, "In God the Lord, we have an everlasting rock" (Isaiah 26:4). He's all-powerful, all-knowing, and all-sufficient.

His perfect peace will exist in both the calm and the storms of life when he is our rock.

> "But Zion said, 'The Lord has abandoned me, and the
> Lord has forgotten me.' 'Can a woman forget her
> nursing child and have no compassion on the son of
> her womb? Even these may forget, but I will not forget
> you. Behold, I have inscribed you on the palms of my
> hands; your walls are continually before me.'"
> —Isaiah 49:14–16

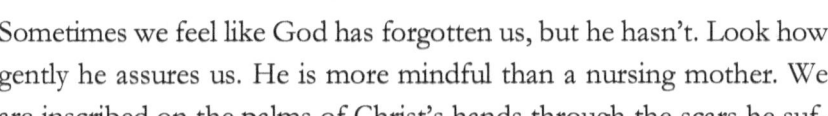

Sometimes we feel like God has forgotten us, but he hasn't. Look how gently he assures us. He is more mindful than a nursing mother. We are inscribed on the palms of Christ's hands through the scars he suffered so each of us could come to him freely.

He doesn't forget. In fact, he thinks of his people continually. When you or I remember something, it usually flits out of our minds quickly as another thought overtakes it. We can only think of one thing at a time, but God can hold each of us in his mind at all times.

A nursing child may think his mother has forgotten him when she leaves him even for a few hours. To that child, the separation might seem unending and cruel.

We might feel that way on this earth. There will be times we can't feel the presence of God, and all seems hopeless. It may feel like he's deserted us here in a world of strangers who can't give us what we need.

But just as the good mother's plan is always to return to the child, the Lord himself will come back and get us. He has not forgotten.

In the meantime, we have the presence of the Holy Spirit living in our hearts, and through him, we are comforted, helped (John 16:7), and taught (John 14:26).

"You are from God, little children, and have
overcome them; because greater is he who is
in you than he who is in the world."
—1 John 4:4

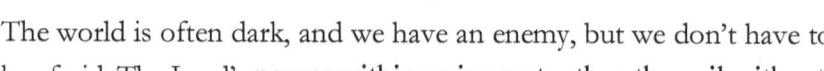

The world is often dark, and we have an enemy, but we don't have to be afraid. The Lord's **power within us is greater than the evil without.**

This doesn't mean we can stop all the evil that happens, but it does mean we can overcome even when we're walking through things caused by evil. We can be "afflicted in every way, but not crushed; perplexed, but not despairing; persecuted, but not abandoned; struck down, but not destroyed" (2 Corinthians 4:8–9).

We can show kindness when others are cruel. We can love when others hate and be peacemakers when others divide. We can reach out when others retreat and give when others take. We can hope when others despair.

No evil or law in the world can make us stop being loving, joyful, peaceful, patient, kind, good, faithful, and self-controlled . . . unless we let it (Galatians 5:22–23).

Satan wants the evil to make us bitter, cruel, angry, anxious, fearful, selfish, unforgiving, hopeless, and indulgent so we will stop following God's path.

We overcome by not letting it overcome us; we triumph over it and destroy Satan's plans when evil doesn't overtake our hearts.

This overcoming doesn't require a gun, a cape, an argument, or anger. Jesus didn't overcome by fighting. He overcame through his death, and we overcome through the death of our flesh (Romans 8:13). As we're raised again in the power of the Holy Spirit, the life we lives will show others the way to the kingdom of God.

As we submit to and obey Christ, he works in us, and we overcome.

"Pleasant words are a honeycomb,
sweet to the soul and healing to the bones."
—Proverbs 16:24

All of us have felt this power. Maybe we're stressed, insecure, frustrated, or exhausted, and someone says something kind. Those words find the hurting place in our hearts, and unexpected tears fill our eyes.

We were trying to hide the hurt, but they saw it, spoke to it, and in doing so, brought a little healing.

We often forget this power when it comes to our own words. Hurtful words come easy. Pleasant words take work and intention.

But since we've all had both kind and hurtful things said to us, we know how difficult it is to rid the hurtful ones from our minds, how hard it is to stop fearing they are true, and how long it takes us to put them aside.

The pleasant words often get lost because we can only remember the harsh ones.

When we speak to others, we're adding to one side of that scale or the other. Something we say may end up in a person's mind forever—pleasant words bringing gentle encouragement and peace or hurtful ones lingering in insecurity and fear.

There are enough unpleasant words in the world. With every word we say, we can either tear others down or build them up.

When we see a hurt in someone, we shouldn't be afraid to speak life there. Let's be intentional about speaking words that build up—words that heal the wounds in others, pleasant words that are sweet to the soul and healing to the body.

"Rejoice always, pray without ceasing, in everything give
thanks; for this is the will of God for you in Christ Jesus."
—1 Thessalonians 5:16–18

Rejoice, pray, give thanks—three things that aren't always easy to do, but we're told to do them constantly.

This means we must be intentional and conscientious about doing them all the time, but especially when things are difficult.

When we're frustrated, irritated, exhausted, or scared, we can choose to sing a worship song, praise the Lord for who he is, take everything to him in prayer, and thank him for what he's done for us already. This sends us to the source of true comfort and serves to remind us of things we often forget in trials—that our God is good, he loves us, and will never leave or forsake us.

Praise while we're in the miry pit is powerful—like Paul and Silas singing in the prison after being beaten, stripped, and chained. God showed up and opened the prison doors for them, but in an action that was probably inexplicable to anyone watching, they chose not to escape.

As they prayed, God gave them insight as to the eternal purpose in their pain and that great purpose became stronger than their need to escape. Many came to salvation because of their rejoicing and praying in the trial (Acts 16:22–30).

Being in the pit isn't always about getting out; sometimes it's about how we can bring others to God from within.

So let's rejoice, pray, and give thanks while we're there, and be open to hearing from the Lord about when it's time to escape the pit or to stay there for the sake of bringing others into glorious eternity with us.

"Lord, my heart is not proud, nor my eyes arrogant; nor
do I involve myself in great matters, or in things too
difficult for me. I have certainly soothed and quieted my
soul; like a weaned child resting against his mother, my
soul within me is like a weaned child. Israel, wait for the
Lord from this time on and forever."
—Psalm 131

Young children believe their mothers know everything, understand everything, and can solve every problem. They don't concern themselves with matters they can't comprehend, because they trust their mothers to do it for them. Even after weaning, when the mother has ceased giving instant nourishment, the child has learned calm confidence—content that sustenance, comfort, and provision are still certain.

In the same way, as young believers, God often grants us quicker and more visible shows of his provision and care. As we mature and learn to be confident in him, sometimes the nourishment comes slower, and it feels he isn't as close.

But just as that weaned child can continue to rely on the good mother's provision even when she's not in sight, we can relax in the knowledge that God is caring for us even when we don't see him and don't understand the circumstances. We don't have to involve ourselves in matters too great for us.

We can hope only in him as a young child runs to his mother with every need.

There are many things too great and difficult for us, but just like the psalmist, we can soothe and quiet ourselves by resting in the Lord and trusting that he will continue to provide and satisfy.

"Blessed is the person who does not walk in the counsel
of the wicked, nor stand in the path of sinners, nor sit in
the seat of scoffers! But his delight is in the law of the
Lord, and on his law he meditates day and night. He will
be like a tree planted by streams of water, which yields
its fruit in its season, and its leaf does not wither;
and in whatever he does, he prospers."
—Psalm 1:1–3

This verse reminds us what will nourish us, what will keep us safely rooted, and what will keep us fruitful even when our circumstances are hard.

If our souls are feeling empty and our faith shaky, it's good to ask:

- Are we listening to the wisdom of unbelievers for our direction?
- Are there areas we haven't surrendered to the Lord?
- Are we dwelling on all the things we think others are doing wrong?
- Are we planting ourselves where God has put us?
- Are we delighting in his Word, learning from it, and applying it to our lives because we know it's the path to the abundant life he's offered us?

If we consider how much we let the voices of the world or our own selfishness influence our thoughts rather than planting ourselves where we're constantly fed by the living water of Jesus and the truths of the Bible, it's often clear why we don't feel nourished.

We live in the world, but we dare not drink from it if we want to thrive in any and all circumstances. We are planted in Christ, and he is where we go for our nourishment and strength if we want to be fruitful and survive the hard seasons without withering.

"But if you do not forgive other people,
then your Father will not forgive your offenses."
—Matthew 6:15

———————◆———————

Forgiveness is hard. We all have people who have hurt us and never shown remorse. It's difficult to work up forgiveness for those people, but Jesus doesn't make it optional.

Matthew 18:23–35 gives the parable of the servant who was forgiven a great debt by the king, then went out and threw a man in jail for owing him something ridiculously small in comparison.

So how do we forgive when we don't feel like forgiving? The same way we love when we don't feel like loving—by choice, in obedience.

As resentments resurface again in our memory, we make the intentional choice to forgive them repeatedly—seventy times seven times if needed—more than we could ever count. We whisper a prayer bringing even our difficulty to the Lord: "I forgive; help my unforgiveness."

And instead of allowing new bitterness to take root, we use those thoughts as prompts for prayer. It's difficult to remain in unforgiveness while we're praying for our enemies (Matthew 5:44). We are called to love them, and that means praying they receive the same mercy Christ has given us.

If we cannot wish that for them, we do not yet understand the depths to which God has forgiven us.

Our feelings may follow our obedience, but even where they do not, we give our hurt to Christ, take the offence to the cross, and leave it there once again.

"We look not at the things which are seen, but at
the things which are not seen; for the things
which are seen are temporal, but the things
which are not seen are eternal.
—2 Corinthians 4:18

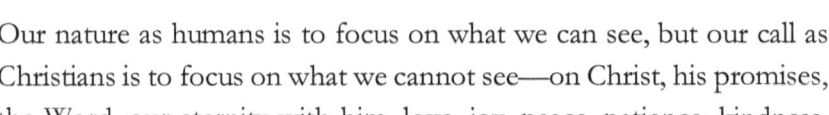

Our nature as humans is to focus on what we can see, but our call as Christians is to focus on what we cannot see—on Christ, his promises, the Word, our eternity with him, love, joy, peace, patience, kindness, goodness, faithfulness, gentleness, and self-control.

When the things we can see dictate our hopes and our fears, we're allowing ourselves to be tossed by transient waves. The seen things will rise and fall constantly in this life, but the unseen things will matter through eternity after everything that we can see has passed away.

When the seen things begin to draw us in, whether it's putting our hope in them, falling into despair over loss, or luring us into sin, remember all they can offer is as fleeting as a wave on the ocean shore . . . as changeable as the shape of a cloud as it passes overhead, and as uncertain as the wind before a storm. No circumstance is forever; moths and rust corrupt and thieves break in and steal (Matthew 6:19).

Living this truth is so freeing. We don't have to bow to the fickle whims of the world; there is no keeping up with the Joneses.

The unseen things cannot be taken from us by any earthly authority (Galatians 5:23); they are our only true possession and inheritance.

Our lives are guaranteed to have eternal meaning no matter what our external, visible circumstances look like when we live them out with character through the Holy Spirit.

"Some praise their chariots and some their horses,
but we will praise the name of the Lord, our God."
—Psalm 20:7

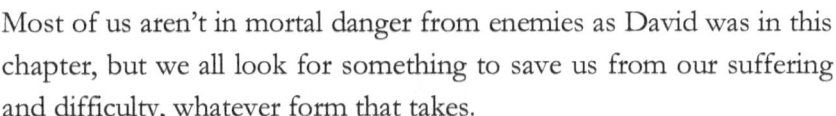

Most of us aren't in mortal danger from enemies as David was in this chapter, but we all look for something to save us from our suffering and difficulty, whatever form that takes.

We often find ourselves hoping in and praising things besides the Lord as our salvation. We look around and think, "If I just had that one thing, I'd be OK. I'd finally be safe, comfortable, and whole."

Maybe it's a house, a raise, or a relationship.

But believing those will save us is building a foundation on shifting sand; they do not have the power we think they do.

Here's the good news: we can be confident and content in the Lord even when we don't have the chariots and horses we think we need. If we can trust him in battle, we can surely trust him with our needs and desires!

As Paul says in Philippians 4:11–13, "I have learned to be content in whatever circumstances I am. I know how to get along with little, and I also know how to live in prosperity; in any and every circumstance I have learned the secret of being filled and going hungry, both of having abundance and suffering need. I can do all things through him who strengthens me."

Trusting God in contentment doesn't mean we will never desire something we don't have; I don't think Paul stopped wanting food when he was hungry. We can continue thinking it would be nice to have the chariots, horses, house, raise, or relationship as long as we don't put our hope in getting them or our trust in them once we do.

> "Remain in me, and I in you. Just as the branch cannot
> bear fruit of itself but must remain in the vine, so neither
> can you unless you remain in me. I am the vine, you are
> the branches; the one who remains in me, and I in him
> bears much fruit, for apart from me you can do nothing."
> —John 15:4–5

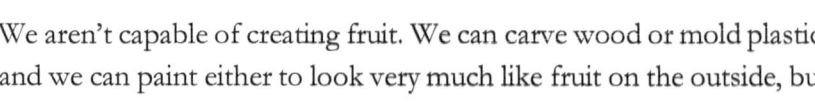

We aren't capable of creating fruit. We can carve wood or mold plastic, and we can paint either to look very much like fruit on the outside, but it will not be nourishing or even edible. It might fool some people at first, but as soon as they try to taste it, they'll discover the truth.

The same is true of spiritual fruit. If we're feverishly trying to appear fruitful yet not staying connected to the Father, we might create something that looks like fruit on the outside, but as soon as someone tries to be nourished by what we're producing, they'll discover the truth. That fruit will be exhaustion, discouragement, pride, bitterness, or some other rotten thing.

Only fruit produced out of a rich intimacy with Christ will be nourishing to others and fill true spiritual need.

If our fruit is nonexistent or rotten, let's check our connection to the vine. Are we spending time in prayer and meditating on God's Word? Are we studying it intentionally so we know how to apply it to our daily lives? Are we looking to worldly wisdom, or are we running to God for his truth so our hearts and minds are transformed and renewed?

Apart from him, all our fruit is useless, but when we remain connected to the vine, we will naturally produce godly fruit in its season.

"Jesus answered them and said, 'Truly, truly, I say to you,
you seek me, not because you saw signs, but because you
ate some of the loaves and were filled. Do not work for
the food that perishes, but for the food that lasts for
eternal life, which the Son of Man will give you."
—John 6:26–27

The idea that if we serve God, we will have all our earthly wants filled
is prevalent in today's Christianity. Some think that if we serve him
well, we are guaranteed a successful professional life, financial wealth
(or at least stability), and good health.

Even those of us who don't believe this outright often have the
subconscious idea that if we're obeying the Lord and trying to serve
him, he should make everything smooth sailing for us.

When hardships hit, we often get angry with him and ask, "Why,
Lord? I was doing my best to live for you!"

If our faith is shaken when this world does not satisfy, then our
faith has really been in this world and the hopes that our service to and
faith in the Lord will keep us "filled" in the here and now.

We've still been working for the food that perishes.

And if that's where our faith is, it will always crumble because the
foundation of this life's fulfillment will always be shakable; it's always
perishing. Whatever satisfaction it can provide will always be temporary.

Christ is the bread of life (John 6:48), and only by making him our
sustenance will we gain eternal life (John 6:58).

> "Then the Lord said to Gideon, 'The people are still too many; bring them down to the water and I will test them for you there. So it shall be that he of whom I say to you, "This one shall go with you," he shall go with you; but everyone of whom I say to you, "This one shall not go with you," he shall not go.'"
> —Judges 7:4

The Lord called Gideon to free his people from the oppression of the Midianites. They were severely outnumbered before they even started; the Midianites had 135,000 warriors and the Israelites only 32,000.

The Lord, however, said they had too many men and proceeded to whittle the army down to 10,000.

Can you imagine being Gideon and looking at those numbers? That's pretty terrible odds.

Then God said they still had too many and cut that number down further to 300 men . . . 300 against 135,000.

This is the kind of battle many of us would advise against or refuse to join. It looked hopeless.

But the Lord wants us to trust him instead of numbers or worldly might. He uses the foolish to shame the wise, the weak to shame the strong (1 Corinthians 1:27).

The battle belongs to the Lord, and we don't have to fear even against impossible odds (2 Chronicles 20:15).

He doesn't need us to have enough power, time, talent, strength, intelligence, or any other resource. He just needs us to face the battle he's given us in obedience and confidence in him.

Don't look at the odds. Look at God.

> "You there! Everyone who thirsts, come to the waters;
> and you who have no money come, buy and eat. Come,
> buy wine and milk without money and without cost.
> Why do you spend money for what is not bread, and
> your wages for what does not satisfy?"
> —Isaiah 55:1–2

Jesus said this again in John 6:27: "Do not work for the food that perishes, but for the food that lasts for eternal life, which the Son of Man will give you." The crowds asked him what kind of work they need to do to receive this enduring food, and he answered, "This is the work of God, that you believe in him whom he has sent" (John 6:29).

We don't have to buy the bread of life and living water. We only have to believe . . . but this belief is not a simple acknowledgement, for "the demons also believe, and shudder" (James 2:19).

Jesus is talking about the kind of belief that affects your life.

Like Noah: "By faith Noah, being warned by God about things not yet seen, in reverence prepared an ark for the salvation of his household" (Hebrews 11:7).

Like Abraham: "By faith Abraham, when he was called, obeyed by going out to a place which he was to receive for an inheritance; and he left, not knowing where he was going" (Hebrews 11:8).

Noah and Abraham followed God into the unknown because they believed him.

That's the kind of belief Jesus is talking about.

Truly believing God will result in following his direction, and following his direction will lead to the nourishment that satisfies our hungry souls.

"Love never fails; but if there are gifts of prophecy, they
will be done away with; if there are tongues, they will
cease; if there is knowledge, it will be done away with."
—1 Corinthians 13:8

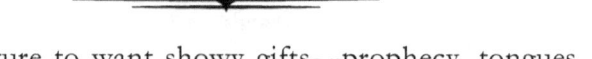

It's human nature to want showy gifts—prophecy, tongues, and knowledge—gifts that bring awe, attention, and awards.

But love is the greatest commandment (Mark 12:30–31); it's the one gift that crosses over into eternity.

The Word tells us these others are transient; none are guaranteed to have eternal impact.

But love—the kind of love that involves every piece of our emotions, desires, motives, thoughts, and will—that is infinite. It has unquestionable impact wherever we live it.

And rather than garnering recognition, power, or impressing others, love often keeps us in the shadows. We're washing feet (John 13:13–15). We're putting ourselves at the end of the table rather than choosing a place of honor (Luke 14:7–11). We're giving more honor to others than we expect for ourselves (Romans 12:10).

Many of us feel incapable of doing very much good because we don't have any obvious talents or gifts. This is a lie from the devil.

Every last one of us can love, and it's the greatest of all the gifts. No one is less valuable than any other because they cannot prophesy, speak in tongues, or because they are not gifted in knowledge.

In fact, if people have those gifts, but don't have love, they're simply making noise (1 Corinthians 13:1). But every one of us can love.

Our heart's prayer should be not to have gifts that look important, but that God would teach us how to love fully.

"Now I want you to know, brothers and sisters,
that my circumstances have turned out
for the greater progress of the gospel."
—Philippians 1:12

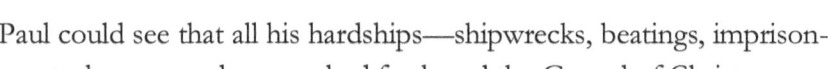

Paul could see that all his hardships—shipwrecks, beatings, imprisonments, hunger, and more—had furthered the Gospel of Christ.

Sometimes we lose heart in our struggles because we can't see what they're accomplishing. How could there be purpose in this terrible thing?

Paul couldn't necessarily see it while those things were happening, but he persevered in obedience, and they "turned out" for the furtherance of the Gospel. Eventually, he could see that all the hard stuff was worth it.

And so will we. We don't have to lose heart in our sufferings.

If we could see how our struggles would bring healing and godly character to us while also furthering the Lord's kingdom and bringing people into eternity with him, we would have the strength to endure.

Since we believe his Word, then we can know this is true. We have assurance that all things—every circumstance, both bad and good—will turn out for good for those who love him and are called to his purpose (Romans 8:28).

Things don't turn out good coincidentally or magically; they turn out that way through God's great providence and sovereignty.

And with the certainty of that truth, we can endure in faith and hope even when we can't see how God could possibly use whatever we're going through for good.

We don't have to wait for hindsight, because we can trust him and know that it's true.

Whatever we're going through will be worth it.

"Whoever exalts himself shall be humbled,
and whoever humbles himself shall be exalted."
—Matthew 23:12

If we try to make sure we receive our due in this world, we will be humbled. But if we do not concern ourselves with recognition, we will be exalted. That doesn't make sense to our human nature; it's hard not to seek acknowledgment we feel we deserve.

And each day includes thousands of moments in which we can exalt ourselves or humble ourselves. We'll usually know which one we're doing if we take the time to check, but if were not sure, we can ask ourselves these questions.

Do we resent doing the work God's placed in front of us? Are we annoyed when others ask for help or something interrupts what we planned to do? Are we doing things hoping that others respond to us in a certain way, or are we content even if they don't acknowledge or notice what we've done? Are we kind even when others make mistakes or act selfishly? Are we judging other people in our thoughts? Are we doing things only because we expect something in return?

On the other side, are we loving people even though we see their flaws? Are we doing our duty to God's glory even when it's hard and we don't feel like it? Are we trusting that God sees our right actions even if others don't notice them? Are we building people up and loving them as Christ loves them? Do we seek to serve or believe we should be served? Are we willing to put others ahead of ourselves?

May we learn to submit to the Holy Spirit, humbling ourselves in every action and every thought.

"My times are in your hand."
—Psalm 31:15

It's so easy to be attached to our schedules, our to-do lists, and our own expectations of what we should accomplish in a day. We get frustrated by interruptions and delays, often allowing them to make us irritable and unkind.

But if our times are in the Lord's hand, then he is not shocked by any interruption.

When a kid bursts into the room while you're praying, God is there. When the hot water heater springs a leak, God is there. When the dog gets sick, God is there. When that unexpected deadline at work pops up, God is there.

Perhaps your child has been discouraged and really needs to feel your love. Perhaps that plumber's fee for the water heater was exactly the amount needed to cover a child's medical bill. Perhaps the client sitting next to us at the vet clinic just lost a spouse, and we can listen to her story. Perhaps fulfilling that unexpected deadline at work will save a coworker's job.

We can choose to see God in the interruptions and bring him there with us, or we can respond with anxiety and a bad attitude, shutting off the work of the Holy Spirit in our hearts and interactions.

He knows what we hope and plan to achieve, but only he knows what we actually need to accomplish.

If we follow our own agendas, which are formed by our own very limited perspectives, we may accomplish many tasks but do very little that matters in eternity.

Only by listening to his still, small voice will we be certain we are doing kingdom work.

"Remind them to be subject to rulers, to authorities, to
be obedient, to be ready for every good deed, to
slander no one, not to be contentious, to be gentle,
showing every consideration for all people."
—Titus 3:1–2

The opposite of this verse would be to live in rebellion, to speak evil of people, to be thoughtless, critical, hard-headed, and rude. It's easy to do that, but quite difficult to do what the Lord has called us to do.

We won't do it by accident. Our nature is to do what we want regardless of authority, to speak and act without thinking, and to be demanding and selfish. To obey this verse, we must be intentional—tame our tongues (James 3:1–12), discipline our bodies (1 Corinthians 9:27), and crucify our flesh (Galatians 5:24–26).

We cannot say everything we feel like saying or do everything we feel like doing.

A practical way to live this out is to institute a pause before we speak or act. When we recognize that something negative is happening and the desire to argue or speak evil arises, instead of just reacting, we can use that pause to prompt prayer and as a chance to bless those who curse us and pray for those who are abusive to us (Luke 6:28).

It will often go against our desires in the moment. It will be hard to follow through instead of giving in to our impulses. But in doing so, we'll demonstrate the same forgiveness Christ extended to us, and we'll slowly become more and more free from the reactions that once enslaved us.

Every difficult situation, every hurtful person, and every selfish inclination becomes an opportunity to practice what we believe and show others the beauty of God's grace.

"For here we do not have a lasting city,
but we are seeking the city which is to come."
—Hebrews 13:14

"Don't take your coat off."

Sometimes this phrase is used when we have an errand for someone who's just walked in the door, but sometimes it's used rudely to mean something like, "You're not welcome here; don't get comfortable."

As Christians, this world often isn't very welcoming or comfortable. We shouldn't expect it to be. John 3:19 says, "the Light has come into the world, and people loved the darkness rather than the Light; for their deeds were evil." If we're walking in the Light, the world will often see us as enemies, but we're called to bear Christ's reproach in our own lives (Hebrews 13:13).

Our ultimate happiness and fulfillment won't be found here.

It's painful to feel displaced and like the world doesn't understand us or want what we have to offer, but we're not alone in that.

It didn't want Jesus either, and he was perfect. Despite rejection, false accusation, and persecution, he gave all of himself, not only to those who loved him, but to the unappreciative, the hateful, and the evil alike.

So when we can't find our place, let's remember that this world isn't our home. We're not supposed to get comfortable, for we "desire a better country, that is, a heavenly one" (Hebrews 11:16). We are "strangers and exiles on the earth" (Hebrews 11:13).

We aren't meant to take our coats off and settle in. We can expect that this world will want to push us out, but the true blessing is coming—the eternal city with no tears, no mourning, and no pain (Revelation 21:4)—and it will be better than anything we can imagine (1 Corinthians 2:9).

November 9

"Serve the Lord with jubilation;
come before him with rejoicing."
—Psalm 100:2

Joy is all over the Bible. "Delight yourself in the Lord" (Psalm 37:4). "Rejoice in the Lord always" (Philippians 4:4). "Be . . . rejoicing in hope" (Romans 12:10–12). These are just a few of the verses imploring us to be joyful.

Joy is also listed second, right after love, in the fruit of the Spirit (Galatians 5:22–23).

It's clearly meant to be a distinguishing mark of our Christian walk.

So why do so many of us live in guilt, fear, bitterness, anger, and overwhelm instead?

My own lack of joy is usually a symptom of focusing on things other than Jesus. Perhaps I've begun placing my hope in my own goodness or success, some pleasure the world offers, some achievement I hope to attain, or some other person.

When our joy becomes dependent upon things other than Jesus, our faith becomes weak, for the joy of the Lord is our refuge (Nehemiah 8:10). That word "refuge" also means our fortress, our rock, and our strength.

So what's the solution?

"Let's rid ourselves of every obstacle and the sin which so easily entangles us, and let's run with endurance the race that is set before us, looking only at Jesus, the originator and perfecter of the faith, who for the joy set before Him endured the cross, despising the shame, and has sat down at the right hand of the throne of God" (Hebrews 12:1–2).

What is the obstacle, sin, or distraction that is stealing our joy? And what are we looking at to provide that joy?

Let's set all of that aside, turn our gaze only to Jesus's example instead, and endure for the eternal joy set before us.

"Give us this day our daily bread."
—Matthew 6:11

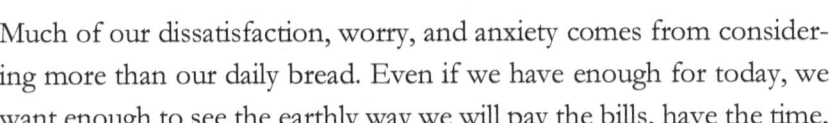

Much of our dissatisfaction, worry, and anxiety comes from considering more than our daily bread. Even if we have enough for today, we want enough to see the earthly way we will pay the bills, have the time, or sustain us for anything that might come in the future.

But God wants us to trust him each moment, and that often means we can't see where the provision, the time, or the hope will come from.

He wants us to trust that he is our portion (Lamentations 3:24; Psalm 142:5; and more) . . . our daily bread for every emotional, spiritual, and physical need. "I am the bread of life" he said (John 6:35).

A portion is what we need at that moment, not everything we will ever need. We can't hoard our time and have more the following day. We can't store up enough Jesus at church on Sunday and expect that to last us through the week.

Think of a dinner portion. It would be useless to have all the food we'll need for the rest of our lives at once. We could never carry it, and even if we could, it would spoil.

Having extra provision becomes a burden, so trusting him for our daily bread is part of the light burden Jesus promises us (Matthew 11:30). We don't have to carry everything we will ever need around with us. We have something better: the Provider himself, and he will take care of us along the way (Matthew 6:34).

Each day, we must choose to seek the Lord and receive what he has for us anew.

"And my message and my preaching were not in
persuasive words of wisdom, but in demonstration of the
Spirit and of power, so that your faith would not rest on
the wisdom of mankind, but on the power of God."
—1 Corinthians 2:4–5

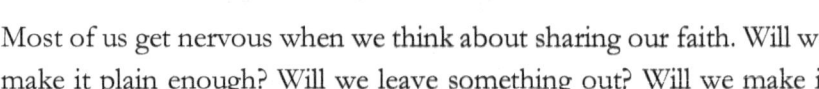

Most of us get nervous when we think about sharing our faith. Will we make it plain enough? Will we leave something out? Will we make it sound enticing enough?

When we focus on these fears, our focus is on ourselves. We are doubting the very power of the faith we try to share.

This verse reminds us that the Gospel will prevail even if we share it ineptly. It is the power of the Spirit that brings people to Christ, not our winsome words.

And when it's hard to overcome that fear, we can lean on the fact that it's okay to pray, "I believe; help my unbelief!"

In Isaiah 55:11, the Lord says, "So will my word be which goes out of my mouth; it will not return to me empty, without accomplishing what I desire, and without succeeding in the purpose for which I sent it."

When we speak the Word of God, it will accomplish the purpose for which the Lord sent it out. That doesn't depend on us. Our part is to know the Word, to accurately handle the truth (2 Timothy 2:15), and to speak it obediently: "Go, therefore and make disciples . . . teaching them to follow all that I commanded you" (Matthew 28:19–20).

Trust God, and don't hold your words back when he prompts you to share his Word or to pray with someone.

"With [the tongue] we bless our Lord and Father, and
with it we curse people, who have been made in the
likeness of God; from the same mouth come both
blessing and cursing. My brothers and sisters, these things
should not be this way. Does a spring send out from the
same opening both fresh and bitter water?"
—James 3:9–11

It's easy to say nice words about God while speaking harshly and negatively about and to others. This is what happens when we speak from the bitter springs of our own humanness instead of drawing from the fresh, overflowing rivers of living water (John 7:38).

Most of us, if we take the time to reflect on our words, know whether we're speaking blessing or cursing. Many times, we're speaking cursing and negativity because we're not being thoughtful about what fills our hearts (Luke 6:45).

When our words are fueled by a heart full of anger, offense, fear, complaint, pride, and bitterness rather than a Christlike love, they've become cursing, and we need to back up and stay silent until we can speak with respect and humility.

We need to learn how to be honest about bad situations without turning it into "cursing." It's easy to fall into using harmful words when we're not speaking in love and carefully considering our tone and intent.

We can discuss negative issues in helpful ways, or we can discuss them in ways that are dismissive and demeaning—with words that tear down or words that lift up.

If we're filling our springs with living water, then blessing rather than cursing will flow from our words even when those words are filled with difficult truths.

"For if anyone thinks that he is something
when he is nothing, he deceives himself."
—Galatians 6:3

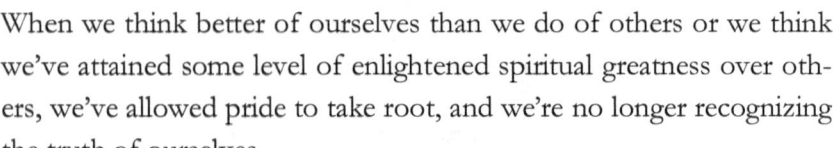

When we think better of ourselves than we do of others or we think we've attained some level of enlightened spiritual greatness over others, we've allowed pride to take root, and we're no longer recognizing the truth of ourselves.

In reality, any goodness that seems to come from us actually comes *through* us from Christ. We are nothing without the Spirit of God working in us, and knowing that should keep us humble.

We do well to remember it when we face those in whom we cannot see goodness. If we could see ourselves as we would be without Christ, we would be no better—and at risk of becoming much worse. The good we do is nothing we can boast of in and of ourselves; we can only boast in Christ and the sacrifice he made for us on the cross (Galatians 6:14).

Some of us may have gifts that put us front and center or that worldly wisdom tells us are more valuable than other gifts. But Romans 12:3–8 says we should not let those gifts make us think more highly of ourselves than we do of anyone else, because each gift is given from God. None is more important than another. When we begin to be arrogant in our own abilities, we become deceived. All our gifts, training, intelligence, talent, and advantages can be counted as rubbish, as Paul says in Philippians 3:4–11. They can all be used for evil if the Holy Spirit is not working in and through us.

It's only our Lord who makes us into something.

"Why are you seeking the living one among the dead?"
—Luke 24:5

Sometimes, we're so focused on the death that we can't see the life that has sprung from it.

The dream died; the effort was unfruitful; the plan failed. So we mourn. We visit our sorrow and dig around in the rubble.

But we can't see what is being planted with that death—what green shoot will sprout from the sacrifice.

It takes supernatural intervention to get us to look up and see that we're searching in the wrong place.

We're looking for what was buried when we should be looking for what was raised—a shoot, a vine, the green bud that will flower and turn into fruit.

The death and burial are painful, and we can mourn them, but they are not more powerful than what God can do.

He says, "Behold, I am going to do something new, now it will spring up; will you not be aware of it?" (Isaiah 43:19). We have to be watching or we might not see it.

Between Jesus's death and the resurrection, there were three long days when all seemed lost—when the disciples went back to being fishermen. It seemed like they'd been wrong about Jesus.

But the third day came and changed everything. Their hope and belief were not in vain! He really was the Messiah. The enemy hadn't won after all.

The pain and loss in our lives is no different. Eventually, something begins to spring up out of the death; it's time to turn from the dead and look to what now lives.

"So do not worry about tomorrow; for
tomorrow will worry about itself. Each day
has enough trouble of its own."
—Matthew 6:34

Sometimes we need to hear a familiar verse in a different package for it to sink in. That happened to me with this one.

I'd been feeling restless and stressed about the what, the how, and the when of whatever the Lord wanted me to do next when the message, "Trust God and do the next thing," began to appear over and over in my life.

That line encapsulates this verse—to be faithful in the moment and trust the Lord with it.

We so often look ahead, stressing about what's to come and whether we'll know what to do or be able to do it.

But as we walk with the Lord, the "next things" line up naturally, and time forces us to take them as they come.

Though our lives do require planning future steps, they never require worrying about those future steps or trying to accomplish them before they arrive.

When we allow ourselves to be distracted by the future, we're neglecting today, never really living our actual lives, but attempting to live our future lives in our minds instead.

This drains today of both the strength we need to fight its battles and the pleasure we could gain from its joys.

When our minds begin to run anxiously into the future, we can bring them back to the present through the Lord's strength, trust him to order our steps, and rest in the fact that this day is the only one we can live right now.

What task has God given us this moment? Let's trust him and do the next thing.

"For my people have committed two evils: they
have abandoned me, the fountain of living waters,
to carve out for themselves cisterns, broken
cisterns that do not hold water."
—Jeremiah 2:13

Most of us have lived this story in one way or another. We run away from God because we think we know a better, faster way of getting what we think we want. We dig our own wells instead of believing him when he says that Jesus is the living water.

Maybe we've dug the well of control, relationships, addiction, shopping, financial security, the respect of our peers, or food. It could be anything.

All of it is more useless than trying to get our water from a cracked well. We might get a sip or two, but it won't last long, and we certainly won't have any to share. We'll have to keep digging deeper for sips that do not sustain, always sliding further down into that hole we've dug.

When the Lord is our source, his unending supply of living water will not only fill us but provide all we need to give and serve sacrificially as he leads us, never fearing we will run out.

So how do we fill our cup from him? Abide in the Word daily. Obey what it says, and go where the Holy Spirit guides. Be a doer, not just a hearer. Pray without ceasing. Give thanks. Take our thoughts captive. Don't worry about tomorrow. Trust him with our needs. Learn who God is. Draw near to him, and he will draw near to us.

When we're feeling empty, we need to ask ourselves what cistern we've been drinking from and turn, instead, to the Lord and his fountain that overflows with the living water that is Jesus!

> "He [King Amaziah] did what was right in
> the sight of the Lord, only not wholeheartedly."
> —2 Chronicles 25:2

In the Bible, we see many stories of people who tried to follow God part-way or who followed him well for a time, then fell away. Each of those stories show us that God desires and, indeed, requires our true and persevering devotion.

King Amaziah was defeated and eventually killed because he took false gods from another culture and began to worship them as his own, despite the true God having helped him win a battle against those very people.

It's a lesson on how easily we can become ensnared by the wiles of this world and that winning one battle does not mean we can take off our spiritual armor. Why would Amaziah have been tempted by gods that did not even protect those he had defeated?

We can ask ourselves the same thing. Why are we tempted by riches, fame, success, and unattainable beauty standards when we can see that the rich, famous, successful, and beautiful are often the emptiest of us all?

The world's idols will never satisfy, and we would do well to remember that God is a jealous god who will not allow us to run after those false gods because he loves us. He is jealous of our devotion, as a good husband is jealous of a man trying to lure his wife away with false promises.

We are to be wholeheartedly faithful to the end (Matthew 24:13; Hebrews 6:11; Hebrews 12:1–2), being sure of our hope in him and not lured away by the false promises of these worldly idols.

"And when you are praying, do not use thoughtless
repetition as the Gentiles do, for they think that
they will be heard because of their many words.
So do not be like them; for your Father knows
what you need before you ask him."
—Matthew 6:7–8

So many of us are nervous to pray in front of people because we don't think our prayers sound good enough. Sometimes we're even hesitant to pray to God in private because we think we won't do it right; we'll get distracted or speak with clumsy words. But God doesn't care about whether our prayers sound fancy, thoughtful, or smart enough, and he already knows about all our weaknesses and distraction. He still wants us to come to him.

When Jesus tells the disciples how to pray in Matthew 6:9–13, the example he gives is about forty seconds long. This is our model prayer—the Lord's prayer.

He wants our prayers to be full of our desire for him and his will, humility, trust in his provision, forgiveness, and hope for the future.

Our prayers—as we see in verse 8—are not even really about making sure we remember every tiny thing we should pray for, because he already knows them. They're about communing with our Father, being in relationship with him, and trusting him. They can be simple and short.

A good father doesn't require his children to speak with ceremony and flounder through unnatural words; he simply rejoices in their desire to be with him and receive his guidance.

"But encourage one another every day, as long as
it is still called 'today,' so that none of you will be
hardened by the deceitfulness of sin."
—Hebrews 3:13

———————◆———————

As believers, we're meant to be there for one another, to encourage each other, and to speak truth in a world that thrives on lies.

This verse tells us what happens if we're not there to encourage one another—we're left open to the temptations of this world and our hearts become hardened. We need to show up, speak truth, and encourage others every day so they're constantly reminded of what is good and true. And we need others to do the same for us.

Without this, believers become easy prey to the short-term visions of what the world tells us will make us happy.

People often wander into the ways of the world because their lives are missing something. What they're missing is Christ, and we are the body of Christ, called to love and help each other remain in truth, to bear one another's burdens, and support one another when we are weak.

And when do we do that? "Today." Always today, because there is no other day in which to do it. Is there someone we can show up for today? Someone the Lord has put on our heart? Someone we know is struggling? A name that crosses our minds for no reason?

Perhaps what they need is for us to check on them, love them, and encourage them in truth and hope. Perhaps that simple act will help them defeat the darts the enemy is shooting at them.

"But the fruit of the Spirit is love, joy, peace, patience,
kindness, goodness, faithfulness, gentleness, self-control;
against such things there is no law."
—Galatians 5:22–23

———◆———

Notice the fruit has nothing to do with tangible outcomes, rewards, or even how others respond to us. It has everything to do with what is being produced in and coming out of us.

Our society judges success by accomplishments, outcomes, and numbers. Unfortunately, the Christian community doesn't seem immune to this. We think unless we can show the results of our work for God in numbers, with a product we've created, or by how many people respond, then we don't have any "fruit."

The truth is all those numbers, products, works, and responses will amount to absolutely nothing if they are not fueled by the love of Christ (1 Corinthians 13) and producing joy, peace, patience, kindness, goodness, faithfulness, gentleness, and self-control through that love.

Rather than asking ourselves, "What have I done for God lately?", we should ask, "What has God done in me lately? How is he growing and changing me? How am I allowing the mirror of the Word to show me areas I need to surrender to him?"

Our fruit cannot be measured by statistics of the good we've endeavored to do, though we may produce products and works and have great numbers and responses. Our call is to stay connected to the vine (John 15) and watch Christ produce fruit in us as we grow in love, obedience, and trust. If the fruit of the Spirit is expressed in our lives, then those around us will be nourished by our presence in ways we could never plan by strategy.

"He will not be disheartened or crushed until he has
established justice on the earth; and the coastlands
will wait expectantly for his law."
—Isaiah 42:4

We frequently grow disheartened and crushed, tired and hopeless, but God doesn't.

He knows he already has the victory. He knows that justice will be established. He sees everything from beginning to end and the glorious forever of those who follow him.

When we're tired and discouraged, isn't it helpful to have someone walking alongside us who we know is confident, hopeful, and has the power to help when we grow weary? Someone who isn't mired down and can encourage us with truth and be there with their comforting presence? In our daily lives, knowing we have a friend supporting us is often enough to keep us going.

That's what the Lord is for us. We have the strongest, truest, most loving companion walking this road with us when we grow faint.

When we're weary and discouraged by the trouble in this world, it should be our practice to remind ourselves that God is walking with us and upholding us all along the way. We can't see what's happening, but he can, and he is always intimately involved in our lives.

We're like children who have been walking a long way and now worry they've become lost, but when we look up to our heavenly Father and see his confident face, etched with comfort and peace rather than fear or concern, we put our hand back in his and trust he knows the way. His purposes will be fulfilled (Psalm 138:8).

"Certainly all mankind standing is a mere breath. Certainly
every person walks around as a fleeting shadow; they
certainly make an uproar for nothing; he amasses riches
and does not know who will gather them."
—Psalm 39:5–6

It's good to remember that we often "make an uproar for nothing."
We are here but for a moment . . . a mere breath and fleeting shadow.

Our turmoil is unnecessary and unhelpful. We spend most of our
time here on this earth in an uproar about what we're building for this
temporary life even though it's like the snap of a finger compared to
the eternity to come.

There is nothing worth building or gaining or achieving here on this
earth more important than the things that will impact eternity—
following the Lord's commands (1 Corinthians 7:19), living out the
fruit of the Spirit (Galatians 5:22), doing the good works he placed us
here to do (Ephesians 2:10), doing justice, loving kindness, and walking
humbly with God (Micah 6:8).

Those are the unseen things that are eternal. Our aim should be to
focus on them rather than on the visible, temporary things (2 Corinthians 4:18) that can be destroyed by moths and rust and thieves (Matthew 6:19).

May we constantly be evaluating what we make an uproar over and
what we seek to amass. Is it something temporary or something that is
going to last forever? What will those things be worth in the end?

There is nothing we can store in barns—or banks or houses—
worth the uproar in our hearts.

> "A bent reed he will not break off and a dimly
> burning wick he will not extinguish; he will
> faithfully bring forth justice."
> —Isaiah 42:3

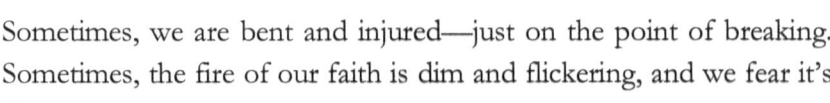

Sometimes, we are bent and injured—just on the point of breaking. Sometimes, the fire of our faith is dim and flickering, and we fear it's about to go out.

Our Lord does not crush us in our weakness. He does not shame us for being hurt and weak.

We often think of him as a taskmaster up in heaven judging us for not being good enough, shouting down reprimands like a harsh parent or a cruel master.

But he is gentle and loving. He says, "Come to me, all who are weary and burdened, and I will give you rest. Take my yoke upon you and learn from me, for I am gentle and humble in heart, and you will find rest for your souls. For my yoke is comfortable, and my burden is light" (Matthew 11:28–30).

He understands that this world is full of hurt, difficulty, evil, and injustice. He was no stranger to these things in his own life, and he assures us that he will not only handle our brokenness and sorrow with care, but justice will also prevail against the evil we face.

When we're bruised and about to break, he wants to tend us gently as a plant on the verge of dying. He is the water and the light to bring us back to life. When we're flickering and sputtering, the breath of the Holy Spirit will fan the flames of our souls to give us new energy and hope (Ezekiel 37:9–14).

> "I am the true vine, and my Father is the
> vinedresser. Every branch in me that does not bear
> fruit, he takes away; and every branch that bears
> fruit, he prunes it so that it may bear more fruit."
> —John 15:1–2

Christ is always working to cut away any branch in us that does not bear fruit.

Like a surgeon performing a procedure to heal us, God is not after our comfort but our spiritual health. The cutting hurts, but it will make us increasingly more like him so that we bear more of his fruit—love, joy, peace, patience, kindness, goodness, faithfulness, gentleness, and self-control.

If some hardship comes upon us and we feel like our right arm has been chopped off, we may ask ourselves if that thing was bringing out the fruits of the Spirit in us or if it was bringing about apathy, callousness, anger, or anxiety.

Not all loss is a pruning for the purpose of correction—we can see that most clearly in Job where it was an attack of the enemy—but any time the Lord prunes, there are two purposes: to take off what is not profitable and to bring about what is better.

The first result is often that we feel we've been butchered. Where before we might've seemed manicured and presentable with lots of green, we may now appear nearly dead—branches cut off on all sides and most of our leaves gone—misshapen and ugly.

Trust that the Lord is doing surgery—not murder—with his knife. The cut branches were a cancer robbing our fruit-producing limbs of what they needed to thrive.

It's hard to trust him in the pruning, but it's always for our good and his glory.

"Servants, be subject to your masters with all respect, not only to those who are good and gentle, but also to those who are harsh. For this finds favor, if for the sake of conscience toward God a person endures grief when suffering unjustly. For what credit is there if, when you sin and are harshly treated, you endure it with patience? But if when you do what is right and suffer for it you patiently endure it, this finds favor with God."
—1 Peter 2:18–20

———————◆———————

This attitude isn't admired in our culture. We glorify defending ourselves at all costs and revel in stories about corrupt bosses or unfair teachers getting payback. It feels like justice.

But God is the greatest proponent of justice, and he says he will bring it in his own time (Romans 12:17–21).

The Bible advises calm respect and diligent work even toward those who don't deserve it.

We take our example from Joseph in slavery, being so faithful that he ended up managing his master's entire house, and from Daniel, a captive forced to serve an evil government in a foreign land and who became a witness to everyone around him.

We find favor with the Lord when we endure injustice with integrity and trust his sovereign plan. When we've been served injustice, it feels like we have a right to slack off or be deceitful, but God says no.

It's always our duty to work diligently and respectfully. And even if obedience to God requires disobeying those unjust leaders as Daniel's daily prayers did, we do so gently, not for the purpose of rebellion, but because our loyalty must be to God first.

We're called to maintain gentle respect and integrity in humility even when faced with harsh injustice.

"For to me, to live is Christ, and to die is gain.
But if I am to live on in the flesh, this will
mean fruitful labor for me."
—Philippians 1:21–22

Sometimes we grow weary of this world and its cares; the evil, brokenness, and pain feel like too much.

As believers, to die is gain. That's true. It's good to long for eternity with our Lord.

But that longing is not to keep us from fully living the life God has ordained for us to live. If our weariness has us retreating and looking inward in fear, anger, bitterness, sadness, or insecurity rather than being about the Father's business, we're missing the abundant life he has for us and neglecting our duty to love him and others well.

When we live out our lives here in joy and peace despite all the troubles—when we are afflicted but not crushed, perplexed but not despairing, persecuted but not abandoned, struck down but not destroyed—the power of God flows through us by the laying down of our lives and submission to the Holy Spirit. The love of Christ will spread to more and more people, and thanksgiving will overflow (2 Corinthians 4:7–15).

There is no servant of Christ walking this earth without good purpose. The feeblest bodies may pray the most effective prayers, and the emptiest pockets may give the most in love. If we live on in this flesh, faithfully walking with him, it will mean fruitful labor that results in eternal joy, not only for us, but for those to whom we shine the light of the Gospel and demonstrate the hope of eternity.

To live is Christ.

Let that be our highest goal.

"You whom I have taken from the ends of the earth and called from its remotest parts, and said to you, 'You are my servant, I have chosen you and have not rejected you. Do not fear, for I am with you; do not be afraid, for I am your God. I will strengthen you, I will also help you, I will also uphold you with my righteous right hand.'"
—Isaiah 41:9–10

It's easy to be dismayed when we realize we can't control our circumstances, when everything seems to be going wrong, and when we can't see how things can be made right.

Just before this verse, Isaiah speaks of the other nations who are looking to each other for help, building their own gods, and turning to their own strength in the face of trouble.

God tells us not to do that. He will strengthen, help, and uphold, but it is not in our power to strengthen, help, or uphold ourselves. To pretend otherwise is just as futile as crafting that golden idol or carving that wooden statue with our own hands then bowing down to it and hoping it will protect us.

Nothing made by our own hands is worthy of our hope, trust, or worship. The visible things we build can all fall in a moment (Matthew 6:19). Systems, structures, insurance, retirement plans, and weapons are never foolproof.

Only our all-powerful God can uphold us because he is the firm foundation. His righteous right hand is immovable, unshakable, and as long as we remain in him (John 15:10), he will not let us go. He will strengthen us, he is holding us, and there is no need to fear.

"For our struggle is not against flesh and blood, but
against the rulers, against the powers, against the
world forces of this darkness, against the spiritual
forces of wickedness in the heavenly places."
—Ephesians 6:12

We often forget we have an enemy. When bad things happen, we look at God and ask him why rather than remembering the devil is always scheming against us.

Even if we don't blame God, we frequently look at other people as the culprits and let our anger and unforgiveness come between us and the love we're supposed to have for them.

The devil gloats when we blame God and other people for his attacks. He rejoices in causing division, hurt, and bitterness. He especially enjoys it when we misrepresent Christ in our anger or turn away from our faith because of something he's caused.

Of course, not every bad thing that happens in our lives is the devil; some of them are consequences of our own sin or discipline from the Lord as he trains godly character into us.

But when the attacks come and the tragedies strike, rather than accusing God or lashing out at others—even if they may be the perpetrators we can see—we must be mindful that we have an enemy we can't see. He's an active predator who prowls around seeking someone to devour (1 Peter 5:8).

This is not cause for fear. No matter how the enemy comes against us—whether through temptation or some other kind of attack—the Spirit within us is stronger than the enemy in this world (1 Corinthians 10:13; 1 John 4:4).

"Even if the fig tree does not blossom, and there is
no fruit on the vines, if the yield of the olive fails,
and the fields produce no food, even if the flock
disappears from the fold, and there are no cattle in
the stalls, yet I will triumph in the Lord, I will
rejoice in the God of my salvation."
—Habakkuk 3:17–18

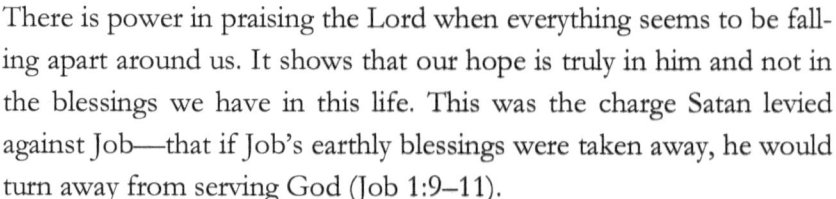

There is power in praising the Lord when everything seems to be falling apart around us. It shows that our hope is truly in him and not in the blessings we have in this life. This was the charge Satan levied against Job—that if Job's earthly blessings were taken away, he would turn away from serving God (Job 1:9–11).

While suffering, Job cried and questioned, grieved and wished he'd never been born, but he never turned from God, though he lost all his possessions and all his family except a bitter wife.

This is our responsibility—that our faith in the Lord would not be based on what we gain or lose in this life. We can be in plenty or in need and still be content (Philippians 4:11–13) because Jesus is the treasure in a field worth trading everything else to gain (Matthew 13:44).

Jesus said, "My kingdom is not of this world" (John 18:36).

So when this world lets us down, we don't have to despair. We can still praise, knowing that the Lord and his promises are still true. We can take joy in him and the salvation he's given us.

Rejoicing in the midst of trouble is a sign to those around us that our faith is not in this world, but in the Lord alone.

"All these died in faith, without receiving the
promises, but having seen and welcomed them
from a distance, and having confessed that they
were strangers and exiles on the earth."
—Hebrews 11:13

We all have times of tragedy, difficulty, and struggle in this life. It's easy in those times to ask, "Why, God? I'm trying to be faithful and serve you."

It's not wrong to talk to God about our doubts and disappointments or even to ask him, "Why?" He's big enough for our questions, and we see David, Job, and others ask him the same thing.

But this verse gives us the ultimate answer: this world isn't our home.

When it seems like we're not receiving the promises, we can know that we will receive them in that "better country"—the heavenly one where God is now preparing a place for us (Hebrews 11:16) beyond all imagination (1 Corinthians 2:9).

We might be strangers and exiles in this life, but Ephesians 2:19–22 reminds us that we are "no longer strangers and foreigners, but [we] are fellow citizens with the saints, and are of God's household, having been built on the foundation of the apostles and prophets, Christ Jesus himself being the cornerstone, in whom the whole building, being fitted together, is growing into a holy temple in the Lord, in whom [we] also are being built together into a dwelling of God in the Spirit."

We don't have to despair when this life is not meeting our expectations.

This isn't our home, but we have one—a glorious, forever home that will realize and exceed all our expectations.

"Do not learn the way of the nations, and do not
be terrified by the signs of the heavens, although
the nations are terrified by them."
—Jeremiah 10:2

———————◆———————

Our world has its ways of handling things, but we shouldn't look to it to learn how to respond when difficult times come.

Our culture has become increasingly fearful, and the voices in the world seem to thrive on shouting that fear out louder and stronger. So much of what we see sensationalizes all the things we could be afraid of to keep us hooked on knowing all the dreadful details, afraid to look away lest we miss something.

We shouldn't fear the things the world fears or respond the way culture influences us to—with distress, doomsaying, anger, hatred, fearmongering, or selfish stockpiling.

So how do we respond?

We love our enemies and pray for those who persecute us (Matthew 5:44).

We know that the Lord will sustain us even when there is much to be anxious about; he is our comfort (Psalm 94:18–19).

We thank him for all the ways he has come through for us in the past so we don't forget his everlasting faithfulness (Psalm 136).

We remind ourselves that what we can see with our eyes is not the whole story; he is always there upholding and defending us (Psalm 37:17; 2 Kings 6:16; Exodus 14:14).

We remember that death and sorrow are not our end. He is making all things new (1 Corinthians 15:54–55; Revelations 21:4–5), and all who follow him have an inheritance reserved in heaven which is imperishable, undefiled, and will not fade away (1 Peter 1:4).

We don't have to be dismayed when things in this world are dark, for Christ has already overcome the world (John 16:33).

December 2

"He must increase, but I must decrease."
—John 3:30

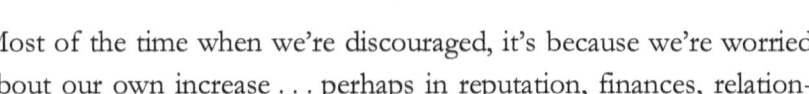

Most of the time when we're discouraged, it's because we're worried about our own increase . . . perhaps in reputation, finances, relationship goals, personal betterment, or success.

We want to see that we matter and that what we do matters, and we tend to gauge that by numbers. Is our bank account growing? How many people seem to be appreciating, noticing, or responding to what we do? Do we have as many friends as so-and-so? Are we getting more followers?

But this is all about our increase. We are checking our worth by worldly standards.

All those things are nice if they happen, but when they become the goal, we have things backwards.

The Lord never says, "Make sure you are very successful in your life and endeavors. That's what glorifies me."

He repeatedly says things like, "The last shall be first" (Matthew 20:16), "whoever wants to become prominent among you shall be your servant" (Matthew 20:26), and "the one who humbles himself will be exalted" (Luke 14:11).

When we decrease, this is no cause for concern, because it's not about us. And according to the Word, doing what he has for us might look very much like being a nobody in a worldly sense.

And this is actually freeing. We don't have to seek to get our dues or be noticed. We don't have to scramble to make an impact.

We can simply quietly serve the Lord, abide in him (John 15), grow in knowledge and discernment (Philippians 1:9), and trust that we are living in his will. If that brings our increase, it isn't wrong, but our own increase should never be the goal.

"He has made everything appropriate in its time."
—Ecclesiastes 3:11

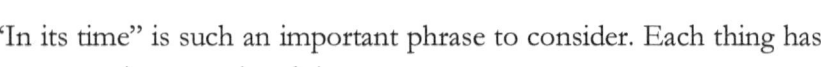

"In its time" is such an important phrase to consider. Each thing has an appropriate, appointed time.

Some trees flower before they have any leaves; some grow the leaves first. Some bushes have flowers for months, and some bloom once for mere days each season.

The largest flower in the world only blooms once approximately every forty years. There's another that can take one hundred years to bloom, then it dies.

This is just one reason why comparison is never helpful.

We can't say the flower that blooms once every forty years is a failure. We can't say that the flower that blooms once a year for a few days is incompetent.

They are each different and uniquely beautiful.

In the same way, one person may seem to have an evergreen career and enjoy win after win. Others may experience success several notable times in their lives. But some people will be the flower that blooms once in forty or one hundred years, and that is not a failure. That is God's ordained purpose.

We seem to think that we should all be on the same track—college, career, family, steady finances, good health. But God has different timelines, different paths, and different purposes for each of us. Each "blooming" will look different.

If you feel that your life has not blossomed the way you hoped, hang on. God will make it appropriate—some versions say "beautiful"— in its time.

"Then on the seventh day they got up early at the
dawning of the day and marched around the city
in the same way seven times; only on that day did
they march around the city seven times."
—Joshua 6:15

Sometimes the Lord asks us to do things that don't make sense in any earthly way.

"March around the city every day? What's that going to do?"

I'm sure they all had questions. Not only that, but they were supposed to do it seven days in a row—seven days during which the people inside the walls of Jericho were likely mocking them, maybe even throwing things at them, and certainly laughing at the ridiculous display which seemed to have no purpose.

Our reaction to this kind of treatment is often to think, "This can't be what God meant. It doesn't make any sense, and I look like a fool."

God had told them to do it each day, but on the seventh day, to do it seven times. By this point, they were probably tired, confused, and a little worried that nothing was going to happen. But they didn't let their lack of understanding stop them. They continued faithfully in what God had called them to do.

When we've followed the Lord into battles we don't understand, we don't have to cower in insecurity when opposition comes. We can trust that the Lord has reasons even when we can't see them. If the Lord asks us to walk in circles that seem to have no purpose, and it looks crazy to outsiders, let's obey him instead of our doubts or the world's jeers.

"She said to him, 'Sir, you have no bucket and the well is
deep; where then do you get this living water?'"
—John 4:11

Jesus was thirsty and had no bucket, but he was offering the Samaritan
woman water that would quench her soul's thirst forever.

From the woman's perspective, she was better off than Jesus was;
she held a bucket in her hands while he had nothing. How did he expect to give her any water at all?

But the living water Christ offered the Samaritan woman was himself—the very same living water each of us draws from the well of the
Holy Spirit.

And we can also dip into this well to share Christ with others no
matter our earthly circumstance.

Other people may have more earthly tools than we do—more
money or talent, more intelligence or education, more beauty or time,
more opportunities or health, more interpersonal skills or fame—but
friends, if they don't have Jesus, we should be the one offering them
something.

They might look at us puzzled—how could we offer them something when our hands are empty?

But the soul's well is too deep for them; no earthly bucket can reach
the water it needs. The Samaritan woman had tried bucket after bucket
of relationship—five husbands and counting—and her heart was still
unsatisfied. The richest man could fill buckets to the brim, but without
Christ, he would be a pauper compared to the humblest believer.

We might lack compared to others in this life, but we can offer them
the wealth of eternal living water that is Christ instead of pining after
their temporary advantages. Those will all count for nothing the moment our souls are required of us.

DECEMBER 6

"I will most gladly spend and
be expended for your souls."
—2 Corinthians 12:15

Paul echoes this statement again in Philippians 2:17: "But even if I am being poured out as a drink offering upon the sacrifice and service of your faith, I rejoice and share my joy with you all."

Just like Jesus, Paul laid his life down willingly to bring others to God. This is just one example that it was not only for Jesus to sacrifice for the kingdom of God, but for all of us as fellow heirs with Christ (Romans 8:17).

That will look different for each of us. Whatever life the Lord has given us, we're called to lay it down. "We know love by this, that he laid down his life for us; and we ought to lay down our lives for the brothers and sisters. But whoever has worldly goods and sees his brother or sister in need, and closes his heart against him, how does the love of God remain in him? Little children, let's not love with word or with tongue, but in deed and truth" (1 John 3:16–18).

This doesn't mean we will do everything anyone asks or expects of us, but it does mean if we're walking in the Spirit, we will give willingly where the Lord leads. We will gladly "spend and be expended," whether in our time, finances, emotion, or physical effort.

This life is not about what we can get out of it, but about what we can pour into others for the sake of the Gospel.

"But when Simon Peter saw this, he fell down at
Jesus' knees, saying, 'Go away from me, Lord, for
I am a sinful man!' For amazement had seized
him and all his companions because of the catch
of fish which they had taken; and likewise also
were James and John, sons of Zebedee, who were
partners with Simon. And Jesus said to Simon,
'Do not fear; from now on you will be catching
people.' When they had brought their boats to
land, they left everything and followed him."
—Luke 5:8–11

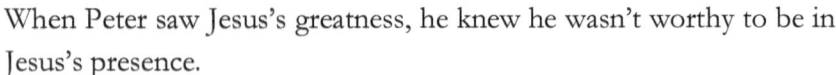

When Peter saw Jesus's greatness, he knew he wasn't worthy to be in Jesus's presence.

Imagine Peter's surprise when Jesus didn't shun him, but instead invited him to join the greatest mission of all.

The understanding that we are not worthy—that the Lord's forgiveness is undeserved—is part of the truth of the Gospel. It's not a reason to hide or run away from him; it's a reason to follow. We're transformed into his image as we believe and live our belief out in obedience (1 John 2:6).

When we come to Jesus in repentance, all our sinfulness is washed away, and we have the indwelling of the Holy Spirit.

Then we must follow as the disciples did—willing to abandon all else as the disciples did if he requires it.

When we're humble before him, he will always say, "Don't be afraid; follow me."

He will give us a purpose and an eternal mission, and he's worth infinitely more than anything we could ever leave behind.

> "Therefore, if you have been raised with Christ,
> keep seeking the things that are above, where
> Christ is, seated at the right hand of God. Set your
> minds on the things that are above, not on the
> things that are on earth. For you have died,
> and your life is hidden with Christ in God."
> —Colossians 3:1–3

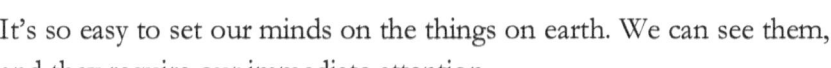

It's so easy to set our minds on the things on earth. We can see them, and they require our immediate attention.

We often think that setting our minds on things above looks like staring whimsically into the clouds or spending all day in prayer, but God is also clear that we are to serve and do our work on this earth with integrity.

So what this really looks like is keeping our hope, desires, and purpose on the things above while yet keeping our hands to the daily work that duty requires of us.

To do this, we must die to our flesh (Romans 8:13) and perform our earthly duties with heavenly intent—in the power of the Holy Spirit and trusting that no matter how unspiritual the task, we can do it while displaying his fruit.

When we're tempted to set our energy and emotions on the things of this world, may we remember that we're already dead, and ask ourselves if those things matter in the life we live above with Christ.

We can put our earthly wants aside and make our lives about abiding in Christ in the day-to-day for the purpose of bringing him glory and showing him to others.

"For the vision is yet for the appointed time; it hurries
toward the goal, and it will not fail. Though it delays, wait
for it; for it will certainly come, it will not delay long."
—Habakkuk 2:3

God gives us all good works to do in this lifetime (Ephesians 2:10).
Some of those good works are simply living life where we are with
faithful integrity, showing others the work of the Spirit in us, and making disciples of those around us.

But sometimes it feels a bit bigger than that; God gives us a hint or
a vision of something that seems beyond us.

And sometimes we're tempted to make that vision come to fruition
by our own efforts . . . like Moses trying to free the Israelites by his
own strength and being exiled from Egypt or like Abraham and Sarah
making their own plan about how to get a son. They did get a son, but
he was not the promised son.

God's way had Moses shepherding in the wilderness as a nobody
for forty years. It had Abraham and Sarah childless for twenty-five
years after the promise.

If God calls us to something big and he hasn't shown us the way to
accomplish it, proceeding according to our own human efforts will always lead to disaster rather than fulfillment.

In the end, Moses freed the Israelites with miracles he never could
have performed without God's power. Abraham and Sarah had a child
after it was beyond the realm of possibility according to all human
standards.

If God gives a way forward, we move in it. If he doesn't, we keep
praying about that vision and trusting that God has given it an appointed time in which he will bring it to pass.

"Each of us is to please his neighbor for his good, to his
edification. For even Christ did not please himself."
—Romans 15:2–3

Most of us spend a lot of time trying to figure out how to make ourselves happy. We may put our desires aside for a time, but there's often
still a voice whispering, "I'll get back to doing what I want later, so it's
okay temporarily."

But when the "temporary" extends longer than we'd hoped, our
desires start rearing their ugly heads. We get annoyed about how long
this "pleasing and edifying my neighbor" is taking rather than getting
our own time for whatever seems pleasing and edifying to us.

But if we would put off our desires for good in favor of following
the Lord's leading in our lives, how much happier and freer we would
be! For "what is the source of quarrels and conflicts among you? Is the
source not your pleasures that wage war in your body's parts?" (James
4:1).

Putting our desires aside is, in the end, freedom from the sins that
so easily plague us. When we do so, we finally find that running this
race with endurance is worth the joy set before us—eternity with the
Lord (Hebrews 12:1–2).

We are also typically quite bad at knowing what will bring us true
and lasting joy; setting aside our own desires leaves us open to all the
unexpected, beautiful places God wants us to go.

Putting the edification of others for their good above our own
wants in favor of the Lord's direction is the path to peace and, ultimately, to more purpose and joy than chasing our desires ever could
provide.

"As the deer pants for the water brooks, so my soul pants
for you, God. My soul thirsts for God, for the living God;
when shall I come and appear before God?"
—Psalm 42:1–2

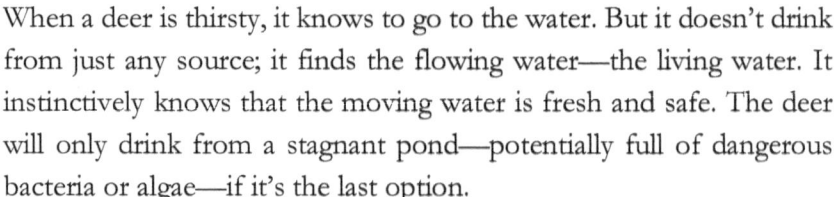

When a deer is thirsty, it knows to go to the water. But it doesn't drink from just any source; it finds the flowing water—the living water. It instinctively knows that the moving water is fresh and safe. The deer will only drink from a stagnant pond—potentially full of dangerous bacteria or algae—if it's the last option.

Our human instincts aren't quite as good. We frequently find ourselves drinking from the stagnant pools of this world rather than water that flows from our living God.

We drink and drink the tainted water and wonder why we're thirsty and ill. The voices of the world tell us we simply haven't drunk enough or we need to try a different pond, so we attempt to quench our heart's desire with more and different worldly things. Satan is just as happy if we drink from the worldly pond of pride or deceitful riches as he is to keep us at the pool of lust or addiction.

But the more we drink from the world, the more our thirst increases; the less satisfied we become. We're poisoning ourselves—sometimes slowly and sometimes fast. Anything other than the overflowing fountain of Jesus Christ will do its deadly work in the end.

When our souls pant from thirst, nothing but the true life-giving nourishment of Christ will do. He's the only source of the spiritual refreshment that will sustain us, and as we come to him, the living water of the Holy Spirit will flow through us and nourish those around us as well.

"So Jesus said to them again, 'Peace be to you; just as the
Father has sent me, I also send you.'"
—John 20:21

We can look at how the Father sent Jesus to know how he sends us.

He sent him humbly, in the form of a baby who had to grow and learn just like we do.

He sent him humbly, as a servant who washed the feet of his own followers.

He sent him humbly, as a sacrifice willing to give up his own life and everything else in this world for the sake of others.

But not only humbly . . .

He sent him in power, as one who did not have to fear evil because he had overcome it.

He sent him in power, the relationship with the Father and the Holy Spirit guiding and enabling him to resist temptation and walk in truth.

He sent him in power, as one who was not controlled by the fear of death.

He sent him in power, as one who stood up to those in authority when they oppressed others.

He sent him in power, with the authority to defeat our enemy who prowls about seeking to devour us.

We have been sent as humble servants with a power that no one can take from us, ready to give up this life at its end, dying to self each moment before that, yet walking in the strength that we can only get from abiding in Christ with every breath.

DECEMBER 13

"Come now, you who say, 'Today or tomorrow we will go
to such and such a city, and spend a year there, and
engage in business, and make a profit.' Yet you do not
know what your life will be like tomorrow. For you are
just a vapor that appears for a little while, and then
vanishes away. Instead, you ought to say, 'If the Lord
wills, we will live and also do this or that.'"
—James 4:13–15

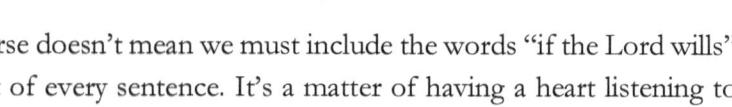

This verse doesn't mean we must include the words "if the Lord wills"
in front of every sentence. It's a matter of having a heart listening to
the Holy Spirit—one that is not boastful or set on its own plans but is
humble and willing to accept a new path as God leads.

Every goal we make in life should be held with open hands, with
the attitude of "your will be done, Lord," and with acceptance if what
he has for us is different than what we hope.

It's okay to plan, hope, and have desires, but we must add—as Jesus
did—the "nevertheless, not my will but yours" (Luke 22:42) to all of
those.

If we resist what God has for us or grow bitter when our plans or
hopes don't come to fruition, we have made ourselves, our desires, and
the things of this world into a god. Our culture may not have many
idols carved from stone or wood, but there are many things we put in
front of our desire for the Lord's will.

Let's live the life God gives us moment by moment instead of
dwelling on the what-ifs, the might've-beens, or the should've-beens.

December 14

"Because of the extraordinary greatness of the revelations,
for this reason, to keep me from exalting myself, there
was given to me a thorn in the flesh, a messenger of Satan
to torment me—to keep me from exalting myself!"
—2 Corinthians 12:7

Paul had a lot of abilities, experiences, and wisdom that could've made him prone to self-importance—not the least being his miraculous conversion on the road to Damascus. Can't you imagine that many pastors in our day would use such a story to build their entire platform and would expect special treatment because of it?

Paul knew that was a danger for him. He was smart, educated, and raised to know the law and the existing Scriptures intimately. He'd been a rising star within the Pharisees before the Lord appeared to him personally. He had many reasons to be arrogant.

But God gave him this thorn in the flesh to keep him humble. We don't know what it was, and it doesn't matter. The point is that sometimes there's a struggle the Lord allows to remain in our lives because he cares more about our character than our comfort.

If giving us what we want or taking a difficulty from us would cause us to become self-righteous, selfish, or anything harmful to Christ's character in us, the Lord will keep us right where we are.

We can pray that our struggles are removed, but even if they're not, perhaps the Lord will reveal how they're growing us in the Holy Spirit and keeping us on his path. Either way, we can trust that all our trials will work something good in and through us when we love and follow the Lord in the midst of them.

"Blessed are those who hunger and thirst for
righteousness, for they will be satisfied."
—Matthew 5:6

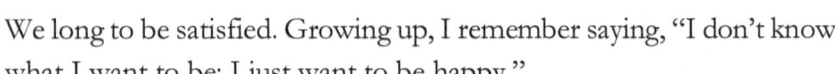

We long to be satisfied. Growing up, I remember saying, "I don't know what I want to be; I just want to be happy."

But we're usually quite bad at knowing what will truly make us happy, and many of us spend years chasing one thing after another grasping for it.

If we could change that statement to, "I don't know what I want to be; I only want to be righteous," our satisfaction and success would be guaranteed.

To seek happiness itself might lead to all sorts of selfishness and debauchery. If we all sought righteousness, we would not only be reaching out to the source of satisfaction and good but helping ensure the satisfaction and good of others.

Righteousness leads to placing others' needs above our own. It keeps us from oppressing the weak and compels us to help them instead.

To hunger and thirst after righteousness is to hunger and thirst after God. He tells us over and over that he will satisfy (Psalm 73:25–26), provide for (Psalm 81:10), protect (Deuteronomy 3:22), and give us more than we need so that we can also reveal his goodness and satisfaction to others (Luke 6:38).

If we all hungered and thirsted for righteousness the way many of us hunger and thirst for happiness, think of the satisfaction that would spread like a wildfire throughout the world! True joy would be the by-product.

Our souls would be satisfied in watching God's plan and purpose come to fruition in our own lives and the lives of those around us.

"Why are you in despair, my soul? And why are you
restless within me? Wait for God, for I will again praise
him for the help of his presence, my God."
—Psalm 42:11

This is a wonderful example of taking our thoughts captive (2 Corinthians 10:5) by talking back to our own minds and preaching to our own hearts. We know that the Lord is where our hope and help come from and that he is our only firm foundation, but we forget. Our soul despairs over our circumstances or grows restless and dissatisfied.

But those feelings don't rule us. We might still feel despair and restlessness, but we choose to act on what we know—that our hope in God is sure, he is fully good and wants good for us, he works all circumstances to good for believers, and our eternity with him is sure.

We too often accept our thoughts and feelings, allowing them to control us instead of standing up to them and telling them the truth of who God is and what he's promised. Philippians 4:8 says to think on the things that are true, honorable, just, pure, lovely, commendable, excellent, and worthy of praise. It says that living like this brings peace and puts us in God's presence (Philippians 4:9).

So when our hearts are despairing or restless, first, we remind them to wait on the Lord, who is our only salvation. Next, we replace those despairing thoughts with things that are true, honorable, and just, etc.

Our emotions do not always lead us in truth. In those times, we focus on what we know, despite what we might feel.

We can always praise him for the help and peace of his presence, because he is always faithful and never leaves us.

"Therefore what benefit were you then deriving
from the things of which you are now ashamed?
For the outcome of those things is death."
—Romans 6:21

When we look at the benefits versus the consequences of the things we're ashamed of, there's no comparison. Yet somehow, we still find it difficult to say no to those things.

What benefit are we deriving? Quick pleasure that is over nearly the second the action is complete.

This is true of almost every appetite—whether it's that doughnut we know is one too many, endlessly scrolling social media, the high from online shopping, the porn addiction we keep going back to, or the nightly drinks we "will quit eventually."

What consequence are we reaping? Slow destruction—emptiness, shame, and spiritual death (often hastening our physical death) along with emotional, relational, financial, and physical problems.

The temptation for those things feels overwhelming. We try to resist, but it seems impossible. We give in because it seems like no one could expend that much willpower forever, and it's true. No one can—but we don't have to.

As we exercise the Spirit rather than the flesh, the Spirit becomes stronger, and the flesh weakens. The desire begins to ease, the nagging want calms, and it slowly becomes easier to say no. It's like walking uphill—it gets harder and harder until you reach the top where the way opens up before you. The walk may not be complete, but it's no longer strenuous.

This usually comes after we've resisted longer than we think we can—long enough for our bodies to overcome their habits, our minds to begin enjoying the freedom from that want, and our hearts to see the Holy Spirit move more clearly as we submit to him through our obedience.

"And we know that God causes all things to work
together for good to those who love God, to those
who are called according to his purpose."
—Romans 8:28

This is one of the most comforting verses in Scripture.

It doesn't say that all things are good; it says that in the lives of believers, God can and will work all things to good purpose even if the things in and of themselves are bad.

Just like he worked Joseph's slavery and imprisonment to the good of all who would've starved from the Egyptian famine.

Just like he used Esther—an orphaned girl who had no choice in becoming one of the king's many wives—to save all of Israel.

Just like Jesus's own crucifixion was for the ultimate and eternal salvation of all mankind.

We live in a world broken by our sin. The badness is here, and it will continue until eternity begins and this world passes away.

The beauty of redemption is that God can enter the badness and transform it. We brought the bad into the world, but in his grace, he allows a way to turn even that to good.

And we don't have to doubt it; the verse says, "we know." We also don't have to wonder if he will do it for this particular thing or not. The verse says, "all things."

When we're in the middle of a difficulty, trauma, or tragedy, it doesn't feel possible that any good can come of it, but the Lord promises it will for those who follow him.

Joseph and Esther couldn't see the end of their stories either, but they were faithful in the middle.

Let's hold on to the Lord and his promises even when we can't see the end.

"Strength and dignity are her clothing,
and she smiles at the future."
—Proverbs 31:25

Do we go out into the world wearing strength and dignity? Do we face the unknown with confidence in our God, showing that we know him to be good, trustworthy, and in control?

We don't have to fear the future when we're walking with the Lord. Like Esther, we can walk into the Lord's plan for us saying, "If I perish, I perish" (Esther 4:16).

Hard things may happen, but when our lives are hidden in Christ (Colossians 3:3), our hope is secure in the eternal promise of a God who cannot lie and does not change. Good things may happen too. God often shows up when we least expect it—when it seems like everything is against us—just like he did for Esther and the Israelites. We don't know what our earthly future holds, but we know God is leading us, and we can walk through it all with strength and dignity because of our trust in him.

The truth is, we can cower at the future, or we can smile at it; it will come with its good and bad all the same. But we know how the story ends, and the Lord gives us what we need along the way.

So let's step into the unknown, the chaos, and the trials with strength, dignity, and confidence in what he has for us. Our ultimate, infinite eternity will outshine it all, and that is worth smiling at.

December 20

"Come to me, all who are weary and burdened, and I
will give you rest. Take my yoke upon you and learn
from me, for I am gentle and humble in heart, and
you will find rest for your souls. For my yoke is
comfortable, and my burden is light."
—Matthew 11:28–30

Just before this in verse 25, Jesus talks about being children of God and how his truth has been revealed to "infants."

As children, the yoke is easy because it is no longer ours. The small child traveling with a good father isn't worried about what to pack, how he will carry it, or whether he knows the way. He trusts that his good father will provide everything needed and will not lead him astray.

Our good Father says not to worry about what we will eat, drink, or wear (Matthew 6:25), yet we worry about it nearly every minute of every day.

He says we shouldn't seek the approval of man (Matthew 6:1; Galatians 1:10; Colossians 3:23), yet we spend half our lives striving to live up to the world's expectations.

He says not to fear those who can kill the body but only he who can destroy the soul (Matthew 10:28), yet we cower when a worldly Goliath stands ready to destroy us.

He says not to be anxious about tomorrow (Matthew 6:34), yet we spend most of today worrying about the future.

We make our burdens heavy by taking on cares God never intended us to bear. But we can be as infants, leaving all those fears with him. Though the crowds jostle and the noise of the journey distracts and frightens, we can go on carefree as long as we're holding tightly to the hand of our Father.

DECEMBER 21

"But Mary said to the angel, 'How will this be, since I am a virgin?' The angel answered and said to her, 'The Holy Spirit will come upon you, and the power of the Most High will overshadow you; for that reason also the holy Child will be called the Son of God.'"
—Luke 1:34–35

As Christ was borne in Mary through the Holy Spirit, he is now borne in all believers.

We may ask, as Mary did, "How will this be?"

The answer is the same: by the power of the Holy Spirit. We are simply to obey and respond as she did, "Behold, I am the servant of the Lord; let it be to me according to your word."

As we love him and submit to his Word, he comes and makes his dwelling place within us (John 14:23); we will see Christ being born in our lives. "Just as we have borne the image of the earthly, we will also bear the image of the heavenly" (1 Corinthians 15:49).

Our old flesh is in opposition to the Spirit (Galatians 5:17; 1 Peter 2:11), but through the Spirit's power now in us, we put to death the deeds of the flesh (Romans 8:13) and use our bodies for righteousness (Romans 6:19), becoming honorable vessels for him (2 Timothy 2:21–22).

Mary's life is a picture of how our humble God has chosen to live within each of us. Our bodies are no longer our own, but we have become the temple of the Holy Spirit (1 Corinthians 6:19).

DECEMBER 22

> "A soothing tongue is a tree of life,
> but perversion in it crushes the spirit."
> —Proverbs 15:4

———◆———

We do not live in a time when having a soothing tongue is encouraged. Most of the voices we hear are loud, harsh, and intent on winning at any cost.

We feel like we won't be heard if we don't match them, but we're called to be soothing rather than antagonistic. That word "soothing" is also translated "wholesome" and "healing." It literally means our words can be curative, like medicine.

That's a beautiful way to use our words—for healing instead of injuring.

It means we use them without that edge of "perversion," which is also translated "crooked, slippery" or "viciousness."

Do we speak only with an aim to heal, or do we also want to poke at faults and tear down? Do we speak truth in love and say what we actually mean, or do we sneak in false words, name-calling, and manipulation?

We can use our words to heal even when disagreeing, or we can use our words to cut others down, belittle, and shame them.

Proverbs 18:21 says, "Death and life are in the power of the tongue." Every word we say is either giving life to those around us or crushing their spirit.

May we all learn to "bridle our tongues" that our faith may be fruitful (James 1:26), and may all our words give life even when we're using them in the defense of truth against evil and injustice.

"Beloved, do not be surprised at the fiery ordeal among
you, which comes upon you for your testing, as though
something strange were happening to you."
—1 Peter 4:12

When things go wrong, we often begin looking for the reason. "What did I do to deserve this?" we ask. "Why is this happening to me?"

We forget that Jesus told us, "In the world you have tribulation, but take courage; I have overcome the world" (John 16:33).

Even he would've preferred not to endure the suffering he did: "My Father, if it be possible, let this cup pass from me; nevertheless, not as I will, but as you will" (Matthew 26:39).

If Jesus himself—perfect and sinless as he is—did not escape the suffering of this fallen world, we should not expect to do so either.

Jesus has overcome the world and the power of death and sin, but we still live in it in these fleshly bodies with all the other fleshly people around us.

While that continues, there will always be a battle. Christ overcame the world in that we no longer must be controlled by its pursuits and desires (Romans 6:5–6), and we no longer need to be terrified of death (1 Corinthians 15:54–57).

We can't always know the reason we are going through difficulties. Sometimes it's discipline meant to purify our hearts, keep us from loving this world, and teach us perseverance. Sometimes it's to bring God glory. Sometimes it's a consequence of sin, whether our own or that of others.

No matter the cause, we can know Jesus, and we can be certain he gives us what we need to walk through those difficulties until our final redemption out of struggle and into the glory of eternity.

"Now to him who is able to do far more abundantly
beyond all that we ask or think, according to
the power that works within us."
—Ephesians 3:20

He can do far more than we can even imagine, but it's "according to the power that works within us."

The Holy Spirit is the "power that works within us," but 1 Thessalonians 5:19 warns that we can quench the Spirit. When we take that into consideration after looking at today's verse, we can see that quenching the Spirit will limit what the Lord does in and through us.

But what does quenching the Spirit mean? The flesh is at war with the Spirit: "For the desire of the flesh is against the Spirit, and the Spirit against the flesh" (Galatians 5:17). So we quench the Spirit by setting our minds on—prioritizing—the flesh.

And the "power at work within us" is proportional to the level of submission to Christ: "the Holy Spirit, whom God has given to those who obey him" (Acts 5:32).

Just like the disciples could not cast out the demons because they could only be cast out by prayer (Mark 9:29), we may be lacking in obedience—whether that be in some task God calls us to, our attitudes, or some unrepented sin—and thereby limiting God's power and voice in our lives.

The more complete our submission to the Spirit and the less we give in to the desires of the flesh—"sexual immorality, impurity, indecent behavior, idolatry, witchcraft, hostilities, strife, jealousy, outbursts of anger, selfish ambition, dissensions, factions, envy, drunkenness, carousing, and things like these" (Galatians 5:19–22)—the more we will see the Holy Spirit's power working within us far more abundantly than we can ask or think.

"In this you greatly rejoice, even though now for a little
while, if necessary, you have been distressed by various
trials, so that the proof of your faith, being more
precious than gold which perishes though tested by fire,
may be found to result in praise, glory, and honor at the
revelation of Jesus Christ; and though you have not seen
him, you love him, and though you do not see him now,
but believe in him, you greatly rejoice with joy
inexpressible and full of glory, obtaining as the
outcome of your faith, the salvation of your souls."
—1 Peter 1:6–9

Perhaps this Christmas season finds us in a place where we cannot see
God in our lives; perhaps we are distressed by trials.

We see him all around in mangers, and others seem to bask in the
joy of his advent, but we cannot.

Let's take comfort in the fact that we can look beyond this
moment—this "little while" of testing—to the glorious revelation on
the other side of the fire, where our faith has been proven, all the
worthless dross of this life burned away, and our love is purified.

Right now, we cannot see him, but because we believe in the
"Immanuel, God with us" without seeing, we can still rejoice with joy
inexpressible in what is to come, knowing that this endurance will result in the salvation of our souls.

We may grieve for what we've lost or what is missing in our lives,
but let's look further to see what we have—the guarantee of eternal joy
in our Savior's presence where all our sorrows are washed away.

"My soul waits in silence for God alone; from him
comes my salvation. He alone is my rock and my
salvation, my stronghold; I will not be greatly shaken."
—Psalm 62:1–2

Seeking help from others or working toward a solution by our own means is not wrong, but our tendency is to seek help in all those other places before we lay it before the Lord. We often live in feverish concern about a thing before we finally hand it over to him and say, "This is too much for me."

But a loving parent doesn't want to wait to help their children until after they've worked themselves into a frenzy of exhaustion trying to do something on their own.

The loving parent is always ready: "Here, let me teach you; let me help you. This is really heavy. Let me carry it."

God is that loving parent. He knows we can't handle all the burdens this world hands us. We aren't meant to. We're meant to cast our burdens and anxieties on our heavenly Father (Psalm 55:22; 1 Peter 5:7).

All of them can be laid at his feet. We don't have to complain, cajole, wear ourselves out, or get angry before God is willing to step in.

How many of our needs would be met through the Lord's provision if we took them to him instead of dragging them around with us everywhere else first?

He is our stronghold, and only in him will we remain unshaken even when the world is unsteady.

"I will cry to God most high,
to God who accomplishes all things for me."
—Psalm 57:2

We often stress about God's purposes for us. Our human nature has us looking at our circumstances, worrying whether we'll be able to accomplish them.

But God is the potter, and we are the clay (Isaiah 45:9–10); he gave us our purpose from the beginning of time (Ephesians 2:10), and he is the one who will fulfill it as we seek him and cry out to him (Numbers 23:19; Philippians 1:6).

The enemy wants us obsessing about whether we are doing what God wants with our gifts and lives. He wants us to agonize in fear and to stay focused on ourselves instead of on God.

The truth is, we aren't capable of accomplishing the Lord's purpose in, through, or for ourselves.

Moses couldn't part the waters and rescue the Israelites from Pharoah. Gideon's three hundred men couldn't have defeated the Midianites great army. Joshua and the Israelites couldn't bring down Jericho's wall.

But God accomplished his purposes in, through, and for each of them nonetheless because they cried out to him and obeyed where he led.

When the Lord gives us something to do, he will make a way. Our job is to be obedient even when obedience has us standing up to insurmountable odds. What looks like defeat can be the Lord's great victory.

This doesn't mean we will always live through that triumph. Each of us has our appointed time to die (Hebrews 9:27), and when that time comes, our death will accomplish his purpose as well and will be no great loss to us as we enter our eternal home without pain or sorrow.

> "You will make known to me the way of life; in
> your presence is fullness of joy; in your right
> hand there are pleasures forever."
> —Psalm 16:11

How many of us agonize over what path to take in life? And not just once, but over and over.

But God assures us so many times of his guidance:

- Ephesians 2:10 says, "We are his workmanship, created in Christ Jesus for good works, which God prepared beforehand so that we would walk in them."
- Isaiah 30:21 says, "Your ears will hear a word behind you, saying, 'This is the way, walk in it,' whenever you turn to the right or to the left."
- Psalm 25:12 says, "He will instruct him in the way he should choose."
- Proverbs 3:5–6 says, "Trust in the Lord with all your heart and do not lean on your own understanding. In all your ways acknowledge him, and he will make your paths straight."
- Jeremiah 33:3 says, "Call to me and I will answer you, and I will tell you great and mighty things, which you do not know."
- James 1:5 says, "If any of you lacks wisdom, let him ask of God, who gives to all generously and without reproach, and it will be given to him."

His way is perfect (Psalm 18:30) and leads to the fullness of joy—not just some joy, but its fullness.

He shows us the way of life; it's in his presence, where, once we join him in eternity, we have pleasures forevermore.

We make it so complicated. We doubt him and stop seeking his presence. We start seeking other things, hurrying, scrambling, and worrying. We forfeit our direction and our joy.

Seek him first (Matthew 6:33); his way is sure and full of joy.

"Then Jesus said to him,
'Go away, Satan! For it is written . . ..'"
—Matthew 4:10

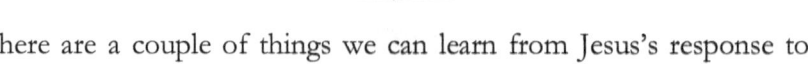

There are a couple of things we can learn from Jesus's response to Satan's temptation.

First, through his connection to the Father, he knew what was or wasn't something he should do. To make your own food when you're hungry (Matthew 4:3) doesn't seem so bad on the surface, but Jesus knew it would be a misuse of his power according to the purpose God had for him. As we submit to, seek, and follow the Lord, the Holy Spirit will reveal this to us as well.

Second, Jesus knew his sure defense came from God's Word. Satan's deception doesn't work if we know and believe what God has truly said in the Bible.

The devil comes at us with the same deceptions he brought to Eve in Eden—"Did God really say . . .?" Our enemy subtly adds to the command that was given (Genesis 3:1) then outright calls God a liar (Genesis 3:4). He tries to convince us God doesn't really want good for us (Genesis 3:5).

But we can defend our hearts and minds with truth. All the crafty messages are defeated when we have the two-edged sword of the Word (Hebrews 4:12) stored up in our hearts (Psalm 119:11).

"It is written" is a tool we should all have at the ready. Whatever temptation is common in our lives, we can study the Word and find Scriptures that apply to it, then memorize them and have them ready when that temptation arrives.

And the more we study, meditate, and memorize the Word in general, the more the Holy Spirit will bring what God has said to mind even when unexpected temptations come our way.

"For the mouth speaks from that which fills the heart."
—Matthew 12:34

What fills our hearts? If we're not sure, we can find out by checking out our words.

What do we talk about? What attitudes come out in our words? That's what we hold in our hearts.

Do we often speak about the lasting things that are important in the kingdom of God, or do we only talk of worldly things? Is the attitude of our speech peace, love, and the other fruits of the Spirit or is it anger, complaint, discontentment, unforgiveness, or bitterness?

If we look at our words and are disappointed by what they reveal about our spirit, it just means we have some heart-change to work on.

Many of us try to change only our outward actions. That's a place to start, and to some extent, we can use willpower to moderate what comes out of our mouths, but what's truly in us will still emerge in times of stress, fear, or anger.

To change from the inside out, we need to work on our hearts and minds and let the Lord work on our spirits.

We do this by taking time to sit with him, praying and meditating on his Word, and living by the truths we say we believe. We need to resist temptation, the lies of the devil, and worldly mindsets. The more we follow the Lord, the more readily we hear his voice (James 4:7–8).

We can store up verses to train our hearts and minds to dwell on biblical truth and goodness when our attitude strays back to fear, anger, or insecurity (Philippians 4:8).

With time, obedience, and intention, the renewing of our minds (Romans 12:2) will bring about the transformation of our hearts and words.

"The end of a matter is better than its beginning;
patience of spirit is better than arrogance of spirit."
—Ecclesiastes 7:8

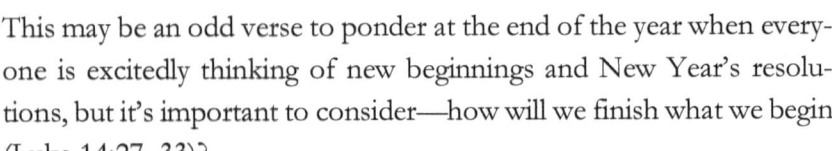

This may be an odd verse to ponder at the end of the year when everyone is excitedly thinking of new beginnings and New Year's resolutions, but it's important to consider—how will we finish what we begin (Luke 14:27–33)?

Because anyone can start. We see it all the time—launching a new endeavor, pursuing a shiny goal—the enthralling rush that accompanies all the plans we make.

It's the same feeling that accompanies young love, which often fizzles as the thrill fades, the difficulties arise, and reality sets in.

I'm afraid we frequently do this in our faith life. I read something that said there was "nothing like" those first days of following Jesus, but this is not how it should be. The end should be better than the beginning.

If we expect those early thrills to carry us through, we will not make it.

We should always be growing in the Spirit, and our love for Christ should deepen in the way the committed love of a marriage deepens as the years go on, even when the flutters have ceased and the trials of life are in full force.

We often begin with arrogance and naivety, but we can only complete with patience, perseverance, and dedication.

We must commit to the long-term rewards instead of the short, to showing up even when we don't feel like it, and to persevering even when we're exhausted.

Let us be people who do not begin in arrogance, but who plan and commit to doing what it takes to finish well, both in faith and in life.

www.ingramcontent.com/pod-product-compliance
Lightning Source LLC
Chambersburg PA
CBHW030353130626
46549CB00004B/1475